JOYCE MEYER

Battlefield
of the
mind

Winning the Battle in Your Mind

FaithWords

New York   Nashville

FaithWords
Hachette Book Group
1290 Avenue of the Americas, New York, NY 10104
faithwords.com
twitter.com/faithwords

First published in October 2016
This edition: May 2017

FaithWords is a division of Hachette Book Group, Inc. The FaithWords name and logo are trademarks of Hachette Book Group, Inc.

The publisher is not responsible for websites (or their content) that are not owned by the publisher.

The Hachette Speakers Bureau provides a wide range of authors for speaking events. To find out more, go to www.hachettespeakersbureau.com or call (866) 376-6591.

Unless otherwise noted, Scriptures are taken from *The Amplified Bible, Classic Edition* copyright © 1965, 1987 by The Zondervan Corporation.

Scripture quotations marked (AMP) are taken from *The Amplified Bible* copyright © 2015 by The Lockman Foundation. Used by permission.

Scripture quotations marked (NIV) are taken from the *Holy Bible: New International Version* ®. Copyright © 1973, 1978, 1984 by International Bible Society. Used by permission of Zondervan Publishing House. All rights reserved.

Scripture quotations marked (MSG) are taken from *The Message*. Copyright © 1993, 1994, 1995, 1996, 2000, 2001, 2002. Used by permission of NavPress Publishing Group.

Scripture quotations marked (NKJV) are taken from the *New King James Version*. Copyright © 1979, 1980, 1982 by Thomas Nelson, Inc., Publishers.

Scripture quotations marked (NLT) are taken from the *Holy Bible*, New Living Translation, Copyright © 1996. Used by permission of Tyndale House Publishers, Inc., Wheaton, Illinois 60189. All rights reserved.

ISBN: 978-1-4555-4285-7

Printed in the United States of America

LSC-C

10 9

Battlefield of the Mind

I would like to dedicate *Battlefield of the Mind*
to my oldest son, David.

I know your personality is enough like mine that you have had
your share of struggles in the mental realm. I see you growing
continually, and I know that you are experiencing the victories
that come from the renewal of the mind.

I love you, David, and I am proud of you.
Keep pressing on!

Contents

CONTENTS

Introduction to the Updated Edition

Battlefield of the Mind was originally published in 1995. It pleases me to tell you that it is still my best-selling book although many years have gone by. The English language edition of the book has sold more than three million copies, and it has been translated in forty-seven languages—and it is still going strong. It has been so instrumental in people's lives that we felt called to create editions for children and teens as well as a daily devotional that are based on the principles of the book. At our ministry, we have had countless testimonies of people who have experienced positive changes in their lives as a result of reading the book and applying its biblical principles. People have been set free from addictions of all kinds, eating disorders, fear, worry, self-hatred and numerous other problems.

I recall a woman who shared that she had spent years in and out of treatment programs for a life-threatening eating disorder. Her parents had spent well over one hundred thousand dollars and she had not improved. She had almost given up the hope of ever getting well until she read *Battlefield of the Mind*. She stated that at times when she was tempted to overeat and then purge herself by vomiting, she would bow in front of the toilet that had been taking her life and pray and read *Battlefield of the Mind* out loud until the temptation passed. Today she is completely free of illness and helping others who have suffered the way she did.

Another story that blessed me tremendously was about a Jewish man who accidentally knocked over a stack of books in a Barnes and Noble bookstore. While picking up the books and trying to restack them, he ended up with *Battlefield of the Mind*. He opened it up expecting to find something he could make fun of and ended up purchasing the book. He hid it from his wife because he did not want her to catch him reading a book by a Christian author. He became interested in the principles he read and bought a Bible that he also hid from his wife. Eventually he discovered that his wife was also secretly reading a Bible she had hidden. They both received Jesus as their Savior and were instrumental in leading other family members to salvation through Jesus as well.

It is life changing when we discover that wrong thoughts are the root of our problems and that we can change our life by changing our thinking. God's word teaches us that our mind must be renewed so we learn to think like God thinks. When we do, then we can enjoy the life that God wants us to have—one of freedom, fruitfulness, peace, and joy.

A whole new world opens up to us when we learn to choose our own thoughts rather than letting the devil fill our minds full of things that will destroy us. We must learn to be responsible for our thoughts and words because they produce our actions. It is impossible for us to behave better unless we think better thoughts.

Our television viewers almost always choose those of our programs that have been on their minds and thoughts as their favorite ones. Why? It is because our minds give us more problems than anything else. We want peace of mind! We want to think healthy, life giving thoughts rather than ones that produce all kinds of misery. *Battlefield of the Mind* teaches us that we can do that and shows us how.

In order to prepare for this special edition of *Battlefield of the Mind* I needed to read the entire book. I really like it!!! I had not read it since I wrote it and was personally encouraged and edified. It is easy to read and contains one of the foundational truths that we must have in order to access the new life we are offered through our relationship with Christ. I have added some new material in this edition that reflects further study and insight that God has given me over the years since it was first published. I've also included updates that show how God has moved in situations that I discussed in the first edition. I am very glad that you are about to read this book because I really believe it will be life changing for you.

I believe this book will benefit you whether you are a new believer in Jesus Christ or have already been walking with God for many years. I pray that you will enjoy it and that it will be a blessing in your life.

PART I:

The Importance of the Mind

Introduction

How can we express the importance of our thoughts sufficiently in order to convey the true meaning of Proverbs 23:7: "For as he [a person] thinks in his heart, so is he"?

The longer I serve God and study His Word, the more I realize the importance of thoughts and words. On a fairly regular basis, I find the Holy Spirit leading me to study in these areas.

I have said, and I believe it is true, that as long as we are on this earth we will need to study in the areas of thoughts and words. No matter how much we know in any area, there are always new things to learn, and there are things we have previously learned that we need to be refreshed in.

For the weapons of our warfare are not physical [weapons of flesh and blood], but they are mighty before God for the overthrow and destruction of strongholds, [Inasmuch as we] refute arguments and theories and reasonings and every proud and lofty thing that sets itself up against the [true] knowledge of God; and we lead every thought and purpose away captive into the obedience of Christ (the Messiah, the Anointed One).
2 CORINTHIANS 10:4,5

What does Proverbs 23:7 really mean? The *King James Version* says, "As he [a man] thinketh in his heart, so is he." Another translation states, "As a man thinks in his heart, so does he become."

The mind is the leader or forerunner of all actions. Romans 8:5 makes it clear: "For those who are according to the flesh and are controlled by its unholy desires set their minds on and pursue those things which gratify the flesh, but those who are according to the Spirit and are controlled by the desires of the Spirit set their minds on and seek those things which gratify the [Holy] Spirit."

Our actions are a direct result of our thoughts. If we have a negative mind, we will have a negative life. If, on the other hand, we renew our mind according to God's Word, we will, as Romans 12:2 promises, prove out in our experience "the good and acceptable and perfect will of God" for our lives.

I have divided this book into three main parts. This first part deals with the importance of thoughts. I want to establish firmly in your heart forever that you need to begin to think about what you are thinking about.

So many people's problems are rooted in thinking patterns that actually produce the problems they experience in their lives. Satan offers wrong thinking to everyone, but we do not have to accept his offer. Learn what types of thinking are acceptable to the Holy Spirit and what types are not acceptable.

Second Corinthians 10:4,5 clearly indicates that we must know the Word of God well enough to be able to compare what is in our mind with what is in the mind of God; any thought that attempts to exalt itself above the Word of God we are to cast down and bring into captivity to Jesus Christ.

I pray that this book will help you to do that.

The mind is the battlefield. It is a vital necessity that we line up our thoughts with God's thoughts. This is a process that will take time and study.

Don't ever give up, because little by little you are changing. The more you change your mind for the better, the more your life will also change for the better. When you begin to see God's good plan for you in your thinking, you will begin to walk in it.

Chapter

1

The Mind
Is the Battlefield

The Mind Is the Battlefield

*F*rom this Scripture we see that we are in a war. A careful study of this verse informs us that our warfare is not with other human beings but with the devil and his demons. Our enemy, Satan, attempts to defeat us with strategy and deceit, through well-laid plans and deliberate deception.

For we are not wrestling with flesh and blood [contending only with physical opponents], but against the despotisms, against the powers, against [the master spirits who are] the world rulers of this present darkness, against the spirit forces of wickedness in the heavenly (supernatural) sphere.

EPHESIANS 6:12

The devil is a liar. Jesus called him "the father of lies and of all that is false" (John 8:44). He lies to you and me. He tells us things about ourselves, about other people and about circumstances that are just not true. He does not, however, tell us the entire lie all at one time.

He begins by bombarding our mind with a cleverly devised pattern of little nagging thoughts, suspicions, doubts, fears, wonderings, reasonings, and theories. He moves slowly and cautiously (after all, well-laid plans take time). Remember, he has a strategy for his warfare. He has studied us for a long time.

He knows what we like and what we don't like. He knows our insecurities, our weaknesses, and our fears. He knows what bothers us most. He is willing to invest any amount of time it takes to defeat us. One of the devil's strong points is patience.

TEARING DOWN STRONGHOLDS

For the weapons of our warfare are not physical [weapons of flesh and blood], but they are mighty before God for the overthrow and destruction of strongholds.

[Inasmuch as we] refute arguments and theories and reasonings and every proud and lofty thing that sets itself up against the [true] knowledge of God; and we lead every thought and purpose away captive into the obedience of Christ (the Messiah, the Anointed One).

2 Corinthians 10:4,5

Through careful strategy and cunning deceit, Satan attempts to set up "strongholds" in our mind. A stronghold is an area in which we are held in bondage (in prison) due to a certain way of thinking.

In this passage, the Apostle Paul tells us that we have the weapons we need to overcome Satan's strongholds. We will learn more about these weapons later, but right now, please notice that once again we see that we are engaged in warfare, spiritual warfare. Verse 5 shows us clearly the location of the battlefield on which this warfare is waged.

The Amplified Bible translation of this verse says that we are to take these weapons and refute arguments. The devil argues with us; he offers us theories and reasonings. All of this activity goes on in the mind.

The mind is the battlefield.

Summary of the Situation

Thus, so far we have seen that:

1. We are engaged in a war.

2. Our enemy is Satan.

3. The mind is the battlefield.

4. The devil works diligently to set up strongholds in our mind.

5. He does it through strategy and deceit (through well-laid plans and deliberate deception).

6. He is in no hurry; he takes his time to work out his plan.

Let's examine his plan more clearly through a parable.

MARY'S SIDE

Mary and her husband, John, are not enjoying a happy marriage. There is strife between them all the time. They are both angry, bitter, and resentful. They have two children who are being affected by the problems in the home. The strife is showing up in their schoolwork and behavior. One of the children is having stomach problems caused by nerves.

Mary's problem is that she doesn't know how to let John be the head of their home. She is bossy—she wants to make all the decisions, handle the finances and discipline the children. She wants to work so she will have her "own" money. She is independent, loud, demanding and a nag.

About now you may be thinking, "I've got her answer. She needs to know Jesus."

She does know Him! Mary received Jesus as her Savior five years ago—three years after she and John were married.

"Do you mean there hasn't been a change in Mary since receiving Jesus as Savior?"

Yes, there has been change. She believes she is going to heaven even though her bad behavior causes her to feel constant condemnation. She has hope now. Before she met Jesus, she was miserable and hopeless; now she is just miserable.

Mary knows that her attitude is wrong. She wants to change. She has received counseling from two people. She takes every opportunity to be prayed for and asks for victory over anger, rebellion, unforgiveness, resentment, and bitterness. Why hasn't she seen more improvement?

The answer is found in Romans 12:2: "Do not be conformed to this world (this age), [fashioned after and adapted to its external, superficial customs], but be transformed (changed) by the [entire] renewal of your mind [by its new ideals and its new attitude], so that you may prove [for yourselves] what is the good and acceptable and perfect will of God, even the thing which is good and acceptable and perfect [in His sight for you]."

Mary has strongholds in her mind. They have been there for years. She doesn't even understand how they got there. She knows she shouldn't be rebellious, bossy, nagging, etc., but she doesn't know what to do to change her nature. It seems that she simply reacts in certain situations in an unseemly way because she can't control her actions.

Mary can't control her actions because she doesn't control her thoughts. She doesn't control her thoughts because she doesn't even know that doing so is an option for her. There are strongholds in her mind that the devil set up early in her life.

Satan begins to initiate his well-laid plans and to sow his deliberate deception at a very young age. In Mary's case, her problems started long ago, in childhood.

As a child Mary had an extremely domineering father who often spanked her just because he was in a bad mood. If she made one wrong move, he would vent his anger on her. For years, she suffered helplessly as her father mistreated her and her mother. He was disrespectful in all his ways toward his wife and daughter. Mary's brother, however, could do no wrong. It seemed as if he was favored just because he was a boy.

By the time she was sixteen, Mary had been brainwashed for years by Satan who had told her lies that went something like this: "Men really think they are something. They are all alike; you can't trust them. They will hurt you and take advantage of you. If you're a man, you've got it made in life. You can do anything you want. You can order people around, be the boss, treat people any way you please and nobody (especially not wives or daughters) can do anything about it."

As a result, Mary's mind was resolved: "When I get away from here, nobody is ever going to push me around again!"

Satan was already waging war on the battlefield of her mind. Play those thoughts over and over in your head a hundred thousand times or more over a period of ten years, and see if you're ready to get married and become a sweet, submissive, adoring wife. Even if by some miracle you should want to be, you won't know how. This is the kind of mess in which Mary finds herself today. What can she do? What can any of us do in such a situation?

THE WEAPONS OF THE WORD

If you abide in My word [hold fast to My teachings and live in accordance with them], you are truly My disciples.

And you will know the Truth, and the Truth will set you free.

John 8:31,32

Here Jesus tells us how we are to win the victory over the lies of Satan. We must get the knowledge of God's truth in us, renew our minds with His Word, then use the weapons of 2 Corinthians 10:4,5 to tear down the strongholds and every high and lofty thing that exalts itself against the knowledge of God.

These "weapons" are the Word received through preaching, teaching, books, CDs, DVDs, conferences, and private Bible study. But we must "abide" (continue) in the Word until it becomes revelation given by inspiration of the Holy Spirit. Continuing is important. In Mark 4:24 Jesus says, "The measure [of thought and study] you give [to the truth you hear] will be the measure [of virtue and knowledge] that comes back to you." I repeat, we must *continue* using the weapon of the Word.

Two other spiritual weapons available to us are praise and prayer. Praise defeats the devil quicker than any other battle plan, but it must be genuine heart praise, not just lip service or a method being tried to see if it works. Also, praise and prayer both involve the Word. We praise God according to His Word and His goodness.

Prayer is relationship with the Godhead. It is coming and asking for help or talking to God about something that bothers us. It is fellowship, friendship, and an opportunity to express gratitude for all that God is and does.

If you want to have an effective prayer life, develop a good personal relationship with the Father. Know that He loves you, that He is full of mercy, that He will help you. Get to know Jesus. He is your Friend. He died for you. Get to know the Holy Spirit. He is with you all the time as your Helper. Let Him help you.

Learn to fill your prayers with the Word of God. Psalm 9:10 says that we seek God on the authority of His Word and the right of our necessity (need).

So, our weapons are the Word used in various ways. We can pray the word, speak the word, sing the word, and study the word. As Paul tells us in 2 Corinthians, our weapons are not carnal (fleshly) weapons; they are spiritual. We need spiritual weapons because we are fighting master spirits, yes, even the devil himself. Even Jesus used the weapon of the Word in the wilderness to defeat the devil. (See Luke 4:1-13.) Each time the devil lied to Him, Jesus responded with, "It is written," and quoted him the Word.

As Mary learns to use her weapons, she will begin to tear down the strongholds that have been built in her mind. She will know the truth that will set her free. She will see that not all men are like her earthly father. Some are, but many are not. Her husband, John, is not. John loves Mary very much.

John's Side

The other side of the story involves John. He, too, has problems that are a contributing factor to the situation he and Mary face in their marriage, home, and family.

John should be taking his position as head of the family. God intends for him to provide spiritual leadership in his home. John is also born again and knows the proper order for family life. He knows that he should not allow his wife to control the household, the finances, the children, and him. He knows all this, but he doesn't do anything about it except feel defeated and retreat into TV and sports.

John is hiding from his responsibility because he hates confrontation. He prefers to take a passive attitude, thinking, "Well, if I just leave this situation alone, perhaps it will work itself out." Or, he excuses himself from taking real action by saying, "I'll pray about it." Of course, prayer is good, but not if it is merely a way of avoiding responsibility.

Let me clarify what I mean when I say that John should assume his God-given position in the home. I don't mean that he should come on like "Mr. Macho," ranting and raving about his authority. Ephesians 5:25 teaches that a man should love his wife as Christ loved the Church. John needs to take responsibility, and with responsibility comes authority. He should be lovingly firm with his wife. He should reassure Mary that even though she was hurt as a child, as she releases herself to God through trusting Him, she will gain confidence that not all men are like her father was.

John should be doing a lot of things; but, like Mary, he also has "mindsets" that open the door for the devil to hold him captive. There is also a battle going on in John's mind. Like Mary, he was verbally abused in childhood. His domineering mother had a sharp tongue and frequently said hurtful things to him, things like, "John, you're such a mess; you'll never amount to anything."

John tried hard to please his mother because he craved her approval (as all children do); but the harder he tried, the more mistakes he made. He had a habit of being clumsy, so his mother told him all the time what a klutz he was. Of course, he dropped things because he was trying so hard to please that it made him nervous, and so he defeated his purpose.

He also experienced some unfortunate rejection from children with whom he desired to be friends. This type of thing happens to most of us at some time in our lives, but it devastated John because he already felt rejected by his mother.

And there was a girl whom he really liked in his early high school years who rejected him for another boy. By the time all of these things had tallied up in John's life, and the devil had worked on him, building strongholds in his mind for years and years, John simply had no courage to be anything but quiet, shy, and withdrawn.

John is a low-key type person who simply chooses not to make waves. For years he has been having thoughts directed into him that go something like this: "There is no point in telling anyone what you think; they won't listen anyway. If you want people to accept you, you just need to go along with whatever they want. Just leave things alone, nothing you say will make any difference anyway."

The few times he tried to stand his ground on an issue, it seemed that he always ended up losing, so he finally decided that confrontation wasn't worth the effort.

"I'm going to lose anyway in the end," he reasoned, "so why even start anything?"

What Is the Answer?

The Spirit of the Lord [is] upon Me, because He has anointed Me [the Anointed One, the Messiah] to preach the good news (the Gospel) to the poor; He has sent Me to announce release to the captives and recovery of sight to the blind, to send forth as delivered those who are oppressed [who are downtrodden, bruised, crushed, and broken down by calamity],

To proclaim the accepted and acceptable year of the Lord [the day when salvation and the free favors of God profusely abound].

Luke 4:18,19

With John's and Mary's conflicting problems, it is not too hard to imagine what their home life is like. Remember, I said there was a lot of strife in it. Strife isn't always open warfare. Many times, strife is an angry undercurrent in the home that everyone knows is there, but nobody deals with. The atmosphere in their home is terrible—it is filled with tension and the devil loves it!

What will happen to John and Mary and their children? Will they make it? They are Christians—it would be a shame to see their marriage fail and their family ruined. Actually, though, it is up to them. John 8:31,32 will be a key Scripture in their decision. If they continue to study God's Word, they will know the truth, and acting on the truth will set them free. *But* they must each face the truth about themselves and their past as God reveals it to them.

The truth is always revealed through the Word; but sadly, people don't always accept it. It is a painful process to face our faults and deal with them. Generally speaking, people justify misbehavior. They allow their past and how they were raised to negatively affect the rest of their lives.

Our past may explain why we're suffering, but we must not use it as an excuse to stay in bondage.

Everyone is without excuse because Jesus always stands ready to fulfill His promise to set the captives free. He will walk us across the finish line of victory in any area if we are willing to go all the way through it with Him.

The Way Out

For no temptation (no trial regarded as enticing to sin), [no matter how it comes or where it leads] has overtaken you and laid hold on you that is not common to man [that is, no temptation or trial has come to you that is beyond human resistance and that is not adjusted and adapted and belonging to human experience, and such as man can bear]. But God is faithful [to His Word and to His compassionate nature], and He [can be trusted] not to let you be tempted and tried and assayed beyond your ability and strength of resistance and power to endure, but with the temptation He will [always] also provide the way out (the means of escape to a landing place), that you may be capable and strong and powerful to bear up under it patiently.

1 Corinthians 10:13

I hope you see from this parable-type example how Satan takes our circumstances and builds strongholds in our lives—how he wages war on the battlefield of the mind. But, thank God, we have weapons to tear down the strongholds. God doesn't abandon us and leave us helpless. First Corinthians 10:13 promises us that God will not allow us to be tempted beyond what we can bear, but with every temptation He will also provide the way out, the escape.

Any one of us may be Mary or John. I am sure that most of us relate in some way to the scenario. Their problems are internal—in their thoughts and attitudes. Their outward behavior is only a result of their inner life. Satan knows well that if he can control our thoughts, he can control our actions.

You may have some major strongholds in your life that need to be broken. Let me encourage you by saying, "God is on your side." There is a war going on, and your mind is the battlefield. But the good news is that God is fighting on your side.

Chapter
2

A Vital Necessity

A Vital Necessity

Chapter

2

This one Scripture alone lets us know how very important it is that we think properly. Thoughts are powerful, and according to the writer of the book of Proverbs, they have creative ability. If our thoughts are going to affect what we become, then it should certainly be a priority that we think right thoughts.

For as he thinks in his heart, so is he.

PROVERBS 23:7

I want to impress on you the absolute necessity of getting your thinking in line with God's Word.

You cannot have a positive life and a negative mind.

THE MIND OF THE FLESH
VERSUS THE MIND OF THE SPIRIT

For those who are according to the flesh and are controlled by its unholy desires set their minds on and pursue those things which gratify the flesh, but those who are according to the Spirit and are controlled by the desires of the Spirit set their minds on and seek those things which gratify the [Holy] Spirit.

Romans 8:5

In the *King James Version* the eighth chapter of Romans teaches us that if we "mind" the things of the flesh, we will walk in the flesh; but if we "mind" the things of the Spirit, we will walk in the Spirit.

Let me put it another way: if we think fleshly thoughts, wrong thoughts, negative thoughts, we cannot walk in the Spirit. Renewed, God-like thinking is a vital necessity to a successful Christian life.

There are times when we humans will be lazy about something if we don't realize how important it is to pay attention to it. But, when we realize it is a matter that will cause great problems if we ignore it, then we take action.

Let us say, for example, that the bank calls and tells you that your account is overdrawn by eight hundred and fifty dollars. You immediately look for the problem. Perhaps in your search you discover that you failed to make a deposit that you thought you had made. You rush to the bank right away with the deposit, so you won't have any further problems.

I would like for you to consider this matter of getting the mind renewed in the same manner.

Your life may be in a state of chaos because of years of wrong thinking. If so, it is important for you to come to grips with the fact that *your life will not get straightened out until your mind does*. You should consider this area one of *vital necessity*. Be serious about tearing down the strongholds Satan has built in your mind. Use your weapons of the Word, praise, and prayer.

BY THE SPIRIT

Not by might, nor by power, but by My Spirit . . . says the Lord of hosts.

Zechariah 4:6

One of the best aids to freedom is asking God for a lot of help—and asking often.

One of your weapons is prayer (asking). You can't overcome your situation by determination alone. You do need to be determined, but determined in the Holy Spirit, not in the effort of your own flesh. The Holy Spirit is your Helper—seek His help. Lean on Him. You can't make it alone.

A VITAL NECESSITY

For the believer, right thinking is a vital necessity. A vital necessity is something that is so important that one simply cannot live without it—like a heartbeat is vital, or blood pressure is vital. These are things without which there is no life.

The Lord impressed this truth on me years ago concerning personal fellowship with Him in prayer and the Word. I was having a terrible time disciplining myself to do these things until He showed me that they are a vital necessity. Just as my physical life is dependent upon my vital signs, so my spiritual life is dependent upon spending regular, quality time with God. Once I learned that fellowship with Him is vital, I gave it priority in my life.

In the same way, once I realized that right thinking is vital to victorious living, I got more serious about thinking about what I was thinking about, and choosing my thoughts carefully.

As You Think, So Are You

Either make the tree sound (healthy and good), and its fruit sound (healthy and good), or make the tree rotten (diseased and bad), and its fruit rotten (diseased and bad); for the tree is known and recognized and judged by its fruit.

Matthew 12:33

The Bible says that a tree is known by its fruit.

The same is true in our lives. Thoughts bear fruit. Think good thoughts, and the fruit in your life will be good. Think bad thoughts, and the fruit in your life will be bad.

Actually, you can look at a person's attitude and know what kind of thinking is prevalent in his life. A sweet, kind person does not have mean, vindictive thoughts. By the same token, a truly evil person does not have good, loving thoughts.

Remember Proverbs 23:7 and allow it to have an impact on your life: for as you think in your heart, so are you. I frequently say, "Where the mind goes, the man follows."

Chapter
3

Don't Give Up!

Don't Give Up!

No matter how bad the condition of your life and your mind, don't give up! Regain the territory the devil has stolen from you. If necessary, regain it one inch at a time, always leaning on God's grace and not on your own ability to get the desired results.

And let us not lose heart and grow weary and faint in acting nobly and doing right, for in due time and at the appointed season we shall reap, if we do not loosen and relax our courage and faint.
GALATIANS 6:9

In Galatians 6:9 the Apostle Paul simply encourages us to keep on keeping on! Don't be a quitter! Don't have that old "give-up" spirit. God is looking for people who will go all the way through with Him.

GO THROUGH

When you pass through the waters, I will be with you, and through the rivers, they will not overwhelm you. When you walk through the fire, you will not be burned or scorched, nor will the flame kindle upon you.

Isaiah 43:2

Whatever you may be facing or experiencing right now in your life, I am encouraging you to go through it and not give up!

Habakkuk 3:19 says that the way we develop hind's feet (a hind is an animal that can climb mountains swiftly) is "to walk [not to stand still in terror, but to walk] and make [spiritual] progress upon" the "high places [of trouble, suffering or responsibility]!"

The way God helps us make spiritual progress is by being with us to strengthen and encourage us to "keep on keeping on" in rough times.

It's easy to quit; it takes faith to go through.

The Choice Is Yours!

I call heaven and earth to witness this day against you that I have set before you life and death, the blessings and the curses; therefore choose life, that you and your descendants may live.

Deuteronomy 30:19

There are thousands upon thousands of thoughts presented to us every day. The mind has to be renewed to follow after the Spirit and not the flesh. Our carnal (worldly, fleshly) minds have had so much practice operating freely that we surely don't have to use any effort to think wrong thoughts.

On the other hand, we have to purposely choose right thinking. After we have finally decided to be like-minded with God, then we will need to *choose* and to *continue to choose* right thoughts.

When we begin to feel that the battle of the mind is just too difficult and that we aren't going to make it, then we must be able to cast down that kind of thinking and *choose* to think that we are going to make it! Not only must we choose to think that we are going to make it, but we must also decide not to quit. Bombarded with doubts and fears, we must take a stand and say, "I will never give up! God is on my side, He loves me, and He is helping me!"

You and I will have many choices to make throughout our lives. In Deuteronomy 30:19 the Lord told His people that He had set before them life and death and urged them to *choose* life. And in Proverbs 18:21 we are told, "Death and life are in the power of the tongue, and they who indulge in it shall eat the fruit of it."

Our thoughts become our words. Therefore, it is vitally important that we *choose* life-generating thoughts. When we do, right words will follow.

Don't Give Up!

When the battle seems endless and you think you'll never make it, remember that you are reprogramming a very carnal, fleshly, worldly mind to think as God thinks.

Impossible? *No!*

Difficult? *Yes!*

But, just think, you have God on your team. I believe He is the best "computer programmer" around. (Your mind is like a computer that has had a lifetime of garbage programmed into it.) God is working on you; at least, He is if you have invited Him to have control of your thoughts. He is reprogramming your mind. Just keep cooperating with Him—and *don't give up!*

It will definitely take time, and it won't all be easy, but you are going in the right direction if you choose God's way of thinking. You will spend your time doing something, so it may as well be going forward and not staying in the same mess for the rest of your life.

Turn and Take Possession!

The Lord our God said to us in Horeb, You have dwelt long enough on this mountain. Turn and take up your journey and go to the hill country of the Amorites. . . .

Behold, I have set the land before you; go in and take possession of the land which the Lord swore to your fathers, to Abraham, to Isaac, and to Jacob, to give to them and to their descendants after them.

Deuteronomy 1:6-8

In Deuteronomy 1:2, Moses pointed out to the Israelites that it was only an eleven-day journey to the border of Canaan (the Promised Land), yet it had taken them forty years to get there. Then in verse 6, he told them, "The Lord God says to us, 'You have dwelt long enough on this mountain.'"

Have you dwelt long enough on the same mountain? Have you spent forty years trying to make an eleven-day trip?

In my own life, I finally had to wake up and realize that I was going nowhere. *I was a Christian without victory.* Like Mary and John, I had many wrong mindsets and many mental strongholds that had been built up over years and years. The devil had lied to me, and I had believed him. Therefore, I had been living in deception.

I had been at the same mountain long enough. I had spent forty years making what could have been a much shorter journey had I known the truth of God's Word.

God showed me that the Israelites stayed in the wilderness because they had a "wilderness mentality"—certain types of wrong thinking that kept them in bondage. We will deal with this subject in a future chapter, but for now, let me urge you to make a quality decision that you are going to get your mind renewed and learn to choose your thoughts carefully. Make up your mind that you will not quit and give up until victory is complete and you have taken possession of your rightful inheritance.

Chapter
4

Little by Little

Little by Little

The renewing of your mind will take place *little by little*, so don't be discouraged if progress seems slow.

Just before they entered the Promised Land, the Lord told the Israelites that He would drive out their enemies before them little by little lest "the beasts of the field" increase among them.

And the Lord your God will clear out those nations before you, little by little; you may not consume them quickly, lest the beasts of the field increase among you.
DEUTERONOMY 7:22

I believe pride is the "beast" that will consume us if we receive too much freedom too quickly. It is actually better to be set at liberty in one area at a time. That way, we appreciate our freedom more; we realize it is truly a gift from God and not something we can make happen in our own strength.

SUFFERING PRECEDES LIBERATION

And after you have suffered a little while, the God of all grace [Who imparts all blessing and favor], Who has called you to His [own] eternal glory in Christ Jesus, will Himself complete and make you what you ought to be, establish and ground you securely, and strengthen, and settle you.

1 Peter 5:10

Why do we need to suffer "a little while"? I believe that from the time we actually realize we have a problem until Jesus delivers us, we endure a type of suffering, but we rejoice even more when freedom comes. When we try to do something on our own, fail, and then realize that we must wait on Him, our hearts overflow with thanksgiving and praise as He rises up and does what we can not do ourselves.

No Condemnation

Therefore, [there is] now no condemnation...for those who are in Christ Jesus, who live [and] walk not after the dictates of the flesh, but after the dictates of the Spirit.

Romans 8:1

Don't receive condemnation when you have setbacks or bad days. Just get back up, dust yourself off, and start again. When a baby is learning to walk, he falls many, many times before he enjoys confidence in walking. However, one thing in a baby's favor is the fact that, even though he may cry awhile after he has fallen, he always gets right back up and tries again.

The devil will try his hardest to stop you in this area of renewing the mind. He knows that his control over you is finished once you have learned to choose right thoughts and reject wrong ones. He will attempt to stop you through discouragement and condemnation.

When condemnation comes, use your "Word weapon." Quote Romans 8:1, reminding Satan and yourself that you do not walk after the flesh but after the Spirit. Walking after the flesh is depending on yourself; walking after the Spirit is depending on God.

When you fail (which you will), that doesn't mean that you are a failure. It simply means that you don't do everything right. We all have to accept the fact that along with strengths we also have weaknesses. Just let Christ be strong in your weaknesses; let Him be your strength on your weak days.

I repeat: *don't receive condemnation.* Your total victory will come, but it will take time because it will come "little by little."

Don't Get Discouraged

Why are you cast down, O my inner self? And why should you moan over me and be disquieted within me? Hope in God and wait expectantly for Him, for I shall yet praise Him, my Help and My God.

Psalm 42:5

Discouragement destroys hope, so naturally the devil always tries to discourage us. Without hope we give up, which is what the devil wants us to do. The Bible repeatedly tells us not to be discouraged or dismayed. God knows that we will not come through to victory if we get discouraged, so He always encourages us as we start out on a project by saying to us, "Don't get discouraged." God wants us to be *en*couraged, not *dis*couraged.

When discouragement or condemnation tries to overtake you, examine your thought life. What kind of thoughts have you been thinking? Have they sounded something like this?

"I'm not going to make it; this is too hard. I always fail, it has always been the same, nothing ever changes. I'm sure other people don't have this much trouble getting their minds renewed. I may as well give up. I'm tired of trying. I pray, but it seems as if God doesn't hear. He probably doesn't answer my prayers because He is so disappointed in the way I act."

If this example represents your thoughts, it is no wonder you get discouraged or come under condemnation. Remember, you become what you think. Think discouraging thoughts, and you'll get discouraged. Think condemning thoughts, and you'll come under condemnation. Change your thinking and be set free! Instead of thinking negatively, think like this:

"Well, things are going a little slow; but, thank God, I'm making some progress. I'm sure glad I'm on the right path that will lead me to freedom. I had a rough day yesterday. I chose wrong thinking all day long. Father, forgive me, and help me to 'keep on keeping on.' I made a mistake, but at least that is one mistake I won't have to make again. This is a new day. You love me, Lord. Your mercy is new every morning.

"I refuse to be discouraged. I refuse to be condemned. Father, the Bible says that You don't condemn me. You sent Jesus to die for me. I'll be fine—today will be a great day. You help me choose right thoughts today."

I'm sure you can already feel the victory in this type of cheerful, positive, God-like thinking.

We like everything instantaneous. We have the fruit of patience inside, but it is being worked to the outside. Sometimes God takes His time about bringing us our full deliverance. He uses the difficult period of waiting to stretch our faith and to let patience have her perfect work (see James 1:4 KJV). God's timing is perfect. He is never late.

Here is another good thought to think: "I believe God. I believe He is working in me no matter what I may feel or how the situation may look. The Lord has begun a good work in me, and He will bring it to full completion" (see Phil. 2:13; 1:6).

It is in this manner that you can effectively use your weapon of the Word to tear down strongholds. I recommend that you not only purposely think right thoughts, but that you go the extra mile and speak them aloud as your confession.

Remember, God is delivering you, *little by little*, so don't be discouraged and don't feel condemned if you make a mistake.

Be patient with yourself!

Chapter
5

Be Positive

Be Positive

*P*ositive minds produce positive lives. Negative minds produce negative lives. Positive thoughts are always full of faith and hope. Negative thoughts are always full of fear and doubt.

It shall be done for you as you have believed.

MATTHEW 8:13

Some people are afraid to hope because they have been hurt so much in life. They have had so many disappointments, they don't think they can face the pain of another one. Therefore, they refuse to hope so they won't be disappointed.

This avoidance of hope is a type of protection against being hurt. Disappointment hurts! So rather than be hurt again, many people simply refuse to hope or to believe that anything good will ever happen to them. This type of behavior sets up a negative lifestyle. Everything becomes negative because the thoughts are negative. Remember Proverbs 23:7: "For as he thinks in his heart, so is he."

Many years ago, I was extremely negative. I always say that if I thought two positive thoughts in a row my mind would get in a cramp. My whole philosophy was this: "If you don't expect anything good to happen, then you won't be disappointed when it doesn't."

I had encountered so many disappointments in life—so many devastating things had happened to me—that I was afraid to believe that anything good might happen. I had a terribly negative outlook on everything. Since my thoughts were all negative, so was my mouth; therefore, so was my life.

When I really began to study the Word and to trust God to restore me, one of the first things I realized was that the negativism had to go.

In Matthew 8:13 Jesus tells us that it will be done for us as we have believed. The *King James Version* says, "as thou hast believed, so be it done unto thee." Everything I believed was negative, so naturally many negative things happened to me.

This doesn't mean that you and I can get anything we want by just thinking about it. God has a perfect plan for each of us, and we can't control Him with our thoughts and words. But, we must think and speak in agreement with His will and plan for us.

If you don't have any idea what God's will is for you at this point, at least begin by thinking, "Well, I don't know God's plan, but I know He loves me. Whatever He does will be good, and I'll be blessed."

Begin to think positively about your life.

Practice being positive in each situation that arises. Even if whatever is taking place in your life at the moment is not so good, expect God to bring good out of it, as He has promised in His Word.

All Things Work for Good

We are assured and know that [God being a partner in their labor] all things work together and are [fitting into a plan] for good to and for those who love God and are called according to [His] design and purpose.

Romans 8:28

This Scripture does not say that all things *are* good, but it does say that all things *work together for good.*

Let's say you're planning to go shopping. You get in the car, and it won't start. There are two ways you can look at this situation. You can say, "I knew it! It never fails. Every time I want to do something, it gets all messed up. I figured this shopping trip would end up a flop; my plans always do." Or you can say, "Well, I wanted to go shopping, but it looks like I can't go right now. I'll go later when the car is fixed. In the meantime, I believe this change in plans is going to work out for my good. There is probably some reason I need to be at home today, so I'm going to enjoy my time there."

In Romans 12:16 the Apostle Paul tells us to readily adjust ourselves to people and things. The idea is that we must learn to become the kind of person who plans things but who doesn't fall apart if that plan doesn't work out.

Recently I had an excellent opportunity to practice this principle. Dave and I were in Lake Worth, Florida. We had been ministering there for three days, and we were packing and getting ready to go to the airport to go home. I had planned to wear slacks and a blouse with flat shoes, so I could be comfortable during the return trip.

I started getting dressed and couldn't find my slacks. We looked all over the place and finally found them in the bottom of the closet. They had slipped off the hanger and were terribly wrinkled. We take a portable clothes steamer with us, and I tried to steam out the wrinkles. I put on the outfit and saw that it was just not going to look right. My only other choice was a dress and high heels.

I could feel my emotions getting upset with the situation. You see, anytime we don't get what we want, our feelings will rise up and try to get us into self-pity and a negative attitude. I recognized immediately that I had a choice to make. I could be irritable because things hadn't worked out the way I wanted them to, or I could adjust myself to the situation and go ahead and enjoy the trip home.

Even a person who is really positive won't have everything work out the way he would like it to all the time. But the positive person can go ahead and decide to enjoy himself no matter what happens. The negative person never enjoys anything.

A negative person is no fun to be with. He brings a gloomy overcast to every project. There is a "heaviness" about him. He is a complainer, a murmurer, and a faultfinder. No matter how many good things are going on, he always seems to spot the one thing that could be a potential problem.

When I was in my days of extreme negativism, I could walk into someone's home that had been newly decorated, and rather than seeing and commenting on all the lovely surroundings, I would spot a corner of wallpaper that was loose or a smudge on the window. I am so glad Jesus has set me free to enjoy the good things in life! I am free to believe that with faith and hope in Him, the bad things can be turned around for good.

If you are a negative person, *don't feel condemned!* Condemnation is negative. I'm sharing these things so you can recognize your problem with being negative and begin to trust God to restore you, not to get you to become negative about your negativism.

The pathway to freedom begins when we face the problem without making excuses for it. I'm sure that if you are a negative person there is a reason for it—there always is. But remember, as a Christian, according to the Bible, you are a new person now.

A New Day!

Therefore if any person is [ingrafted] in Christ (the Messiah) he is a new creation (a new creature altogether); the old [previous moral and spiritual condition] has passed away. Behold, the fresh and new has come!

2 Corinthians 5:17

As "a new creation," you don't have to allow the old things that happened to you to keep affecting your new life in Christ. You're a new creature with a new life in Christ. You can have your mind renewed according to the Word of God. Good things are going to happen to you.

Rejoice! It's a new day!

The Work of the Holy Spirit

However, I am telling you nothing but the truth when I say it is profitable (good, expedient, advantageous) for you that I go away. Because if I do not go away, the Comforter (Counselor, Helper, Advocate, Intercessor, Strengthener, Standby) will not come to you [into close fellowship with you]; but if I go away, I will send Him to you [to be in close fellowship with you].

And when He comes, He will convict and convince the world and bring demonstration to it about sin and about righteousness (uprightness of heart and right standing with God) and about judgment.

John 16:7,8

The hardest part of being set free from negativism is facing the truth and saying, "I'm a negative person, and I want to change. I can't change myself, but I believe God will change me as I trust Him. I know it will take time, and I'm not going to get discouraged with myself. *God has begun a good work in me, and He is well able to bring it to full completion*" (see Phil. 1:6).

Ask the Holy Spirit to convict you each time you start to get negative. That is part of His job. John 16:7,8 teaches us that the Holy Spirit will convict us of sin and convince us of righteousness. When the conviction comes, ask God to help you. Don't think you can change yourself. Lean on Him.

Even though I was extremely negative, God let me know that if I would trust Him, He would cause me to be very positive. I was having a hard time trying to keep my mind in a positive pattern. Now, I can't stand negativism. It's like a person who smokes. Many times, a smoker who has quit smoking has no tolerance for cigarettes. I'm that way. I smoked for many years, but after I quit, I couldn't even stand the smell of smoke.

I'm the same way about being negative. I was a very negative person. Now, I can't stand negativism at all; it is almost offensive to me. I guess I've seen so many good changes in my life since I've been delivered from a negative mind that now I'm opposed to anything negative.

I face reality, and I encourage you to do the same. If you are sick, don't say, "I'm not sick," because that's just not true; but you can say, "I believe God is healing me." You don't have to say, "I'll probably get worse and end up in the hospital"; instead, you can say, "God's healing power is working in me right now; I believe I'll be all right."

It is unwise to refuse to face reality; however if our reality is negative we can still have a positive attitude toward it. Always be ready mentally to face whatever comes, believing that God works good out of all things.

A READY MIND

These were more noble than those in Thessalonica, in that they received the word with all readiness of mind, and searched the scriptures daily, whether those things were so.

Acts 17:11 KJV

The Bible says that we are to have a ready mind. That means that we are to have minds that are open to the will of God for us, whatever that will may be.

For example, recently a young lady whom I know experienced the sorrow of a broken engagement. She and the young man were praying about whether or not the Lord would have them continue dating, even though they had decided not to get married at that time. The young lady wanted the relationship to continue and was thinking, hoping, and believing that her former fiancé would call and feel the same way.

I advised her to have a "ready mind" in case things didn't work out that way. She said, "Well, isn't that being negative?"

No, it isn't!

Negativism would be to think, "My life is over; no one will ever want me. I have failed, so now I'll be miserable forever!"

Being positive would be to say, "I'm really sad this thing has happened, but I'm going to trust God. I hope my boyfriend and I can still date. I'm going to ask and believe for our relationship to be restored; but more than anything, I want God's perfect will. If things don't turn out the way I want them to, *I'll survive*, because Jesus lives in me. It may be hard for a while, but I trust the Lord. I believe that in the end everything will work out for the best."

This is facing facts, having a ready mind, and still being positive.

This is what I consider to be a healthy, well-balanced attitude.

THE FORCE OF HOPE

[For Abraham, human reason for] hope being gone, hoped in faith that he should become the father of many nations, as he had been promised, So [numberless] shall your descendants be.

He did not weaken in faith when he considered the [utter] impotence of his own body, which was as good as dead because he was about a hundred years old, or [when he considered] the barrenness of Sarah's [deadened] womb.

No unbelief or distrust made him waver (doubtingly question) concerning the promise of God, but he grew strong and was empowered by faith as he gave praise and glory to God.

Romans 4:18-20

Dave and I believe that our ministry in the Body of Christ will grow each year. We always want to help more people. But we also realize that if God has a different plan, and if we end up at the end of a year with no growth (everything the same as when we started), we cannot let that situation control our joy.

We believe *for* many things, but beyond them all, we believe *in* Someone. That Someone is Jesus. We don't always know what is going to happen. We just know it will always work out for our good!

The more positive you and I become, the more we will be in the flow of God. God is certainly positive, and to flow with Him, we must also be positive.

You may have really adverse circumstances. You may be thinking, "Joyce, if you knew my situation, you wouldn't even expect me to be positive." Being positive in a positive situation is easy. Anyone can do that. But, when we are positive in a negative situation it shows a genuine trust in God and a spiritual maturity that pleases and glorifies God.

I encourage you to reread Romans 4:18-20 in which it is reported that Abraham, after sizing up his situation (he didn't ignore the facts), considered (thought about briefly) the utter impotence of his own body and the barrenness of Sarah's dead womb. Although all human reason for hope was gone, he hoped in faith.

Abraham was very positive about a very negative situation!

Hebrews 6:19 tells us that hope is the anchor of the soul. Hope is the force that keeps us steady in a time of trial. Don't ever stop hoping. If you do, you're going to have a miserable life. If you are already having a miserable life because you have no hope, start hoping. Don't be afraid. I can't promise you that things will always turn out exactly the way you want them to. I can't promise you that you'll never be disappointed. But, even in disappointing times, if they do come, you can hope and be positive. Put yourself in God's miracle-working realm.

Expect a miracle in your life.

Expect good things!

EXPECT TO RECEIVE! TO RECEIVE, EXPECT!

And therefore the Lord [earnestly] waits [expecting, looking, and longing] to be gracious to you; and therefore He lifts Himself up, that He may have mercy on you and show loving-kindness to you. For the Lord is a God of justice. Blessed (happy, fortunate, to be envied) are all those who [earnestly] wait for Him, who expect and look and long for Him [for His victory, His favor, His love, His peace, His joy, and His matchless, unbroken companionship]!

Isaiah 30:18

This passage has become one of my favorite Scriptures. If you will meditate on it, it will begin to bring great hope. In it, God is saying that He is looking for someone to be gracious (good) to, but it cannot be someone with a sour attitude and a negative mind. It must be someone who is expecting (looking and longing for God to be good to him or her).

Evil Forebodings

What are "evil forebodings"?

Shortly after I began to study God's Word, I was combing my hair one morning in the bathroom when I realized that in the atmosphere around me was a vague, threatening feeling that something bad was going to happen. I became aware that I had actually had that feeling with me most of my life.

I asked the Lord, "What is this feeling I always have?"

"Evil forebodings," was the word He put into my heart.

I did not know what that meant, nor had I ever heard of it. Shortly thereafter, I found the phrase in Proverbs 15:15: "All the days of the desponding and afflicted are made evil [by anxious thoughts and forebodings], but he who has a glad heart has a continual feast [regardless of circumstances]."

I realized at that time that most of my life had been made miserable by evil thoughts and forebodings. Yes, I had circumstances that were very difficult, but even when I didn't, I was still miserable because my thoughts were poisoning my outlook and robbing me of ability to enjoy life and see good days. Even if nothing bad was happening at the time, I always vaguely sensed that something bad was about to happen. Because of that I was unable to really enjoy my life.

KEEP YOUR TONGUE FROM EVIL!

For let him who wants to enjoy life and see good days [good—whether apparent or not] keep his tongue free from evil and his lips from guile (treachery, deceit).

1 Peter 3:10

This verse plainly tells us that enjoying life and seeing good days, and having a positive mind and mouth, are linked together.

No matter how negative you are or how long you have been that way, I know you can change because I did. It took time and "heaping helpings" of the Holy Spirit, but it was worth it.

It will be worth it to you too. Whatever happens, trust in the Lord—and be positive! Don't ever let evil forebodings hang around in your atmosphere; instead resist them aggressively in the name of Jesus Christ.

Chapter
6

Mind-Binding Spirits

Mind-Binding Spirits

*I*once reached a place in my walk with God where I was having a hard time believing certain things that I had previously believed. I didn't understand what was wrong with me, and as a result, I got confused. The longer the predicament went on, the more confused I became. The unbelief seemed to be growing by leaps and bounds. I began to question my call; I thought I was losing the vision God had given me for the ministry. I was miserable (unbelief always produces misery). My mind was sluggish and I felt as if I could not believe God no matter how hard I tried.

Be careful for nothing; but in every thing by prayer and supplication with thanksgiving let your requests be made known unto God.

And the peace of God, which passeth all understanding, shall keep your hearts and minds through Christ Jesus.
PHILIPPIANS 4:6,7 KJV

Two days in a row I heard this phrase coming up out of my spirit: "*mind-binding spirits.*" The first day I didn't think much about it. However, the second day, as I began a time of intercession, I heard it again for about the fourth or fifth time: "*mind-binding spirits.*" Although I was unfamiliar with that phrase, it made sense considering how I felt mentally.

I knew from all the people to whom I had ministered that multitudes of believers have trouble with their minds. I thought the Holy Spirit was leading me to pray for the Body of Christ against a spirit called "Mind Binding." So I began to pray and come against mind-binding spirits in Jesus' name. After only a couple of minutes of praying, I felt a tremendous deliverance come to my own mind. It was quite dramatic. The thought of evil spirits lurking around is rather creepy, but they exist. Jesus called demons by name and commanded them to leave.

Delivered From Mind-Binding Spirits

Nearly every deliverance God has brought to me has been progressive and has come about by believing and confessing the Word of God. John 8:31,32 and Psalm 107:20 are my testimony. In John 8:31,32 Jesus says, "If you abide in My word, ...you are truly My disciples. And you will know the Truth, and the Truth will set you free." Psalm 107:20 says of the Lord, "He sends forth His word and heals them and rescues them from the pit and destruction."

But this time I felt and knew immediately that something had happened in my mind. Within minutes I was able to believe again in areas I had been struggling with just prior to my time of prayer.

I'll give you an example. Before being attacked by the mind-binding evil spirits, I believed that according to the Word of God, the fact that I was a woman from Fenton, Missouri, whom no one knew, wouldn't make any difference in my life or ministry (Gal. 3:28). When God was ready, *He* would open doors that no one could close (see Rev. 3:8), and I would preach all over the world the practical, liberating messages He had given me.

I believed I would have the privilege of sharing the gospel throughout the nation by radio and eventually by television (not because of me, but in spite of me). I knew that, according to the Scriptures, God chooses weak and foolish things to confound the wise (see 1 Cor. 1:27). I believed that the Lord was going to use me to heal the sick. I believed that our children would be used in ministry. I believed all sorts of wonderful things that God had placed in my heart. Most of them seemed foolish to reason or mental understanding, but God put them in my heart and gave me supernatural faith to believe what in the natural was unbelievable.

However, when the evil spirits attacked me, I couldn't seem to believe much of anything. I thought things like, "Well, I probably just made all that up. I just believed it because I wanted to, but it probably won't ever happen." But when the spirits left, the ability to believe came rushing back. This experience clarified to me even more than before just how aggressively the devil comes against our mind. He knows if he can control our thoughts that he can control our life.

Pay attention to the condition of your mind and keep it free, peaceful, and full of faith.

DECIDE TO BELIEVE

So too the [Holy] Spirit comes to our aid and bears us up in our weakness; for we do not know what prayer to offer nor how to offer it worthily as we ought, but the Spirit Himself goes to meet our supplication and pleads in our behalf with unspeakable yearnings and groanings too deep for utterance.

Romans 8:26

As Christians, we need to learn to *decide* to believe. God often gives us faith (a product of the Spirit) for things that our minds just can't always seem to come into agreement with. The mind wants to understand everything—the why, the when, and the how of it all. Often, when that understanding is not given by God, the mind refuses to believe what it cannot understand.

It frequently happens that a believer *knows* something in his heart (his inner man), but his mind wars against it.

I had decided long before to believe what the Word says, and to believe the *rhema* (the revealed Word) that God gave me (the things He spoke to me or the promises He gave me personally), even if I didn't understand why, when, or how it would come to pass in my life. As children of God, one of the privileges we have is believing the impossible.

But this thing I had been battling was different; it was beyond decision. I was bound by these mind-binding spirits and just couldn't bring myself to believe.

Thank God that through the Holy Spirit He showed me how to pray, and His power prevailed.

I'm sure that you are reading this book right now because you were led to it. You too may be having problems in this area. If so, I encourage you to pray in Jesus' name. By the power of His blood, come against all evil spirits that hinder godly thoughts. If you feel your mind is sluggish, lazy, and unable to believe, then speak against "mind-binding spirits." Pray this way not just one time but any time you experience difficulty in this area.

The devil never runs out of fiery darts to throw against us when we are trying to go forward. Lift up your shield of faith and remember James 1:2-8 which teaches us that we can ask God for wisdom in trials and He will give it to us and will show us what to do.

I had a problem, a fiery dart I had not encountered before. But God showed me how to pray, and I was set free.

You will be too.

Chapter

7

Think About
What You're Thinking About

Think About What You're Thinking About	Chapter 7

The Word of God teaches us what we should spend our time thinking about.

I will meditate on Your precepts and have respect to Your ways [the paths of life marked out by Your law].

PSALM 119:15

The psalmist said that he thought about or meditated on the precepts of God. That means that he spent a lot of time pondering and thinking on the ways of God, His instructions and His teachings. Psalm 1:3 says that the person who does this "shall be like a tree firmly planted [and tended] by the streams of water, ready to bring forth its fruit in its season; its leaf also shall not fade or wither; and everything he does shall prosper [and come to maturity]."

It is very beneficial to think about God's Word. The more time a person spends meditating on the Word, the more he will reap from the Word.

BE CAREFUL WHAT YOU THINK!

Be careful what you are hearing. The measure [of thought and study] you give [to the truth you hear] will be the measure [of virtue and knowledge] that comes back to you—and more [besides] will be given to you who hear.

Mark 4:24

What a great Scripture! It tells us that the more time we spend thinking about the Word we read and hear, the more power and ability we will have to do it—the more revelation knowledge we will have about what we have read or heard. Basically this tells us that we will get from the Word of God what we put into it.

Notice especially the promise that the amount of thought and study we devote to the Word will determine the amount of virtue and knowledge that will come back to us.

Vine's *An Expository Dictionary of Biblical Words* says that in certain Scriptures of the *King James Version* the Greek word *dunamis* meaning "power" is translated "virtue."[1] According to *The New Strong's Exhaustive Concordance of the Bible*, another translation of *dunamis* is "ability."[2] Most people do not delve into the Word of God very deeply. As a result, they get confused about why they are not powerful Christians living victorious lives.

The truth is that most of them really don't put much effort of their own into the study of the Word. They may go out and hear others teach and preach the Word. They may listen to sermon CDs or read the Bible occasionally, but they are not really dedicated to making the Word a major part of their lives, including spending time thinking about it.

The flesh is basically lazy, and many people want to get something for nothing (with no effort on their part); however, that really is not the way it works. I will say it again, *a person will get out of the word what he is willing to put into it.*

MEDITATE ON THE WORD

Blessed (happy, fortunate, prosperous, and enviable) is the man who walks and lives not in the counsel of the ungodly [following their advice, their plans and purposes], nor stands [submissive and inactive] in the path where sinners walk, nor sits down [to relax and rest] where the scornful [and the mockers] gather.

But his delight and desire are in the law of the Lord, and on His law (the precepts, the instructions, the teachings of God) he habitually meditates (ponders and studies) by day and by night.

Psalm 1:1,2

According to Webster, the word *meditate* means "1. To reflect on: PONDER. 2. To plan or intend in the mind...To engage in contemplation."[3] Vine's *An Expository Dictionary of Biblical Words* says that *meditate* means "primarily, 'to care for,' ...'to attend to, practice,' ...'be diligent in,' ...to practice is the prevalent sense of the word, ...'to ponder, imagine,' ...'to premeditate.'"[4]

Proverbs 4:20 says, "My son, attend to my words; consent and submit to my sayings." If we put Proverbs 4:20 together with these definitions of the word "meditate," we see that we attend to God's Word by meditating on it, by pondering on it, by contemplating it, by rehearsing or practicing it in our thinking. The basic idea is that if we want to do what the Word of God says, we must spend time thinking about it.

Remember the old saying, "Practice makes perfect"? We really do not expect to be experts at anything in life without a lot of practice, so why would we expect Christianity to be any different?

MEDITATION PRODUCES SUCCESS

This Book of the Law shall not depart out of your mouth, but you shall meditate on it day and night, that you may observe and do according to all that is written in it. For then you shall make your way prosperous, and then you shall deal wisely and have good success.

Joshua 1:8

If you want to be a success and to prosper in all your dealings, the Bible says you must meditate on the Word of God day and night.

How much time do you spend thinking about the Word of God? If you are having problems in any area of your life, an honest answer to this question may disclose the reason why.

For most of my life, I didn't think about what I was thinking about. I simply thought whatever fell into my head. I had no revelation that Satan could inject thoughts into my mind. Much of what was in my head was either lies that Satan was telling me or just plain nonsense—things that really were not worth spending my time thinking about. The devil was controlling my life because he was controlling my thoughts.

THINK ABOUT WHAT YOU'RE THINKING ABOUT!

Among these we as well as you once lived and conducted ourselves in the passions of our flesh [our behavior governed by our corrupt and sensual nature], obeying the impulses of the flesh and the thoughts of the mind.

Ephesians 2:3

Paul warns us here that we are not to be governed by our sensual nature or to obey the impulses of our flesh, the thoughts of our carnal mind.

Although I was a Christian, I was having trouble because I had not learned to control my thoughts. I thought about things that kept my mind busy but were not productive in a positive way.

I needed to change my thinking!

One thing the Lord spoke to my heart when He began to teach me about the battlefield of the mind became a major turning point for me. He said, "Think about what you're thinking about." As I began to do so, it was not long before I began to see why I was having so much trouble in my life.

My mind was a mess!

I was thinking all the wrong things.

I went to church, and had done so for years, but I never actually thought about what I heard. It went in one ear and out the other, so to speak. I read some Scriptures in the Bible every day, but never thought about what I was reading. I was not *attending* to the Word. I was not giving any thought and study to what I was hearing. Therefore, no virtue or knowledge was coming back to me.

MEDITATE ON THE WORKS OF GOD

We have thought of Your steadfast love, O God, in the midst of Your temple.

Psalm 48:9

The psalmist David talked frequently about meditating on all the wonderful works of the Lord—the mighty acts of God. He said that he thought on the name of the Lord, the mercy of God, the love of God and many other such things.

When he was feeling depressed, he wrote in Psalm 143:4,5, "Therefore is my spirit overwhelmed and faints within me [wrapped in gloom]; my heart within my bosom grows numb. I remember the days of old; I meditate on all Your doings; I ponder the work of Your hands."

We see from this passage that David's response to his feelings of depression and gloom was not to meditate on the problem. Instead, he actively came against the problem by *choosing* to remember the good times of past days—pondering the doings of God and the works of His hands. In other words, he thought on something good, and it helped him overcome depression.

Never forget this: *your mind plays an important role in your victory.*

I know that it is the power of the Holy Spirit working through the Word of God that brings victory into our lives. But a large part of the work that needs to be done is for us to line up our thinking with God and His Word. If we refuse to do this or choose to think it is unimportant, we will never experience victory.

BE TRANSFORMED BY RENEWING YOUR MIND

Do not be conformed to this world (this age), [fashioned after and adapted to its external, superficial customs], but be transformed (changed) by the [entire] renewal of your mind [by its new ideals and its new attitude], so that you may prove [for yourselves] what is the good and acceptable and perfect will of God, even the thing which is good and acceptable and perfect [in His sight for you].

Romans 12:2

In this passage the Apostle Paul is saying that if we want to see God's good and perfect will proven out in our lives, we can—*if we* have our minds renewed. Renewed to what? Renewed to God's way of thinking. By this process of new thinking we will be changed or transformed into what God intends for us to be. Jesus has made this transformation possible by His death and resurrection. It becomes a reality in our lives by this process of the renewal of the mind.

Let me say at this point, to avoid any confusion, that right thinking has *nothing* to do with salvation. Salvation is based solely on the blood of Jesus, His death on the cross and His resurrection. Many people will be in heaven because they truly accepted Jesus as their Savior, but many of these same people will never have walked in victory or enjoyed the good plan God had for their lives because they did not get their mind renewed according to His Word.

For years, I was one of those people. I was born again. I was going to heaven. I went to church and followed a form of religion, but I really had no victory in my life. The reason is because I was thinking on the wrong things.

THINK ON THESE THINGS

For the rest, brethren, whatever is true, whatever is worthy of reverence and is honorable and seemly, whatever is just, whatever is pure, whatever is lovely and lovable, whatever is kind and winsome and gracious, if there is any virtue and excellence, if there is anything worthy of praise, think on and weigh and take account of these things [fix your minds on them].

Philippians 4:8

The Bible presents a lot of detailed instruction on what kinds of things we are to think about. I am sure that you can see from these various Scriptures that we are instructed to think on good things, things that will build us up and not tear us down.

Our thoughts certainly affect our attitudes and moods. Everything the Lord tells us is for our own good. He knows what will make us happy and what will make us miserable. When a person is full of wrong thoughts he is miserable, and I have learned from personal experience that when someone is miserable, he usually ends up making others miserable also.

You should take inventory on a regular basis and ask yourself, "What have I been thinking about?" Spend some time examining your thought life.

Thinking about what you're thinking about is very valuable because Satan usually deceives people into thinking that the source of their misery or trouble is something other than what it really is. He wants them to think they are unhappy due to what is going on *around* them (their circumstances), but the misery is actually due to what is going on *inside* them (their thoughts).

For many years I really believed that I was unhappy because of things others were doing or not doing. I blamed my misery on my husband and my children. If they would be different, if they would be more attentive to my needs, if they would help around the house more, then, I thought, I would be happy. It was one thing and then another for years. I finally faced the truth, which was that none of these things had to make me unhappy if I chose to have the right attitude. My thoughts were what was making me miserable.

Let me say it one final time: *think about what you are thinking about.* You may locate some of your problems and be on your way to freedom very quickly.

PART II:

Conditions of the Mind

Introduction

*I*n what condition is your mind?

Have you noticed that the condition of your mind changes? One time you may be calm and peaceful, and another time anxious and worried. Or

But we have the mind of Christ (the Messiah) and do hold the thoughts (feelings and purposes) of His heart.
1 CORINTHIANS 2:16

you may make a decision and be sure about it, then later find your mind in a confused condition concerning the very thing you were previously so clear and certain about.

There have been times in my own life when I have experienced these things, as well as others. There have been times when I seemed to be able to believe God without any trouble, and then there have other times when doubt and unbelief haunted me mercilessly.

Because it seems that the mind can be in so many different conditions, I began to wonder, when is my mind normal? I wanted to know what normal was so I could learn to deal with the abnormal thinking patterns immediately upon their arrival.

For example, a critical, judgmental, and suspicious mind should be considered abnormal for a believer. However, for a major portion of my life, it was normal for me—although it should not have been. It was what I was used to, and even though my thinking was very wrong and was causing a lot of problems in my life, I did not know that there was anything wrong with what I was thinking.

I did not know that I could do anything about my thought life. I was a believer, and had been for years, but I had no teaching at all about my thought life or about the proper condition for a believer's mind to be in.

Our minds are not born again with the New Birth experience—they have to be renewed (see Rom. 12:2). As I have said several times, the renewal of the mind is a process that requires time. Do not be devastated, even if you read the next part of this book and discover that most of the time your mind is in a condition that is abnormal for someone claiming Christ as Savior. Recognizing the problem is the first step toward recovery.

In my own case, I began to get a lot more serious about my relationship with the Lord several years ago, and it was at that time that He began revealing to me that many of my problems were rooted in wrong thinking. My mind was in a mess! I doubt that it was ever in the condition it should have been—and if it was, it did not last long.

I felt overwhelmed when I began to see how much wrong thinking I was addicted to. I would try to cast down the wrong thoughts that came into my mind, and they would come right back. But, little by little, freedom and deliverance did come.

Satan will aggressively fight against the renewal of your mind, but it is vital that you press on and continue to pray and study in this area until you gain measurable victory.

When is your mind normal? Is it supposed to wander all over the place, or should you be able to keep it focused on what you're doing? Should you be upset and confused, or should you be peaceful and reasonably sure of the direction you should be taking in life? Should your mind be full of doubt and unbelief, should you be anxious and worried, tormented by fear? Or is it the privilege of the child of God to cast all his care upon Him (see 1 Pet. 5:7)?

The Word of God teaches us that we have the mind of Christ. What do you think His mind was like when He lived on the earth—not only as the Son of God but also as the Son of Man?

Prayerfully proceed into the next part of *Battlefield of the Mind*. I believe it will open your eyes to normal and abnormal mindsets for the person who is a disciple of Jesus and who has determined to walk in victory.

Chapter
8

When Is My Mind Normal?

When Is My Mind Normal?

Notice that Paul prays that you and I will gain wisdom by having "the eyes of (our) heart" enlightened. Based on several things I have studied, I describe "the eyes of the heart" as the mind.

As Christians, in what condition should our mind be? In other words, what should be the normal state of the mind of the believer? In order to answer that question, we must look at the different functions of the mind and the spirit.

According to the Word of God, the mind and the spirit work together: this is what I call the principle of "the mind aiding the spirit."

[For I always pray to] the God of our Lord Jesus Christ, the Father of glory, that He may grant you a spirit of wisdom and revelation [of insight into mysteries and secrets] in the [deep and intimate] knowledge of Him,

By having the eyes of your heart flooded with light, so that you can know and understand the hope to which He has called you, and how rich is His glorious inheritance in the saints (His set-apart ones).

EPHESIANS 1:17,18

To better understand this principle, let's see how it works in the life of the believer.

THE MIND-SPIRIT PRINCIPLE

For what person perceives (knows and understands) what passes through a man's thoughts except the man's own spirit within him? Just so no one discerns (comes to know and comprehend) the thoughts of God except the Spirit of God.

1 Corinthians 2:11

When a person receives Christ as His personal Savior, the Holy Spirit comes to dwell in him. The Bible teaches us that the Holy Spirit knows the mind of God. Just as a person's own spirit within him is the only one who knows his thoughts, so the Spirit of God is the only One Who knows the mind of God.

Since the Holy Spirit dwells in us, and since He knows the mind of God, one of His purposes is to reveal to us God's wisdom and revelation. That wisdom and revelation is imparted to our spirit, and our spirit then enlightens the eyes of our heart, which is our mind. The Holy Spirit does this so we can understand on a practical level what is being ministered to us spiritually.

NORMAL OR ABNORMAL?

As believers, we are spiritual, and we are also natural. The natural does not always understand the spiritual; therefore, it is vitally necessary for our minds to be enlightened concerning what is going on in our spirits. The Holy Spirit desires to bring us this enlightenment, but *the mind often misses what the spirit is attempting to reveal because it is too busy*. A mind that is too busy is abnormal. The mind is normal when it is at rest—not blank, but at rest.

The mind should not be filled with reasoning, worry, anxiety, fear, and the like. It should be calm, quiet, and serene. As we proceed into this second section of the book you will observe several abnormal conditions of the mind and possibly recognize them as frequent conditions of your own mind.

It is important to understand that the mind needs to be kept in the "normal" condition described in this chapter.

Compare it with the usual condition of our minds and you will see why we frequently have very little revealed to us by the Holy Spirit, and why far too often we feel ourselves lacking in wisdom and revelation.

Remember, the Holy Spirit attempts to enlighten the mind of the believer. The Holy Spirit gives information from God to the person's spirit, and if his spirit and mind are aiding one another, then he can walk in divine wisdom and revelation. But if his mind is too busy, it will miss what the Lord is attempting to reveal to him through his spirit.

The Still, Small Voice

And he said, Go forth, and stand upon the mount before the LORD. And, behold, the LORD passed by, and a great and strong wind rent the mountains, and brake in pieces the rocks before the LORD; but the LORD was not in the wind: and after the wind an earthquake; but the LORD was not in the earthquake:

And after the earthquake a fire; but the LORD was not in the fire: and after the fire a still small voice.

1 Kings 19:11,12 KJV

For years I prayed for revelation, asking God to reveal things to me by His Spirit Who lived within me. I knew that request was scriptural. I believed the Word and felt sure I should be asking and receiving. Yet, much of the time I felt like what I called a "spiritual dunce." Then I learned that I was not receiving much of what the Holy Spirit wanted to reveal to me simply because my mind was so wild and busy that it was missing the information being offered.

Imagine two people in a room together. One is trying to whisper a secret to the other. If the room is filled with a loud noise, even though the message is being communicated, the one waiting for the secret information will miss it simply because the room is so noisy he can't hear. Unless he is paying close attention, he may not even realize that he is being spoken to.

That's the way it is with communication between God's Spirit and our spirit. The ways of the Holy Spirit are gentle; most of the time He speaks to us as He did to the prophet in this passage—in "a still small voice." It is therefore vital that we learn to keep ourselves in a condition conducive to hearing.

The Spirit and the Mind

Then what am I to do? I will pray with my spirit [by the Holy Spirit that is within me], but I will also pray [intelligently] with my mind and understanding.

1 Corinthians 14:15

Perhaps a better way to understand this principle of "mind-aiding spirit" is to think of prayer. In this verse the Apostle Paul said that he prayed both with his spirit and with his mind.

I understand what Paul is talking about because I do the same thing. I frequently pray in the spirit (in an unknown tongue); after I have prayed that way for a while, often something will come to my mind to pray in English (my known tongue). I believe in this way the mind aids the spirit. They work together to get the knowledge and wisdom of God to me in a way that I can understand it.

This also works in the reverse. There are times when I want to pray, so I make myself available to God for prayer. If there is no particular stirring in my spirit, I simply begin to pray out of my mind. I pray about issues or situations that I am aware of. Sometimes these prayers seem really flat—there is no help coming from my spirit. I seem to be struggling, so I go on to something else that I already know about.

I continue in this fashion until the Holy Spirit within me takes hold with me on some issue. When He does, then I know I have hit on something that He wants me to pray about, not just something I am trying to pray about. In this way my mind and my spirit are working together, aiding one another in accomplishing the will of God.

TONGUES AND INTERPRETATION

Therefore, the person who speaks in an [unknown] tongue should pray [for the power] to interpret and explain what he says. For if I pray in an [unknown] tongue, my spirit [by the Holy Spirit within me] prays, but my mind is unproductive [it bears no fruit and helps nobody].

1 Corinthians 14:13,14

Another example of the way the spirit and the mind work together is the gift of tongues with interpretation. If you are not familiar with the gifts of the Holy Spirit, I strongly encourage you to study them in Scripture and keep an open mind to God in this area. Pray and ask

Him to teach you about all the supernatural gifts of the Holy Spirit and even to lead you to good resources that will help you study and gain understanding. One Corinthians chapters 12, 13, and 14 are a good place to begin.

When I speak in tongues, my mind is unfruitful until God gives either me or someone else the understanding of what I am saying; then my mind becomes fruitful.

Please keep in mind that the gifts are not tongues and translation. Translation is an exact word-for-word account of the message, whereas in interpretation one person gives an understanding of what another has said, but in the interpreter 's own style as expressed through his own particular personality.

Let me give you an example: Sister Smith may stand up in church and give a message in an unknown tongue. It has come from her spirit, and neither she nor anyone else knows what she has said. God may cause me to understand what the message was, but perhaps in a general way. As I step out in faith, and begin to interpret what was spoken, I make the message understandable to all. But it comes through me in my own unique way of expression.

Praying in the spirit (in an unknown tongue), and interpretation (of that unknown tongue) is a marvelous way to understand the principle of "mind-aiding spirit." The spirit is speaking something, and the mind is given understanding.

Now just think about this: if Sister Smith speaks in an unknown tongue, and God is looking for someone to give forth the interpretation, He will have to pass me by if my mind is too wild and busy to listen. Even if He tries to give the interpretation to me, I will not receive it.

When I was young in the Lord and learning about spiritual gifts, I prayed almost exclusively in tongues. After quite some time had passed, I began to feel bored with my prayer life. As I talked to the Lord about it, He let me know that I was bored because I had no understanding of what I was praying about. Although I realize that I do not *always* have to understand what I am saying when I pray in the spirit, I have learned that this type of prayer is out of balance and not the most fruitful if I *never* have any understanding.

PEACEFUL, ALERT MIND

You will guard him and keep him in perfect and constant peace whose mind [both its inclination and its character] is stayed on You, because he commits himself to You, leans on You, and hopes confidently in You.

Isaiah 26:3

I hope you can readily see from these examples that your mind and your spirit certainly do work together, and the two are closely linked to one another. *Therefore, it is of utmost importance that your mind be maintained in a normal condition.* Otherwise, it cannot aid your spirit in helping you live a spirit-filled life.

Satan, of course, knows this fact, so he attacks your mind, waging war against you on the battlefield of your mind. He wants to overload and overwork your mind by filling it with every kind of wrong thought so it cannot be free and available to the Holy Spirit working through your own human spirit.

The mind should be kept peaceful. As the prophet Isaiah tells us, when the mind is stayed on the right things, it will be at rest.

Yet the mind should also be alert. This becomes impossible when it is loaded down with things it was never intended to carry.

Think it over: how much of the time is your mind normal?

Chapter
9

A Wandering, Wondering Mind

A Wandering, Wondering Mind

*I*n the previous chapter we stated that a mind too busy is abnormal. Another condition of the mind that is abnormal is for it to be wandering all over the place. An inability to concentrate indicates mental attack from the devil.

Wherefore gird up the loins of your mind.
1 PETER 1:13 KJV

Many people have spent years allowing their minds to wander because they have never applied principles of discipline to their thought life.

Quite often people who cannot seem to concentrate think they are mentally deficient. However, an inability to concentrate can be the result of years of letting the mind do whatever it wants to do, whenever it wants to do it. A lack of concentration can also be a symptom of vitamin deficiency. Certain B-vitamins enhance concentration Therefore, if you have an inability to concentrate, ask yourself if you're eating right and are nutritionally sound.

Extreme fatigue can also affect concentration. I have found that when I am excessively tired Satan will try to attack my mind because he knows it is more difficult to resist him during these times. The devil wants you and me to think that we are mentally deficient so we will not attempt to do anything to cause him problems. He wants us to passively accept whatever lies he tells us.

One of our daughters had difficulty concentrating during her childhood years. Reading was difficult for her because concentration and comprehension go hand in hand. Many children and even some adults don't comprehend what they read. Their eyes scan the words on the page, but their minds do not really understand what is being read.

Often a lack of comprehension is the result of a lack of concentration. I know that, for myself, I can read a chapter in the Bible or a book and all of a sudden realize that I do not know what I have read at all. I can go back and read it again, and it all seems new to me because, even though my eyes were scanning the words on the page, my mind had wandered off somewhere else. Because I did not stay focused on what I was doing, I failed to comprehend what I was reading.

Often the real problem behind a lack of comprehension is a lack of attention caused by a wandering mind. Recently Dave and I and a couple we are friends with in Utah were riding in the car together. Simultaneously the other couple and I heard Dave say, "I bless myself." We laughed when we all realized that even though Dave had sneezed loudly, none of us consciously heard him because we had all gone somewhere else in our minds. I spoke up and said, "Sorry I didn't hear you; I was in the office in St. Louis." The man in the back-seat laughed and said, "I was in Florida taking care of some business." His wife laughed too and said, "I was in Dallas in my office handling a situation."

In a few moments of time the three of us had all gone to another state mentally. It showed us how quickly the mind can wander from what is really happening where we are. We laughed because Dave had to bless himself, since none of us were mentally there. It was funny, but it was also eye-opening to realize how we can lose awareness of what is happening around us by not focusing on the present.

A Wandering Mind

Keep your foot [give your mind to what you are doing].
Ecclesiastes 5:1

I believe the expression "keep your foot" means "don't lose your balance or get off track." The amplification of this phrase indicates that one stays on track by keeping his mind on what he is doing.

I had a wandering mind and had to train it by discipline. It was not easy, and sometimes I still have a relapse. While trying to complete some project, I will suddenly realize that my mind has just wandered off onto something else that has nothing to do with the issue at hand. I have not yet arrived at a place of perfect concentration, but at least I understand how important it is not to allow my mind to go wherever it wishes, whenever it desires.

Webster's dictionary defines the word *wander* as: "1. To move about aimlessly: ROAM. 2. To go by an indirect route or at no set pace: AMBLE. 3. To proceed in an irregular course or action: MEANDER.... 5. To think or express oneself unclearly or incoherently." [1]

If you are like me, you can be sitting in a church service listening to the speaker, really enjoying and benefiting from what is being said, when suddenly your mind begins to wander. After a while you "wake up" to find that you don't remember a thing that has been going on. Even though your body stayed in church, your mind has been at the shopping center browsing through the stores or home in the kitchen cooking dinner.

Remember, in spiritual warfare the mind is the battlefield. That is where the enemy makes his attack. He knows very well that even though a person attends church, if he can't keep his mind on what is being taught, he will gain absolutely nothing by being there. The devil knows that a person cannot discipline himself to complete a project if he cannot discipline his mind and keep it on what he is doing.

This mind-wandering phenomenon also occurs during conversation. There are times when my husband, Dave, is talking to me and I listen for a while; then all of a sudden I realize that I have not heard a thing he has been saying. Why? Because I allowed my mind to wander off on something else. My body was standing there appearing to listen, yet in my mind I heard nothing.

For many years, when this sort of thing happened, I would pretend that I knew exactly what Dave was saying. Now I stop and say,

"Can you back up and repeat that? I let my mind wander off, and I did not hear a thing you said."

In this way, I feel that at least I am dealing with the problem. Confronting issues is the only way to get on the victorious side of them!

I have decided that if the devil went to the trouble to attack me with a wandering mind, then perhaps something was being said that I needed to hear.

One way to combat the enemy in this area is by taking advantage of the recorded messages provided by most churches. If you haven't yet learned to discipline your mind to keep it on what is being said in church, then buy a recording of the sermon each week and listen to it as many times as you need in order to get the message.

The devil will give up when he sees that you are not going to give in.

Remember, Satan wants you to think that you are mentally deficient—that something is wrong with you. But the truth is, you just need to begin disciplining your mind. Don't let it run all over town, doing whatever it pleases. Begin today to "keep your foot," to keep your mind on what you're doing. You will need to practice for a while. Breaking old habits and forming new ones always takes time, but it is worth it in the end. The present moment is the greatest gift we have from God, but if *we* are not present we miss it.

A WONDERING MIND

Truly I tell you, whoever says to this mountain, Be lifted up and thrown into the sea! and does not doubt at all in his heart but believes that what he says will take place, it will be done for him.

For this reason I am telling you, whatever you ask for in prayer, believe (trust and be confident) that it is granted to you, and you will [get it].

Mark 11:23,24

Faced with one thing or another, I frequently began to hear myself say, "I wonder." For example:

"I wonder what the weather will be like tomorrow."

"I wonder what I should wear to the party."

"I wonder what kind of grades Danny [my son] will get on his report card."

"I wonder how many people will show up at the seminar."

The dictionary partially defines the word *wonder* in the noun form as "a feeling of puzzlement or doubt" and in the verb form as "to be filled with curiosity or doubt."[2]

I have come to learn that I am much better off doing something positive than just wondering all the time about everything imaginable. Instead of wondering what kind of grades Danny will get, I can believe that he will make good grades. Rather than wondering what I should wear to the party, I can decide what to wear. Instead of wondering about the weather or about how many people will attend one of my meetings, I can just turn the matter over to the Lord, trusting Him to work out all things for good regardless of what happens.

UPDATE: Our son Danny did not like school and struggled all the way through so I did a lot of wondering about him and his future. I thought you would enjoy knowing that he is currently the CEO at Joyce Meyer Ministries. All my wondering was wasted time. God knew His future and had everything under control.

Although some wondering about things is normal, if it is excessive it can leave a person in indecision, and indecision causes confusion. Wondering, indecision and confusion prevent an individual from receiving from God, by faith, the answer to his prayer or need.

Notice that in Mark 11:23,24 Jesus did not say, "Whatever you ask for in prayer, *wonder* if you will get it." Instead, He said, "Whatever you ask for in prayer, *believe* that you will receive it—and you will!"

As Christians, as *believers,* we are to believe—not doubt!

Chapter
10

A Confused Mind

A Confused Mind

We have discovered that wondering and confusion are relatives. Wondering, rather than being definite in thought, can and does cause doubt and confusion.

James 1:5-8 are excellent Scriptures that help us understand how to overcome wondering, doubt, and confusion and to receive what we need from God. To me, the "man of two minds" (the *King James Version* calls him "a double-minded man") is the picture of confusion as he constantly goes back and forth, back and forth, never deciding on anything. As soon as he thinks he has made a decision, here comes wondering, doubt, and confusion to get him operating once again in two minds. He is uncertain about everything.

I lived much of my life like that, not realizing that the devil had declared war against me and that my mind was the battlefield. I was totally confused about everything, and didn't understand why.

If any of you is deficient in wisdom, let him ask of the giving God [Who gives] to everyone liberally and ungrudgingly, without reproaching or faultfinding, and it will be given him.

Only it must be in faith that he asks with no wavering (no hesitating, no doubting). For the one who wavers (hesitates, doubts) is like the billowing surge out at sea that is blown hither and thither and tossed by the wind.

For truly, let not such a person imagine that he will receive anything [he asks for] from the Lord.

[For being as he is] a man of two minds (hesitating, dubious, irresolute), [he is] unstable and unreliable and uncertain about everything [he thinks, feels, decides].

JAMES 1:5-8

REASONING LEADS TO CONFUSION

O ye of little faith, why reason ye among yourselves?
Matthew 16:8 KJV

Thus far, we have talked about wondering and we will talk more about doubt in the next chapter. Right now I would like to elaborate a little more on confusion.

A large percentage of God's people are admittedly confused. Why? As we have seen, one reason is wondering. Another is reasoning. The dictionary partially defines the word *reason* in the noun form as an "underlying fact or motive that provides logical sense for a premise or occurrence" and in the verb form as "to use the faculty of reason: think logically."[1]

A simple way to say it is, reasoning occurs when a person tries to figure out the "why" behind something. Reasoning causes the mind to revolve around and around a situation, issue, or event attempting to understand all its intricate component parts. We are reasoning when we dissect a statement or teaching to see if it is logical, and disregard it if it is not.

Satan frequently steals the will of God from us due to reasoning. The Lord may direct us to do a certain thing, but if it does not make sense—if it is not logical—we may be tempted to disregard it. What God leads a person to do does not always make logical sense to his mind. His spirit may affirm it and his mind reject it, especially if it would be out of the ordinary or unpleasant or if it would require personal sacrifice or discomfort. It is always nice if the spirit and mind agree, but if they don't, we should always choose to follow the spirit.

DON'T REASON IN THE MIND, JUST OBEY IN THE SPIRIT

But the natural man receiveth not the things of the Spirit of God: for they are foolishness unto him: neither can he know them, because they are spiritually discerned.

1 Corinthians 2:14 KJV

Here is a practical, personal illustration that I hope will help bring more understanding on this issue of reasoning in the mind versus obedience in the spirit.

One morning as I was getting dressed to minister in a weekly meeting that I conducted near my hometown, I started thinking about the woman who ran our ministry of helps there and how faithful she had been. A desire rose up in my heart to do something to bless her in some way.

"Father, Ruth Ann has been such a blessing to us all these years," I prayed, "what can I do to bless her?"

Immediately, my eyes fell on a new red dress that was hanging in my closet, and I knew in my heart the Lord was prompting me to give that dress to Ruth Ann. Although I'd bought it three months earlier, I had never worn it. As a matter of fact, it was still hanging under the plastic bag I'd brought it home in. I really liked it, but every time I thought about wearing it, for some reason I just had no desire to put it on.

Remember, I said that when my eyes fell on the red dress, I *knew* I should give it to Ruth Ann. However, I really did not *want* to give it up, so I immediately began to reason in my mind that God could not be telling me to give her the red dress because it was brand new, never worn, rather expensive—and I had even purchased red and silver earrings to match it!

Had I kept my carnal mind out of the situation and continued to be sensitive to God in my spirit, everything would have gone nicely, but we humans have an ability to deceive ourselves through reasoning when we really don't want to do what God is saying. Within a couple of minutes I had forgotten the whole thing and had gone on about my business. The bottom line was that I did not want to give the dress away because it was new and I liked it. My mind reasoned that the desire I felt could not be God, but that the devil was trying to take from me something I enjoyed.

Some weeks later I was getting ready for another meeting at the same location, just as before, when once again Ruth Ann's name came up in my heart. I began to pray for her. I repeated the whole scene again, saying, "Father, Ruth Ann has been such a blessing to us, what can I do to bless her?" Immediately, I saw the red dress again and I got a sinking feeling in my flesh because I now remembered the other incident (which I had quickly and totally forgotten).

This time there was no squirming out of it; either I had to face the fact that God was showing me what to do and do it, or I simply had to say, "I know what You are showing me, Lord, but I am just not going to do it." I love the Lord too much to willfully, knowingly disobey Him, so I began to talk to Him about the red dress.

Within minutes I realized that on the previous occasion I had reasoned my way right out of the will of God, and it had taken only a moment to do it. I had thought that I couldn't be hearing from the Lord because the dress was new. Yet now I realized that the Bible says nothing about giving away only old things! It would be more of a sacrifice for me to give the dress away because it was new, but it would also be more of a blessing to Ruth Ann.

As I opened up my heart to God, He began to show me that I had purchased the dress for Ruth Ann to begin with; that was the reason I could never bring myself to wear it. The Lord had intended to use me as His agent to bless her all the time. But I'd had my own idea about the dress and, until I was willing to lay down my idea, I could not be led by the Spirit.

This particular incident taught me a lot. The realization of how easily we can be led by our heads and allow reasoning to keep us out of God's will provoked in me a "reverential" fear of reasoning.

Remember, according to 1 Corinthians 2:14, the natural man does not understand the spiritual man. My carnal mind (my natural man) did not understand giving away a new dress I had never worn, but my spirit (my spiritual man) understood it well.

I hope this example will bring more understanding to you in this area and help you walk in the will of God more than ever before.

(By the way, I know you're probably wondering if I ever gave Ruth Ann the red dress. Yes, I did, and now she works in our office full time and still wears the red dress to work occasionally.)

UPDATE: After Ruth Ann wore the red dress for several years, she returned it to me as a gift. It is very much out of style now, but I keep it to remind me of the time I reasoned my way out of obeying God over what is now a worn-out, out-of-style piece of red material that nobody will ever wear again.

BE A DOER OF THE WORD!

But be doers of the Word [obey the message], and not merely listeners to it, betraying yourselves [into deception by reasoning contrary to the Truth].

James 1:22

Any time we see what the Word says and refuse to do it, reasoning has somehow gotten involved and deceived us into believing something other than the truth. We cannot spend excessive time trying to understand (mentally) everything the Word says. If we bear witness in the spirit, we can move ahead and do it.

I have found out that God wants me to obey Him, whether or not I feel like it, want to, or think it is a good idea.

When God speaks, through His Word or in our inner man, we are not to reason, debate, or ask ourselves if what He has said is logical.

When God speaks, we are to mobilize—not rationalize.

TRUST GOD, NOT HUMAN REASON

Lean on, trust in, and be confident in the Lord with all your heart and mind and do not rely on your own insight or understanding.

Proverbs 3:5

In other words, do not rely on reasoning. Reasoning opens the door for deception and brings much confusion.

I once asked the Lord why so many people are confused and He said to me, "Tell them to stop trying to figure everything out, and they will stop being confused." I have found it to be absolutely true. Reasoning and confusion go together.

You and I can ponder a thing in our heart, we can hold it before the Lord and see if He desires to give us understanding, but the minute we start feeling confused, we have gone too far.

Reasoning is dangerous for many reasons, but one of them is this: we can reason and figure something out that seems to make sense to us. But what we have reasoned to be correct may still be incorrect.

The human mind likes logic and order and reason. It likes to deal with what it understands. Therefore, we have a tendency to put things into neat little bins in the compartments of our mind, thinking, "This must be the way it is because it fits so nicely here." We can find something our minds are comfortable with and still be totally wrong.

The Apostle Paul said in Romans 9:1, "I am speaking the truth in Christ. I am not lying; my conscience [enlightened and prompted] by the Holy Spirit bearing witness with me." Paul knew he was doing the right thing, not because his reasoning said it was right, but because it bore witness in his spirit.

As we have seen, the mind does, at times, aid the spirit. The mind and the spirit do work together, but the spirit is the more noble organ and should always be honored above the mind.

If we know in our spirit that a thing is wrong, we should not allow reasoning to talk us into doing it. Also, if we know something is right, we must not allow reasoning to talk us out of doing it.

God gives us understanding on many issues, but we do not have to understand everything to walk with the Lord and in obedience to

His will. There are times when God leaves huge question marks as tools in our lives to stretch our faith. Unanswered questions crucify the flesh life. It is difficult for human beings to give up reasoning and simply trust God, but once the process is accomplished, the mind enters into a place of rest.

Reasoning is one of the "busy activities" in which the mind engages that prevents discernment and revelation knowledge. There is a big difference in head knowledge and revelation knowledge.

I don't know about you, but I want God to reveal things to me in such a way that I *know* in my spirit that what has been revealed to my mind is correct. I don't want to reason, to figure, and to be logical, rotating my mind around and around an issue until I am worn out and confused. I want to experience the peace of mind and heart that comes from trusting in God, not in my own human insight and understanding.

You and I must grow to the place where we are satisfied to know the One Who knows, even if we ourselves do not know.

RESOLVE TO KNOW NOTHING BUT CHRIST

As for myself, brethren, when I came to you, I did not come proclaiming to you the testimony and evidence or mystery and secret of God [concerning what He has done through Christ for the salvation of men] in lofty words of eloquence or human philosophy and wisdom;

For I resolved to know nothing (to be acquainted with nothing, to make a display of the knowledge of nothing, and to be conscious of nothing) among you except Jesus Christ (the Messiah) and Him crucified.

1 Corinthians 2:1,2

This was Paul's approach to knowledge and reasoning, and I have come to understand and appreciate it. It took a long time, but I finally realized that in many instances, the less I know the happier I am. Sometimes we find out so much it makes us quite miserable.

I was always a very curious, inquisitive person. I had to have everything figured out in order to be satisfied. God began to show me that my constant reasoning was the basis of my confusion and that it was preventing me from receiving what He wanted to give me. He said, "Joyce, you must lay aside carnal reasoning if you ever expect to have discernment."

I realize now that I felt more secure if I had things figured out. I did not want any loose ends in my life. I wanted to be in control—and when I did not understand things, I felt out of control and frightened. But I was lacking something. I had no peace of mind and was physically worn out from reasoning.

This type of continual wrong mental activity will even make your physical body tired. It can leave you exhausted!

God required me to give it up, and I strongly suggest the same thing for anyone who is addicted to reasoning. Yes, I said *addicted* to reasoning. We can become addicted to wrong mental activity just as someone else can get addicted to drugs or alcohol or nicotine. I was addicted to reasoning and when I gave it up I had withdrawal symptoms. I felt lost and frightened because I did not know what was going on. I even felt bored.

I had spent so much of my mental time reasoning that when I gave it up, I had to become accustomed to my mind being so peaceful. For a while it seemed boring, but now I love it. While I used to run my mind all the time over and over on everything, now I can't tolerate the pain and labor of reasoning.

Reasoning is not the normal condition in which God wants our mind to reside.

Be aware that when the mind is filled with reasoning, it is not normal; at least not for the Christian who intends to be victorious— the believer who intends to win the war that is fought on the battlefield of the mind.

Chapter
11

A Doubtful
and Unbelieving Mind

A Doubtful and Unbelieving Mind

Chapter

11

We usually talk about doubt and unbelief together as if they are one and the same. Actually although they can be connected, the two are very different things.

O you of little faith, why did you doubt?

MATTHEW 14:31

And He marveled because of their unbelief.

MARK 6:6

Vine's Expository Dictionary of Old and New Testament Words partially defines *doubt* in the verb form as "to stand in two ways...implying uncertainty which way to take; ...said of believers whose faith is small....being anxious, through a distracted state of mind, of wavering between hope and fear."[1]

The same dictionary notes that one of the two Greek words translated as *unbelief* "is always rendered 'disobedience' in the R.V." (the Revised Version of the King James translation).[2]

As we look then at these two powerful tools of the enemy, we see that doubt causes a person to waver between two opinions, whereas unbelief leads to disobedience.

I think it is going to be helpful to be able to recognize exactly what the devil is trying to attack us with. Are we dealing with doubt or with unbelief?

DOUBT

How long will you halt and limp between two opinions?
1 Kings 18:21

I heard a story that will shed light on doubt.

There was a man who was sick and who was confessing the Word over his body, quoting healing Scriptures and believing for his healing to manifest. While doing so, he was intermittently attacked with thoughts of doubt.

After he had gone through a hard time and was beginning to get discouraged, God opened his eyes to the spirit world. This is what he saw: a demon speaking lies to him, telling him that he was not going to get healed and that confessing the Word was not going to work. But he also saw that each time he confessed the Word, light would come out of his mouth like a sword, and the evil spirit would cower and fall backward.

As God showed him this vision, the man then understood why it was so important to keep speaking the Word. He saw that he did have faith, which is why the evil spirit was attacking him with doubt.

Doubt is not something God puts in us. The Bible says that God gives every man a "measure of faith" (Rom. 12:3 KJV). God has placed faith in our heart, but the devil tries to negate our faith by attacking us with doubt.

Doubt comes in the form of thoughts that are in opposition to the Word of God. This is why it is so important for us to know the Word of God. If we know the Word, then we can recognize when the devil is lying to us. Be assured that he lies to us in order to steal what Jesus purchased for us through His death and resurrection.

DOUBT AND UNBELIEF

[For Abraham, human reason for] hope being gone, hoped in faith that he should become the father of many nations, as he had been promised, So [numberless] shall your descendants be.

He did not weaken in faith when he considered the [utter] impotence of his own body, which was as good as dead because he was about a hundred years old, or [when he considered] the barrenness of Sarah's [deadened] womb.

No unbelief or distrust made him waver (doubtingly question) concerning the promise of God, but he grew strong and was empowered by faith as he gave praise and glory to God.

Fully satisfied and assured that God was able and mighty to keep
His word and to do what He had promised.

Romans 4:18-21

When I am in a battle, knowing what God has promised and yet
being attacked with doubt and unbelief, I like to read or meditate on
this passage.

Abraham had been given a promise by God that He would cause
him to have an heir from his own body. Many years had come and
gone and still there was no child as a result of Abraham and Sarah's
relationship. Abraham was still standing in faith, believing what God
had said would come to pass. As he stood, he was being attacked
with thoughts of doubt, and the spirit of unbelief was pressing him
to disobey God.

Disobedience in a situation like this can simply be to give up
when God is prompting us to press on. Disobedience is disregarding
the voice of the Lord, or whatever God is speaking to us personally,
not just transgressing the Ten Commandments.

Abraham continued to be steadfast. He kept praising and giving
glory to God. The Bible states that as he did so, he grew strong in
faith.

You see, when God tells us something or asks us to do something, the faith to believe it or to do it comes with the word from
God. It would be ridiculous for God to expect us to do something
and not give us the ability to believe that we can do it. Satan knows
how dangerous we will be with a heart full of faith, so he attacks us
with doubt and unbelief.

*It is not that we don't have faith, it is just that Satan is trying to
destroy our faith with lies.*

Let me give you an example. It concerns the time when I received
my call to the ministry. It was an ordinary morning like any other,
except that I had been filled with the Holy Spirit three weeks earlier.

I had just finished listening to my first recorded teaching. It was a message titled "Cross Over to the Other Side." I was stirred in my heart and amazed that anyone could teach for one whole hour from one Scripture and that all of his teaching would be interesting.

As I was making my bed, I suddenly felt an intense desire well up in me to teach God's Word. Then the voice of the Lord came to me saying, "You will go all over the place and teach My Word, and you will have a large teaching tape ministry." I did not hear an audible voice, but one in my heart that enabled me to believe that I could do what God was showing me.

There would have been no natural reason at all for me to believe that God had actually spoken to me, or that I could or ever would do what I thought I had just heard. I had many problems within myself. I would not have appeared to be "ministry material," but God chooses the weak and foolish things of the world to confound the wise (see 1 Cor. 1:27 KJV). He looks on the heart of man and not the flesh (see 1 Sam. 16:7). If the heart is right, God can change the flesh.

Although there was nothing in the natural to indicate that I should believe, when the desire came over me, I was filled with faith that I could do what the Lord wanted me to do. When God calls, He gives desire, faith, and ability to do the job. But, I also want to tell you that during the years I spent in training and waiting, the devil regularly attacked me with doubt and unbelief.

God places dreams and visions in the hearts of His people; they begin as little "seeds." Just as a woman has a seed planted into her womb when she becomes pregnant, so we become "pregnant," so to speak, with the things God speaks and promises. During the "pregnancy," Satan works hard to try and get us to "abort" our dreams. One of the tools he uses is doubt; another is unbelief. Both of these work against the mind.

Faith is a product of the spirit; it is a spiritual force. The enemy doesn't want you and me to get our mind in agreement with our spirit. He knows that if God places faith in us to do a thing, and we get positive and start consistently believing that we can actually do it, then we will do considerable damage to his kingdom.

KEEP WALKING ON THE WATER!

But the boat was by this time out on the sea, many furlongs [a furlong is one-eighth of a mile] distant from the land, beaten and tossed by the waves, for the wind was against them.

And in the fourth watch [between 3:00-6:00 a.m.] of the night, Jesus came to them, walking on the sea.

And when the disciples saw Him walking on the sea, they were terrified and said, It is a ghost! And they screamed out with fright.

But instantly He spoke to them, saying, Take courage! I AM! Stop being afraid! And Peter answered Him, Lord, if it is You, command me to come to You on the water.

He said, Come! So Peter got out of the boat and walked on the water, and he came toward Jesus.

But when he perceived and felt the strong wind, he was frightened, and as he began to sink, he cried out, Lord, save me [from death]!

Instantly Jesus reached out His hand and caught and held him, saying to him, O you of little faith, why did you doubt?

And when they got into the boat, the wind ceased.

Matthew 14:24-32

I emphasized the last verse because I want to call your attention to the program the enemy lined out in this passage. Peter stepped out at the command of Jesus to do something he had never done before. As a matter of fact, no one had ever done it except Jesus.

It required faith!

Peter made a mistake; he spent too much time looking at the storm. He became frightened. Doubt and unbelief pressed in on him, and he began to sink. He cried out to Jesus to save him, and He did. But notice that the storm ceased as soon as *Peter got back into the boat!*

Remember in Romans 4:18-21 where Abraham did not waver when he considered his impossible situation? Abraham knew the conditions, but unlike Peter, his circumstances did not seem to hinder his faith. He probably didn't think about them much or talk about them. He kept His mind and conversation on God. You and I can be aware of our circumstances and yet, purposely, keep our mind on something that will build us up and edify our faith.

That is why Abraham stayed busy giving praise and glory to God. We glorify God when we continue to do what we know is right even in adverse circumstances. Ephesians 6:14 teaches us that in times of spiritual warfare, we are to tighten the belt of truth around us.

When the storm comes in your life, dig in both heels, set your face like flint, and be determined in the Holy Spirit to stay out of the boat! We might say, "Step out and stay out." Very often the storm ceases as soon as you quit and go back into what you think is a place of safety and security.

The devil brings storms into your life to intimidate you. During a storm, remember that the mind is the battlefield. Don't make your decisions based on your thoughts or feelings, but check with your spirit. When you do, you will find the same vision that was there in the beginning.

No Wavering Allowed!

If any of you is deficient in wisdom, let him ask of the giving God [Who gives] to everyone liberally and ungrudgingly, without reproaching or faultfinding, and it will be given him.

Only it must be in faith that he asks with no wavering (no hesitating, no doubting). For the one who wavers (hesitates, doubts) is like the billowing surge out at sea that is blown hither and thither and tossed by the wind.

For truly, let not such a person imagine that he will receive anything [he asks for] from the Lord.

James 1:5-7

I heard a pastor tell a story about how confused he became trying to decide what to do when he graduated from Bible college. God had placed it strongly in his heart to return to St. Louis, Missouri, and start a local church after graduation, which he intended to do. However, when it was time to go, he had approximately fifty dollars in his pocket, a wife, one child, and another on the way. Obviously, his circumstances were not very good.

In the midst of trying to make his decision, he received two very good offers to join the staff of other large, well-established ministries. His salary would have been good. The ministry opportunities were attractive and, if nothing else, just the honor of working for either of these ministries would have bolstered his ego. The longer he deliberated, the more confused he became. (It sounds like Mr. Doubt was visiting him, doesn't it?)

At one time he had known exactly what he wanted to do, and now he was *wavering* between options. Since his circumstances did not favor going back to St. Louis, it was tempting to accept one of the other offers, but he could not get peaceful about either course of action. He finally asked the advice of one of the pastors who had offered him a job, and the man wisely said, "Go somewhere, get quiet and still, then turn your head off. Look into your heart, see what is there, and do it!"

When he followed the pastor's advice, he quickly found that in his heart was the church in St. Louis. He did not know how he could do it with what he had in hand, but he went forth obediently, and the results were wonderful.

Today that pastor, Rick Shelton, is the founder and senior pastor of Life Christian Center in St. Louis, Missouri. Thousands of lives have been blessed and transformed over the years through its ministry. I was an associate pastor there for five years, and my ministry was birthed during that time. Just think how much the devil would have stolen through doubt and unbelief if Pastor Shelton had been led by his head instead of his heart.

DOUBT IS A CHOICE

In the early dawn the next morning, as He was coming back to the city, He was hungry.

And as He saw one single leafy fig tree above the roadside, He went to it but He found nothing but leaves on it [seeing that in the fig tree the fruit appears at the same time as the leaves]. And He said to it, Never again shall fruit grow on you! And the fig tree withered up at once.

When the disciples saw it, they marveled greatly and asked, How is it that the fig tree has withered away all at once?

And Jesus answered them, Truly I say to you, if you have faith (a firm relying trust) and do not doubt, you will not only do what has been done to the fig tree, but even if you say to this mountain, Be taken up and cast into the sea, it will be done.

And whatever you ask for in prayer, having faith and [really] believing, you will receive.

Matthew 21:18-22

When His disciples marveled and asked Jesus how He was able to destroy the fig tree with just a word, He said to them in essence, "*If you have faith and do not doubt*, you can do the same thing that I have done to the fig tree—and even greater things than this" (see John 14:12).

We have already established that faith is the gift of God, so we know that we have faith (Rom. 12:3). But doubt is a choice. It is the devil's warfare tactic against our minds.

Since you can choose your own thoughts, when doubt comes you should learn to recognize it for what it is, say "No, thank you"—and keep on believing!

The *choice* is yours!

Unbelief Is Disobedience

And when they were come to the multitude, there came to him a certain man, kneeling down to him, and saying, Lord, have mercy on my son: for he is lunatick, and sore vexed: for ofttimes he falleth into the fire, and oft into the water.

And I brought him to thy disciples, and they could not cure him.

Then Jesus answered and said, O faithless and perverse generation, how long shall I be with you? how long shall I suffer you? bring him hither to me.

And Jesus rebuked the devil; and he departed out of him: and the child was cured from that very hour. Then came the disciples to Jesus apart, and said, Why could not we cast him out? And Jesus said unto them, Because of your unbelief.

Matthew 17:14-20 KJV

Remember that unbelief leads to disobedience.

Perhaps Jesus had taught His disciples certain things to do in these cases, and their unbelief caused them to disobey Him; therefore, they were unsuccessful.

In any case, the point is that unbelief, like doubt, will keep us from doing what God has called and anointed us to accomplish in life. It will also keep us from experiencing the sense of peace that He wants us to enjoy as we find rest for our souls in Him (see Matt. 11:28,29 KJV).

A Sabbath Rest

Let us therefore be zealous and exert ourselves and strive diligently to enter that rest [of God, to know and experience it for ourselves], that no one may fall or perish by the same kind of unbelief and disobedience [into which those in the wilderness fell].

Hebrews 4:11

If you read the entire fourth chapter of the book of Hebrews, you will find it speaking about a Sabbath rest that is available to God's people. Under the Old Covenant, the Sabbath was observed as a day of rest. Under the New Covenant, this Sabbath rest spoken of is a spiritual place of rest where the believer can abide. It is the privilege of every believer to refuse to worry or have anxiety. As believers, you and I can enter the rest of God and stay there.

Careful observation of Hebrews 4:11 reveals that we will never enter that rest except through believing, and we will forfeit it through unbelief and disobedience. Unbelief will keep us in "wilderness living," but Jesus has provided a permanent place of rest, one that can be inhabited only through living by faith.

LIVING FROM FAITH TO FAITH

For therein is the righteousness of God revealed from faith to faith: as it is written, The just shall live by faith.
Romans 1:17 KJV

I remember an incident that may drive this point home very clearly. One evening I was walking around my house trying to do some household things, and I was very miserable. I did not have any joy—there was no peace in my heart. I kept asking the Lord, "What's wrong with me?" I often felt that way, and I sincerely wanted to know what my problem was. I was trying to follow all the things I was learning in my walk with Jesus, but something surely seemed to be missing.

About that time the phone rang and, while I was talking, I thumbed through a box of Scripture cards someone had sent me. I wasn't really looking at any of them, just flipping them around while I was on the phone. When I hung up, I decided to choose one at random and see if I could get any encouragement from it.

I pulled out Romans 15:13: "May the God of your hope so fill you with all joy and peace in believing [through the experience of your faith] that by the power of the Holy Spirit you may abound and be overflowing (bubbling over) with hope."

I saw it!

My whole problem was doubt and unbelief. I was making myself unhappy by believing the devil's lies. I was being negative. I could not have joy and peace because I was not believing. It is impossible to have joy and peace and live in unbelief.

Make a decision to believe God and not the devil!

Learn to live from faith to faith. According to Romans 1:17, that is the way the righteousness of God is revealed. The Lord had to reveal to me that instead of living from faith to faith I would often live from faith to doubt to unbelief. Then I would go back to faith for a while, and later, return to doubt and unbelief. Back and forth I would go from one to the other. That's why I was having so much trouble and misery in my life.

Remember, according to James 1:7,8 (KJV), the double-minded man is unstable in all his ways and never receives what he wants from the Lord. Make up your mind that you will not be double-minded; don't live in doubt!

God has a great life planned for you. Don't let the devil steal it from you through lies! Instead, "refute arguments and theories and reasonings and every proud and lofty thing that sets itself up against the [true] knowledge of God; and...lead every thought and purpose away captive into the obedience of Christ (the Messiah, the Anointed One)" (2 Cor. 10:5).

Chapter
12

An Anxious and Worried Mind

An Anxious and Worried Mind

A nxiety and worry are both attacks on the mind intended to distract us from serving the Lord. The enemy also uses both of these torments to press our faith down, so it cannot rise up and help us live in victory.

Fret not thyself in any wise.
PSALM 37:8 KJV

Some people have such a problem with worry that it might even be said that they are addicted to worrying. If they do not have something of their own to worry about, they will worry over someone else's situation. I had this problem, so I am well qualified to describe the condition.

Because I was constantly worrying about something, I never enjoyed the peace that Jesus died for me to have.

It is absolutely impossible to worry and live in peace at the same time.

Peace is not something that can be put on a person; it is a fruit of the Spirit (see Gal. 5:22), and fruit is the result of abiding in Jesus (see John 15:4 KJV). Abiding relates to entering the "rest of God" spoken of in the fourth chapter of Hebrews as well as other places in the Word of God. Jesus gave us His peace (see John 14:27), but He said we must not allow ourselves to be fearful, intimidated and unsettled. In other words, peace is present in us, but it must be chosen over what our fleshly mind thinks. We can choose to be peaceful by choosing to think on things that promote peace rather than things that open a door for worry and anxiety.

There are several words in the Bible that refer to worry, depending on what translation is being read. The *King James Version* does not use the word "worry." In addition to "fret not" (Ps. 37:8), other sample phrases used to warn against worry are "take no thought"

(Matt. 6:25), "be careful for nothing" (Phil. 4:6), and "casting all your care" (1 Pet. 5:7). I generally use *The Amplified Bible*, which includes several different translations of these and other phrases relating to the subject. In order to simplify the teaching in the rest of this chapter, I will refer to the condition as "worry."

WORRY DEFINED

Webster defines the word *worry* as follows: "—vi. 1. To feel uneasy or troubled.... —vt. 1. To cause to feel anxious, distressed, or troubled.... —n.... 2. A source of nagging concern."[1] I have also heard it defined as to torment oneself with disturbing thoughts.

When I saw the part about tormenting oneself with disturbing thoughts, I decided right then and there that I am smarter than that. I believe every Christian is. I think believers have more wisdom than to sit around and torment themselves.

Worry certainly never makes anything better, so why not give it up?

Another part of the definition, from *The Random House Unabridged Dictionary*, also enlightened me: "To seize by the throat with teeth and shake or mangle, as one animal does another, or to harass by repeated biting and snapping."[2]

Pondering this definition, I made the following correlation: the devil uses worry to do to us precisely what is described above. When we have had a bout with worry for even a few hours, that is exactly how we feel—as if someone has had us by the throat and shaken us until we are totally worn out and mangled. The repetition of thoughts that come and won't let up are like the repeated biting and snapping described in this definition.

Worry is definitely an attack from Satan upon the mind. There are certain things the believer is instructed to do with his mind, and the enemy wants to make sure that they are never done. So the devil attempts to keep the mental arena busy enough with the wrong kinds of thinking so that the mind never gets around to being used for the purpose for which God designed it.

We will be discussing the right things to do with the mind in a later chapter, but for now let's continue our study of worry until we get a full revelation on just how useless it really is.

Matthew 6:25-34 are excellent Scriptures to read when we feel a "worry attack" coming on. Let's look at each of these verses separately to see what the Lord is saying to us about this vital subject.

IS NOT LIFE GREATER THAN THINGS?

Therefore I tell you, stop being perpetually uneasy (anxious and worried) about your life, what you shall eat or what you shall drink; or about your body, what you shall put on. Is not life greater [in quality] than food, and the body [far above and more excellent] than clothing?

Matthew 6:25

Life is intended to be of such high quality that we enjoy it immensely. In John 10:10, Jesus said, "The thief comes only in order to steal and kill and destroy. I came that they may have and enjoy life, and have it in abundance (to the full, till it overflows)." Satan attempts to steal that life from us in many ways—one of them being worry.

In Matthew 6:25 we are being taught that there is nothing in life that we are to worry about—not any aspect of it! The quality of life that God has provided for us is great enough to provide all of the things we need, but if we worry about the things, then we lose them as well as the life He intended us to have.

AREN'T YOU MORE VALUABLE THAN A BIRD?

Look at the birds of the air; they neither sow nor reap nor gather into barns, and yet your heavenly Father keeps feeding them. Are you not worth much more than they?

Matthew 6:26

It might do all of us good to spend some time watching birds. That's what our Lord told us to do.

If not every day, then at least every now and then we need to take the time to observe and remind ourselves how well our feathered friends are cared for. They literally do not know where their next meal is coming from; yet, I have personally never seen a bird sitting on a tree branch having a nervous breakdown due to worry.

The Master's point here is really very simple, *"Are you not worth more than a bird?"*

Even if you are wrestling with a poor self-image, surely you can believe that you are more valuable than a bird, and look how well your heavenly Father takes care of them.

What Do You Gain by Worrying?

And who of you by worrying and being anxious can add one unit of measure (cubit) to his stature or to the span of his life?

Matthew 6:27

The point is quickly made that worry is useless. It does not accomplish any good thing. If that is so, then why worry, why be so anxious?

Why Be So Anxious?

And why should you be anxious about clothes? Consider the lilies of the field and learn thoroughly how they grow; they neither toil nor spin.

Yet I tell you, even Solomon in all his magnificence (excellence, dignity, and grace) was not arrayed like one of these.

But if God so clothes the grass of the field, which today is alive and green and tomorrow is tossed into the furnace, will He not much more surely clothe you, O you of little faith?

Matthew 6:28-30

Using the illustration of one of His creations, the Lord makes the point that if a flower, which does nothing, can be so well taken care of and look so good that it outshines even Solomon in all his majesty, then surely we can believe that we will be taken care of and provided for.

THEREFORE, DON'T WORRY OR BE ANXIOUS!

Therefore do not worry and be anxious, saying, What are we going to have to eat? or, What are we going to have to drink? or, What are we going to have to wear?

Matthew 6:31

I like to amplify this verse a bit and include one more question, "What are we going to do?"

I think Satan sends out demons whose job it is to do nothing but repeat that phrase in the believer's ear all day long. They fire off difficult questions, and the believer wastes his precious time attempting to come up with answers he does not have. The devil is constantly waging war on the battlefield of the mind, hoping to engage the Christian in long, drawn-out, tormenting combat. Our answer to the devil's question about what we are going to do should simply be, "I don't know yet what I am going to do in my situation, but God does know and that is good enough for me. He will give me direction at the right time."

Notice that part of verse 31 in which the Lord instructs us not to worry or be anxious. Remember that out of the abundance of the heart the mouth speaks (see Matt. 12:34 KJV). The enemy knows that if he can get enough of the wrong things going on in our mind, they will eventually begin to come out of our mouth. Our words are very important because they confirm our faith—or in some instances our lack of faith.

SEEK GOD, NOT GIFTS

For the Gentiles (heathen) wish for and crave and diligently seek all these things, and your heavenly Father knows well that you need them all.

> But seek (aim at and strive after) first of all His kingdom and His
> righteousness (His way of doing and being right), and then all
> these things taken together will be given you besides.
>
> Matthew 6:32,33

It is clear that God's children are not to be like the world! The world seeks after things, but we are to seek the Lord. He has promised that if we will do that, He will add to us all these things He knows we need.

We must learn to seek God's face and not His hand!

Our heavenly Father delights in giving His children good things, but only if we are not seeking after them. *Seek* is a strong word meaning to pursue, crave, and go after with all of your might. It is permissible to want things, but we should only *seek* God, because without Him nothing else has any value at all.

God knows what we need before we ask. If we will simply make our requests known to Him (see Phil. 4:6 KJV), He will bring them to pass in His own good timing. Worry will not help our cause at all. It will, in fact, hinder our progress.

TAKE ONE DAY AT A TIME

> So do not worry or be anxious about tomorrow, for tomorrow
> will have worries and anxieties of its own. Sufficient for each day
> is its own trouble.
>
> Matthew 6:34

I like to describe worry or anxiety as spending today trying to figure out tomorrow. Let's learn to use the time God has given to us for what He intended.

Life is to be lived—here and now!

Sadly, very few people know how to live each day to the fullest. But you can be one of them. Jesus said that Satan, the enemy, comes to steal your life. (see John 10:10). Don't allow him to do it any longer! Don't spend today worrying about tomorrow. You have enough things going on today; it needs all of your attention. God's grace is on you to handle whatever you need for today, but tomorrow's grace will not come until tomorrow comes—so don't waste today!

Don't Fret or Have Anxiety

Do not fret or have any anxiety about anything, but in every circumstance and in everything, by prayer and petition (definite requests), with thanksgiving, continue to make your wants known to God.

Philippians 4:6

This is another good Scripture to consider when a "worry attack" comes.

I highly recommend speaking the Word of God out of your mouth. It is the two-edged sword that must be wielded against the enemy (see Heb. 4:12; Eph. 6:17 KJV). A sword in its sheath won't do any good during an attack.

God has given us His Word, *use it!* Learn Scriptures like this one and when the enemy attacks, counter his attack with the same weapon that Jesus used: *the Word!*

Cast Down Imaginations

Refute arguments and theories and reasonings and every proud and lofty thing that sets itself up against the [true] knowledge of God; and...lead every thought and purpose away captive into the obedience of Christ (the Messiah, the Anointed One).

2 Corinthians 10:5

When the thoughts being offered you do not agree with God's Word, the best way to shut the devil up is to speak the Word.

The Word coming forth out of a believer's mouth, with faith to back it up, is the single most effective weapon that can be used to win the war against worry and anxiety.

CAST YOUR CARES UPON GOD

Therefore humble yourselves [demote, lower yourselves in your own estimation] under the mighty hand of God, that in due time He may exalt you,

Casting the whole of your care [all your anxieties, all your worries, all your concerns, once and for all] on Him, for He cares for you affectionately and cares about you watchfully.

1 Peter 5:6,7

When the enemy tries to give us a problem, we have the privilege of casting it upon God. The word "cast" actually means to pitch or throw. You and I can pitch or throw our problems to God and, believe me, He can catch them. He knows what to do with them.

This passage lets us know that to humble ourselves is not to worry. A person who worries still thinks that in some way he can solve his own problem. Worry is the mind racing around trying to find a solution to its situation. The proud man is full of himself, while the humble man is full of God. The proud man worries; the humble man waits.

Only God can deliver us, and He wants us to know that, so that in every situation our first response is to lean on Him and to enter His rest.

THE REST OF GOD

O our God, will You not exercise judgment upon them? For we have no might to stand against this great company that is coming against us. We do not know what to do, but our eyes are upon You.

2 Chronicles 20:12

I love this verse! The people in it had come to the place of realizing three things for certain:

1. They had no might against their enemies.

2. They did not know what to do.

3. They needed to have their eyes focused on God.

In verses 15 and 17 of that same passage, we see what the Lord said to them once they came to this realization and freely acknowledged it to Him: "Be not afraid or dismayed at this great multitude; for the battle is not yours, but God's.... You shall not need to fight in this battle; take your positions, stand still, and see the deliverance of the Lord."

What is our position? It is one of worship and abiding in Jesus and entering the rest of God. It is one of waiting on the Lord continually with our eyes focused upon Him, doing what He directs us to do and otherwise having a "reverential fear" of moving in the flesh.

Concerning entering God's rest I would like to say this: there is no such thing as "the rest of God" without opposition. It's easy to have peace when there's nothing to be upset about. Unbelievers also have peace during easy times. But "the rest of God" is the gift that keeps believers peaceful during times of trouble. It is a gift from Him to His children.

To illustrate, let me share a story I once heard involving two artists who were asked to paint pictures of peace as they perceived it. One painted a quiet, still lake, far back in the mountains. The other painted a raging, rushing waterfall, which had a birch tree leaning out over it with a bird resting in a nest on one of the branches.

Which one truly depicts peace? The second one does, because there is no such thing as peace without opposition. The first painting represents stagnation. The scene it sets forth may be serene; a person might be motivated to want to go there to recuperate. It may offer a pretty picture, but it does not depict "the rest of God."

Jesus said, "Peace I leave with you; My [own] peace I now give and bequeath to you. Not as the world gives do I give to you" (John 14:27). His peace is a spiritual peace, and His rest is one that operates in the midst of the storm—not in its absence. Jesus did not come to remove all opposition from our lives, but rather to give us a different approach to the storms of life. We are to take His yoke upon us and learn of Him (see Matt. 11:29). That means that we are to learn His ways, to approach life in the same way He did.

Jesus did not worry, and we do not have to worry either!

If you are waiting to have nothing to worry about before you stop worrying, then I probably should tell you that you will have to wait a long time, because that time may *never* come. I am not being negative. I am being honest! We live in a world filled with turmoil. It is around us, but it does not have to be in us.

Matthew 6:34 suggested that we not worry about tomorrow because each day will have sufficient trouble of its own. Jesus Himself said that, and He certainly was not negative. Being at peace, enjoying the rest of God in the midst of the storm, gives much glory to the Lord because it proves that His ways work.

WORRY, WORRY, WORRY!

I wasted many years of my life worrying about things that I could do nothing about. I would like to have those years back and be able to approach them in a different way. However, once you have spent the time God has given you, it is impossible to get it back and do things another way.

My husband, on the other hand, never worried. There was a time when I would get angry at him because he would not worry with me—and join me in talking about all the gloomy possibilities if God did not come through and meet our needs. I would sit in the kitchen, for example, and pore over the bills and checkbook, getting more upset by the moment, because the bills were more than the money. Dave would be in the next room playing with the children, watching television while they jumped up and down on his back and put rollers in his hair.

I can remember saying to him in an unpleasant tone, "Why don't you come out here and do something instead of playing while I try to figure this mess out!" When he responded with, "What would you like me to do?" I could never think of anything; it just made me angry that he would dare to enjoy himself while we were facing such a desperate financial situation.

Dave would calm me down by reminding me that God had always met our needs, that we were doing our part (which was tithing, giving offerings, praying, and trusting), and that the Lord would continue to do His part. (I should clarify that Dave was trusting while I was worrying.) I would go in the room with him and the children and a short while later the thoughts would creep back into my mind, "But what are we going to do? How are we going to pay these bills? What if…"

And then I would see all these disasters on the movie screen of my imagination—foreclosure of the mortgage, repossession of the car, embarrassment in front of relatives and friends if we had to ask for financial help, and on and on. Have you ever been to that "movie" or had those kinds of thoughts run through your mind constantly? Of course you have, otherwise you probably would not be reading this book.

After entertaining the thoughts the devil was offering me for a while, I would wander back out into the kitchen, get out all the bills, the calculator and the checkbook, and start going over the whole mess again. I guess I thought if I looked long enough and hard enough that I could find an answer, but only God had the answer. The more I would go over and over the bills, the more upset I would become. Then we would repeat the same scene! I would yell at Dave and the children for having a good time while I was taking all the "responsibility"!

Actually what I was experiencing was not responsibility, it was care—something God had specifically told me to cast on Him.

I look back now and realize that I wasted all those evenings that God gave me in my early married life. The time He gives us is a precious gift. But I gave it to the devil. Your time is your own. Use it wisely; you won't pass this way again.

God met all our needs, and He did it in a variety of ways. He never let us down—not one time. God is faithful!

DON'T WORRY—TRUST GOD

Let your character or moral disposition be free from love of money [including greed, avarice, lust, and craving for earthly possessions] and be satisfied with your present [circumstances and with what you have]; for He [God] Himself has said, I will not in any way fail you nor give you up nor leave you without support. [I will] not, [I will] not, [I will] not in any degree leave you helpless nor forsake nor let [you] down (relax My hold on you)! [Assuredly not!]

Hebrews 13:5

This is an excellent Scripture to use to encourage yourself when you have concern about whether or not God will come through and meet your needs.

In this passage, the Lord is letting us know that we do not need to have our minds set on money, wondering how we are going to take care of ourselves, because He will take care of these things for us. He has promised never to fail us or forsake us.

Do your part, but do not try to do God's part. The load is too heavy to bear—and if you're not careful, you will break under the weight of it.

Don't worry. "Trust (lean on, rely on, and be confident) in the Lord and do good; so shall you dwell in the land and feed surely on His faithfulness, and truly you shall be fed" (Ps. 37:3).

That's a promise!

Chapter
13

A Judgmental, Critical,
and Suspicious Mind

A Judgmental, Critical, and Suspicious Mind

13

Much torment comes to people's lives because of judgmental attitudes, criticism, and suspicion. Multitudes of relationships are destroyed by these enemies. Once again, the mind is the battlefield.

Judge not, that ye be not judged.

MATTHEW 7:1 KJV

Thoughts—just "I think"—can be the tool the devil uses to keep a person lonely. People do not enjoy being around anyone who needs to voice an opinion about everything. Sometimes we are more concerned about telling people what we think than we are about listening, learning, and building good relationships.

To illustrate, I once knew a woman whose husband was a very wealthy businessman. He was generally very quiet, and she wanted him to talk more. He knew a great deal about a lot of things. She would get angry at him when they were in a group of people and someone would start a conversation on a subject about which her husband could have knowledgeably contributed much insight. He could have told them everything he knew, but he wouldn't.

One evening after he and his wife had returned home from a party, she chastised him, saying, "Why didn't you speak up and tell those people what you knew about what they were talking about? You just sat there and acted as if you didn't know anything at all!"

"I already know what I know," he replied. "I try to be quiet and listen so I can find out what others know."

I would imagine that this was precisely why he was wealthy. He was also wise! Few people gain wealth without wisdom. And few people have friends without using wisdom in relationships.

Being judgmental, opinionated, and critical are three sure ways to see relationships dissolve. Satan, of course, wants you and me to be lonely and rejected, so he attacks our minds in these areas. This chapter, hopefully, will help us recognize wrong thought patterns as well as learn how to deal with suspicion.

JUDGING DEFINED

In *Vine's Expository Dictionary of Old and New Testament Words*, one of the Greek words translated as *judgment* is partially defined as "a decision passed on the faults of others" and is cross-referenced to the word "condemnation."[1] According to this same source, one of the Greek words translated *judge* is partially defined as "to form an opinion" and is cross-referenced to the word "sentence."[2]

God is the only One Who has the right to condemn or sentence, therefore, when we pass judgment on another, we are, in a certain sense, setting ourselves up as God in his life.

I don't know about you, but that puts a little "godly fear" in me. I have a lot of nerve, but I am not interested in trying to be God! These areas were once a major problem in my personality, and I believe I will be able to share some things God has taught me that will help you.

Criticism, opinions, and judgment all seem to be relatives, so we will discuss them together as one giant problem.

I was critical because I always seemed to see what was wrong instead of what was right. Some personalities are more given to this fault than others. Some of the more jovial personality types do not want to see anything but the "happy or fun" things in life, so they really don't pay much attention to the things that could spoil their enjoyment. The more melancholy personality or the controlling personality often sees what is wrong first; generally, people with this type personality are generous in sharing their negative opinions and outlook with others.

We must realize that we have our own way of seeing things. We like to tell people what *we* think, and that is exactly the point—what I think may be right for me, but not necessarily right for you, and vice versa. We all know, of course, that "Thou shalt not steal" is right for everyone, but I am speaking here of the thousands of things we encounter every day that are neither right nor wrong necessarily but are simply personal choices. I might add that these are choices that people have a right to make on their own without outside interference.

My husband and I are extremely different in our approach to many things. How to decorate a house would be one of those things. It isn't that we don't like anything the other one chooses, but if we go out to shop for household things together, it seems Dave always likes one thing and I like something else. Why? Simply because we are two different people. His opinion is just as good as mine, and mine is just as good as his; they are simply different.

It took me years to understand that there wasn't something wrong with Dave just because he did not agree with me. And, of course, before I learned better, I usually let him know that I thought there was something wrong with him because he did not share my opinion. Obviously, my attitude caused much friction between us and hurt our relationship.

Pride: An "I" Problem

I warn everyone among you not to estimate and think of himself more highly than he ought [not to have an exaggerated opinion of his own importance], but to rate his ability with sober judgment, each according to the degree of faith apportioned by God to him.

Romans 12:3

Judgment and criticism are fruit of a deeper problem—pride. When the "I" in us is bigger than it should be, it will always cause the kinds of problems we are discussing. The Bible repeatedly warns us about being high-minded.

Whenever we excel in an area, it is only because God has given us a gift of grace for it. If we are high-minded or have an exaggerated opinion of ourselves, then it causes us to look down on others and value them as "less than" we are. This type of attitude or thinking is extremely detestable to the Lord, and it opens many doors for the enemy in our lives.

HOLY FEAR

Brethren, if any person is overtaken in misconduct or sin of any sort, you who are spiritual [who are responsive to and controlled by the Spirit] should set him right and restore and reinstate him, without any sense of superiority and with all gentleness, keeping an attentive eye on yourself, lest you should be tempted also.

Bear (endure, carry) one another's burdens and troublesome moral faults, and in this way fulfill and observe perfectly the law of Christ (the Messiah) and complete what is lacking [in your obedience to it].

For if any person thinks himself to be somebody [too important to condescend to shoulder another's load] when he is nobody [of superiority except in his own estimation], he deceives and deludes and cheats himself.

Galatians 6:1-3

Careful examination of these Scriptures quickly reveals to us how we are to respond to the weakness we observe in others. It sets forth the mental attitude we are to maintain within ourselves. We must have a "holy fear" of pride and be very careful of judging others or of being critical of them.

WHO ARE WE TO PASS JUDGMENT?

Who are you to pass judgment on and censure another's household servant? It is before his own master that he stands or falls. And he shall stand and be upheld, for the Master (the Lord) is mighty to support him and make him stand.

Romans 14:4

Think of it this way: let's say your neighbor came to your door and began instructing you on what your children should wear to school and what subjects she felt they should take. How would you respond? Or, suppose your neighbor stopped in to tell you that she didn't like the way you cleaned your home. What would you say to your neighbor? Surely you would tell her to mind her own business.

This is exactly the point this Scripture is making. Each of us belongs to God, and even if we have weaknesses, He is able to make us stand and to justify us. We answer to God, not to each other; therefore, we are not to judge one another in a critical way.

The devil stays very busy assigning demons to place judgmental, critical thoughts in people's minds. I can remember when it was entertaining for me to sit in the park or the shopping mall and simply watch all the people go by as I formed a mental opinion of each of them: their clothing, hairstyles, companions, etc. Now, we cannot always prevent ourselves from having opinions, but we do not have to express them. I believe we can even grow to the point where we do not have so many opinions, and those we do have are not of a critical nature.

I frequently tell myself, "Joyce, it's none of your business." A major problem is brewing in your mind when you ponder your opinion until it becomes a judgment. The problem grows bigger the more you think about it until you begin to express it to others, or even to the one you're judging. It has then become explosive and has the ability to do a great deal of harm in the realm of relationship as well as in the spiritual realm. You may be able to save yourself future problems by simply learning to say, "This is none of my business."

Judgment and criticism were rampant in my family, so I "grew up with them," so to speak. When that is the case—as it may be for you—it is like trying to play ball with a broken leg. I was trying to "play ball" with God; I wanted to do things His way, to think and act His way, but I couldn't. It took many years of misery before I learned about the strongholds in my mind that had to be dealt with before my behavior could change.

Remember, your actions won't change until your mind does.

Matthew 7:1-6 are some of the classic Scriptures on the subject of judgment and criticism. When you are having trouble with your mind in this area, read these and other Scriptures. Read them, then read them over aloud, and use them as weapons against the devil who is attempting to build a stronghold in your mind. He may be operating out of a stronghold that has already been there for many years.

Let's take a look at this passage and I will comment on each part of it as we go through it.

SOWING AND REAPING JUDGMENT

Do not judge and criticize and condemn others, so that you may not be judged and criticized and condemned yourselves.

For just as you judge and criticize and condemn others, you will be judged and criticized and condemned, and in accordance with the measure you [use to] deal out to others, it will be dealt out again to you.

Matthew 7:1,2

These Scriptures plainly tell us that we will reap what we sow (see Gal. 6:7). Sowing and reaping does not apply only to the agricultural and financial realms, it also applies to the mental realm. We can sow and reap an attitude as well as a crop or an investment.

One pastor I know often says that when he hears that someone has been talking about him in an unkind or judgmental way, he asks himself, "Are they sowing, or am I reaping?" Many times we are reaping in our lives what we have previously sown into the life of another.

Physician, Heal Thyself!

> Why do you stare from without at the very small particle that is in your brother's eye but do not become aware of and consider the beam of timber that is in your own eye?
>
> Or how can you say to your brother, Let me get the tiny particle out of your eye, when there is the beam of timber in your own eye?
>
> You hypocrite, first get the beam of timber out of your own eye, and then you will see clearly to take the tiny particle out of your brother's eye.
>
> Matthew 7:3-5

The devil loves to keep us busy, mentally judging the faults of others. That way, we never see or deal with what is wrong with us!

We cannot change others; only God can. We cannot change ourselves either, but we can cooperate with the Holy Spirit and allow Him to do the work. Step One to any freedom, however, is to face the truth the Lord is trying to show us.

When we have our thoughts and conversation on what is wrong with everyone else, we are usually being deceived about our own conduct. Therefore, Jesus commanded that we not concern ourselves with what is wrong with others when we have so much wrong with ourselves. Allow God to deal with you first, and then you will learn the scriptural way of helping your brother grow in His Christian walk.

Love One Another

> Do not give that which is holy (the sacred thing) to the dogs, and do not throw your pearls before hogs, lest they trample upon them with their feet and turn and tear you in pieces.
>
> Matthew 7:6

I believe this Scripture is referring to our God-given ability to love each other.

If you and I have an ability and a command from God to love others, but instead of doing that, we judge and criticize them, we have taken the holy thing (love) and cast it before dogs and hogs (demon spirits). We have opened a door for them to trample on holy things and turn and tear us to pieces.

We need to see that "the love walk" is protection for us against an evil attack. I do not believe the devil can do much harm to someone who really walks in love.

When I became pregnant with our fourth child, I was a Christian, filled with the Holy Spirit, called into ministry and a diligent Bible student. I had learned about exercising my faith for healing. Yet, during the first three months of the pregnancy, I was very, very sick. I lost weight and energy. I spent most of my time lying on the couch, nauseated and so tired I could barely move.

This situation was really confusing to me since I had felt wonderful during my other three pregnancies. I hadn't known much of God's Word then, even though I was in church, and did not actively use my faith for anything. Now, I was very familiar with God's promises, yet I was sick—and no amount of prayer to God or resisting the devil was removing the problem!

One day as I lay in bed listening to my husband and children having a good time in the backyard, I aggressively asked God, "What in the world is wrong with me? Why am I so sick? And why am I not getting well?"

The Holy Spirit prompted me to read Matthew 7. I asked the Lord what that passage had to do with me and my health. I kept feeling that I should read it again and again. Finally, God opened my remembrance to an event that had taken place a couple of years earlier.

I had led and taught a home Bible study to which a young lady came whom we will call Jane. Jane attended the course faithfully until she became pregnant, but then it became very difficult for her to join us regularly because she was always tired and feeling bad.

As I lay in my bed that day, I recalled that another "Christian sister" and I had talked about, judged, and criticized Jane because she "just would not press through" her circumstances and be diligent in coming to Bible study. We never offered to help her in any way. We just formed an opinion that she was a weakling and was using her pregnancy as an excuse to be lazy and self-indulgent.

Now, I was in the same set of circumstances that Jane had been two years earlier. God showed me that although I had been healthy during my first three pregnancies, I had opened a huge door for the devil by my judgment and criticism. I had taken my pearls, the holy thing (my ability to love Jane), thrown it before the dogs and hogs, and now they had turned and were tearing me to pieces. I can tell you, I was quick to repent. As soon as I did, my health was restored, and I was fine throughout the remainder of my pregnancy.

From this incident I learned an important lesson about the dangers of judging and criticizing others. I would like to be able to say that after that experience I never made another mistake of that nature, but I am sorry to say that I have made many such mistakes since then. Each time, God has had to deal with me, for which I am grateful.

We *all* make mistakes. We *all* have weaknesses. The Bible says that we are not to have a hard-hearted, critical spirit toward each another, but instead to forgive one another and to show mercy to one another just as God for Christ's sake has done for us (see Eph. 4:32).

JUDGING BRINGS CONDEMNATION

Therefore you have no excuse or defense or justification, O man, whoever you are who judges and condemns another. For in posing as judge and passing sentence on another, you condemn yourself, because you who judge are habitually practicing the very same things [that you censure and denounce].

Romans 2:1

In other words, the very same things that we judge others for, we do ourselves.

The Lord gave me a very good example once to help me understand this principle. I was pondering why we would do something ourselves and think it was perfectly all right, but judge someone else who does it. He said, "Joyce, you look at yourself through rose-colored glasses, but you look at everyone else through a magnifying glass."

We make excuses for our own behavior, but when someone else does the same thing we do, we are often merciless. Doing unto others as we want them to do to us (see Matt. 7:12) is a good life principle that will prevent a lot of judgment and criticism, if followed.

A judgmental mind is an offshoot of a negative mind—thinking about what is wrong with an individual instead of what is right.

Be positive and not negative!

Others will benefit, but you will benefit more than anyone.

GUARD YOUR HEART

Keep and guard your heart with all vigilance and above all that you guard, for out of it flow the springs of life.
Proverbs 4:23

If you want to have life flowing to you and from you, guard your heart.

Certain types of thoughts are "unthinkable" for a believer—judgment and criticism among them. All the things that God tries to teach us are for our own good and happiness. Following His way brings fruitfulness; following the devil's way brings rottenness.

BE SUSPICIOUS OF SUSPICION

Love bears up under anything and everything that comes, is ever ready to believe the best of every person.
1 Corinthians 13:7

I can honestly say that obedience to this Scripture has always been a challenge for me. I was brought up to be suspicious. I was actually taught to distrust everyone, especially if they pretended to be nice, because they must want something.

In addition to being taught to be suspicious of others and their motives, I had several very disappointing experiences with people, not only before I became an active Christian, but afterward as well. Meditating on the components of love and realizing that love always believes the best has helped me greatly to develop a new mindset.

When your mind has been poisoned, or when Satan has gained strongholds in your mind, it has to be renewed according to God's Word. This is done by learning the Word and meditating (pondering, muttering to yourself, thinking on) it.

We have the wonderful Holy Spirit in us to remind us when our thoughts are going in the wrong direction. God does this for me when I am having suspicious thoughts instead of loving thoughts. The natural man thinks, "If I trust people, I'll be taken advantage of." Perhaps, but the benefits will far outweigh any negative experiences.

Trust and faith bring joy to life and help relationships grow to their maximum potential.

Suspicion cripples an entire relationship and usually destroys it.

The bottom line is this—God's ways work; man's ways don't. God condemns judgment, criticism, and suspicion, and so should we. Love what God loves and hate what He hates. Allow what He allows and disallow what He disallows.

A balanced attitude is always the best policy. That doesn't mean that we are not to use wisdom and discernment in our dealings with others. We don't have to throw open our life to everyone we meet, giving every person we encounter a chance to crush us. On the other hand, we don't have to look at everyone with a negative, suspicious eye, always expecting to be taken advantage of by others.

Trust God Completely and Man Discreetly

But when He was in Jerusalem during the Passover Feast, many believed in His name [identified themselves with His party] after seeing His signs (wonders, miracles) which he was doing.

But Jesus [for His part] did not trust Himself to them, because He knew all [men];

And He did not need anyone to bear witness concerning man [needed no evidence from anyone about men], for He Himself knew what was in human nature. [He could read men's hearts.]

John 2:23-25

One time after I had been involved in a disappointing church situation, God brought John 2:23-25 to my attention.

This passage is speaking of Jesus' relationship with His disciples. It plainly says that He did not trust Himself to them. It does not say that He was suspicious of them or that He had no trust in them; it just explains that because He understood human nature (which we all have), He did not trust Himself to them in an unbalanced way.

I learned a good lesson. I had been hurt badly in the situation at church because I had become too involved with a group of ladies and had got out of balance. Every time we get out of balance, we open a door for the devil.

First Peter 5:8 says, "Be well balanced (temperate, sober of mind), be vigilant and cautious at all times; for that enemy of yours, the devil, roams around like a lion roaring [in fierce hunger], seeking someone to seize upon and devour."

I learned that I had been leaning on the ladies in this group and placing in them a trust that belongs only to God. We can go only so far in any human relationship. If we go beyond wisdom, trouble will brew, and we will be hurt.

Always place your ultimate trust in the Lord. Doing so will open the door for the Holy Spirit to let you know when you're crossing over the line of balance.

Some people think they have discernment when actually they are just suspicious. There is a true gift of the Spirit called the discerning of spirits (see 1 Cor. 12:10 KJV). It discerns good and bad, not just bad. Suspicion comes out of the unrenewed mind; discernment comes out of the renewed spirit.

Pray for true gifts—not flesh that masquerades as gifts of the Spirit. True spiritual discernment will provoke prayer, not gossip. If a genuine problem is being discerned by a genuine gift, it will follow the scriptural pattern for dealing with it, not fleshly ways that only spread and compound the problem.

PLEASANT WORDS ARE SWEET AND HEALING

The mind of the wise instructs his mouth, and adds learning and persuasiveness to his lips. Pleasant words are as a honeycomb, sweet to the mind and healing to the body.

Proverbs 16:23,24

Words and thoughts are like bone and marrow—so close, it is hard to divide them (see Heb. 4:12).

Our thoughts are silent words that only we and the Lord hear, but those words affect our inner man, our health, our joy, and our attitude. The things we think on often come out of our mouth. And, sad to say, sometimes they make us look foolish. Judgment, criticism, and suspicion never bring joy.

Jesus said that He came in order that we might have and enjoy life (see John 10:10). Begin to operate in the mind of Christ, and you will step into a whole new realm of living.

Chapter
14

A Passive Mind

A Passive Mind

*T*his statement is certainly true concerning the area of passivity. Most Christians are not even familiar with the term, nor do they know how to recognize the symptoms.

My people are destroyed for lack of knowledge.

HOSEA 4:6

Passivity is the opposite of activity. It is a dangerous problem because the Word of God clearly teaches that we must be alert, cautious and active (see 1 Pet. 5:8)—that we are to fan the flame and stir up the gift within us (see 2 Tim. 1:6).

I have read various definitions of the word "passivity," and I describe it as a lack of feeling, a lack of desire, general apathy, lukewarmness, and laziness. Evil spirits are behind passivity. The devil knows that inactivity, failure to exercise the will, will spell the believer's ultimate defeat. As long as a person is moving against the devil by using his will to resist him, the enemy will not win the war. However, if he enters into a state of passivity, he is in serious trouble.

So many believers are emotionally ruled that an absence of feeling is all that is needed to stop them from doing what they have been taught to do. They praise if they feel like it, give if they feel like it, keep their word if they feel like it—and if they don't feel like it, they don't.

EMPTY SPACE IS A PLACE!

Neither give place to the devil.

Ephesians 4:27 KJV

The place we give Satan is often empty space. An empty, passive mind can be easily filled with all kinds of wrong thoughts.

A believer who has a passive mind and who does not resist these wrong thoughts often takes them as his own thoughts. He doesn't realize that the evil spirit has injected them into his mind because there was empty space there to fill.

One way to keep wrong thoughts out of your mind is to keep your mind full of right thoughts. The devil can be cast out, but he goes and wanders in dry places for a season. When he returns to his old home and finds it empty, the Bible says in Luke 11:24-26 that he comes back, brings others with him, and the person's last condition is worse than his first.

I am not saying that every person who has an evil thought has an evil spirit. But an evil spirit is often behind evil thoughts. An individual can cast down imaginations repeatedly, but they will always come right back until he learns to fill up the empty space with right thinking. When the enemy returns, he will then find no place in that person.

There are aggressive sins, or sins of commission, and there are passive sins, which are sins of omission. In other words, there are wrong things that we do, and there are right things that we don't do. For example, a relationship can be destroyed by speaking thoughtless words, but it can also be destroyed by the omission of kind words of appreciation that should have been spoken but never were.

A passive person thinks he is doing nothing wrong because he is doing nothing. Confronted with his error, he will say, "I didn't do anything!" His analysis is correct, but his behavior is not. The problem arose precisely *because* he did nothing.

Overcoming Passivity

My husband Dave had some problems years ago with passivity. There were certain things that he was active in. He went to work every day, played golf on Saturday, and watched football on Sunday. Beyond that, it was very hard to motivate him to do anything else.

If I needed a picture hung on the wall, it might take him three or four weeks to get it done. This caused great friction between us. It seemed to me that he did what he wanted to, and beyond that he did nothing.

Dave loved the Lord and as he sought Him about this problem, God directed him to some information about passivity and its dangers. He found that evil spirits were behind his non-action. There were certain areas in which he had no problems because he had maintained his will in those areas, but in other areas he had basically, through non-activity, given his will over to the enemy. He was oppressed in those areas and had moved into a place where he had no desire, no "want to," no motivation at all to help him accomplish certain tasks.

Study of the Word of God and prayer were two other areas where he was passive. Since I knew that he was not seeking God for direction, it was hard for me to listen to him. I had a problem with rebellion anyway, and you can see how the devil used our weaknesses against each other. Many people are divorced over just such problems. They really don't understand what is wrong.

I was actually too aggressive. I was always running out ahead of God, in the flesh, "doing my own thing" and expecting the Lord to bless it. Dave did not do much of anything except wait on God, which severely irritated me. We laugh now when we think of how we both used to be, but it was not funny then and had God not gotten our attention, we might have been one of those divorce statistics.

Dave would tell me that I was always out ahead of God, and I would respond by saying that he was ten miles behind God. I was too aggressive, and Dave was too passive.

When a believer is inactive in any area in which he has capability or talent, that particular area begins to atrophy or become immobilized. The longer he does nothing, the less he wants to do anything. One of the best examples is physical exercise.

I am currently on a good exercise program, and the more I exercise, the easier it gets. When I first started, it was very hard. It hurt each time I followed the program, because I had been inactive and passive concerning exercise for a long time. The longer I did nothing, the worse my physical condition became. I was getting weaker and weaker due to non-use of my muscles.

Dave began to see what his problem was! He was dealing with evil spirits that were oppressing him because of long-term inactivity. As the Holy Spirit revealed this truth to him, Dave determined that he would once again be active and aggressive, not lazy or procrastinating.

Making the decision was the easy part; putting it into action was the hard part. It was hard because each of the areas in which he had been passive now had to be "exercised" until it was strong again.

He began to get up at 5:00 A.M. to read the Word and pray before he went to work. *The battle was on!* The devil does not want to give up ground that he has gained, and he won't give it up without a fight. Dave would get up to spend time with God and would fall asleep on the couch. Even though there were mornings when he fell asleep, he was still making progress simply because he was getting up out of bed and attempting to build a prayer life.

There were times when he was bored. There were days when he felt that he was making no progress, that he was not understanding what he was reading anyway, or that his prayers were not getting through. But he persisted because of the Holy Spirit's revelation about this condition called "passivity."

I began to notice that when I needed Dave to hang a picture or fix something around the house, he responded immediately. He was beginning to do his own thinking again and to make his own decisions. Many times he did not feel like doing it or even want to do it in the natural. But he went beyond his feelings and fleshly desires. The more he took action based on what he knew to be right, the more freedom he enjoyed.

I will be honest and tell you that it was not easy for him. He was not free in a few days or even a few weeks. Passivity is one of the most difficult conditions to overcome because, as I have mentioned, there are no feelings to lend support.

Dave persisted with God's help, and now he is not passive at all. He is the administrator for our ministry, oversees all of our radio and television outreach and has responsibility for all the financial aspects of the ministry. He travels full time with me and makes the decisions concerning our travel schedule. He is also an excellent family man. He prays and spends time regularly in God's Word. In short, he is a man to be respected and admired.

He still plays golf and watches sports, but he also does the other things he is supposed to do. Knowing him now and seeing all that he accomplishes, no one would think that he was ever as passive as he once was.

The condition of passivity can be overcome. But the first step to overcoming passivity in actions is to overcome passivity in the mind. Dave could not make progress until he made a decision and changed his way of thinking.

RIGHT ACTION FOLLOWS RIGHT THINKING

Do not be conformed to this world (this age), [fashioned after and adapted to its external, superficial customs], but be transformed (changed) by the [entire] renewal of your mind [by its new ideals and its new attitude].

Romans 12:2

There is a dynamic principle shown throughout God's Word, and no person will ever walk in victory unless he understands and operates in it: *right action follows right thinking.*

Let me put it another way: *you will not change your behavior until you change your thoughts.*

In God's order of things, right thinking comes first, and right action follows. I believe that right action or correct behavior is a "fruit" of right thinking. Most believers struggle trying to do right, but fruit is not the product of struggle. Fruit comes as a result of abiding in the vine (see John 15:4 KJV). And abiding in the vine involves being obedient (see John 15:10 KJV).

I always use Ephesians 4:22-24 when teaching on this principle. Verse 22 says, "Strip yourselves of your former nature [put off and discard your old unrenewed self] which characterized your previous manner of life and becomes corrupt through lusts and desires that spring from delusion."

Verse 24 continues the thought by saying, "And put on the new nature (the regenerate self) created in God's image, [Godlike] in true righteousness and holiness."

So we see that verse 22 basically tells us to stop acting improperly, and verse 24 tells us to begin acting properly.

But verse 23 is what I call "the bridge Scripture." It tells us how to get from verse 22 (acting improperly) to verse 24 (acting properly): "And be constantly renewed in the spirit of your mind [having a fresh mental and spiritual attitude]."

It is impossible to get from wrong behavior to right behavior without *first* changing thoughts. A passive person may want to do the right thing, but he never will do so unless he purposely activates his mind and lines it up with God's Word and will.

An example that comes to mind involves a man who once asked for prayer at one of my seminars. He had a problem with lust. He really loved his wife and did not want their marriage to be destroyed, but his problem needed to be solved or he would surely ruin his marriage.

"Joyce, I have a problem with lust," he said. "I just cannot seem to stay away from other women. Will you pray for my deliverance? I have been prayed for many times, but I never seem to make any progress."

This is what the Holy Spirit prompted me to tell him, "Yes, I will pray for you, but you must be accountable for what you are allowing to show on the picture screen of your mind. You cannot visualize pornographic pictures in your thinking, or imagine yourself with these other women, if you ever want to enjoy freedom."

Like this man, others have come to realize, on the spot, why they are not experiencing a breakthrough even though they want to be free: *they want to change their behavior—but not their thinking.*

The mind is often an area where people "play around with sin." Jesus said in Matthew 5:27,28, "You have heard that it was said, You shall not commit adultery. But I say to you that everyone who so much as looks at a woman with evil desire for her has already committed adultery with her in his heart." The way for sinful action is paved through sinful thinking.

A woman who attended my first home Bible study had committed her life to the Lord and wanted her home and marriage to be straightened out. Everything in her life was a mess—home, children, marriage, finances, physical condition, etc. She openly said that she did not love her husband; in fact, she actually despised him. Knowing that her attitude was not godly, she was willing to love him, but she just could not seem to tolerate being around him.

We prayed, she prayed, everyone prayed! We shared Scripture with her and gave her recorded teachings to listen to. We did everything we knew to do and even though she was seemingly following our advice, she made no progress. *What was wrong?* During a counseling session, it was revealed that she had been a daydreamer all of her life. She was always imagining a fairy tale existence in which she was the princess and Prince Charming came home from work with flowers and candy, sweeping her off her feet with his devotion to her.

She spent her days thinking like this, and when her tired, overweight, sweaty, dirty husband came home from working hard all day (with one tooth missing), she despised him.

Think about this situation for a moment. The woman was born again, and yet her life was a mess. She wanted to obey God and live for Him, and she also wanted to love her husband because she knew it was God's will. She was willing to have victory in her life and marriage, but her mind was defeating her. There was no way she could overcome her disgust for her husband until she began to operate out of a "sound mind."

She was mentally living in a world that did not exist and never would. Therefore, she was totally unprepared to deal with reality. She had a passive mind, and since she was not choosing her own thinking according to the Word of God, the evil spirits injected thoughts into her mind.

As long as she thought they were her own thoughts and enjoyed them, she would never experience victory. She changed her thinking, and her life began to change. She changed her mental attitude toward her husband, and he began to change his appearance and his behavior toward her.

Set Your Mind on What Is Above

If then you have been raised with Christ [to a new life, thus sharing His resurrection from the dead], aim at and seek the [rich, eternal treasures] that are above, where Christ is, seated at the right hand of God.

And set your minds and keep them set on what is above (the higher things), not on the things that are on the earth.

Colossians 3:1,2

Once again we see the same principle: if you want to live the resurrection life that Jesus has provided, then seek that new, powerful life by setting your mind and keeping it set on things above, not on things on the earth.

The Apostle Paul is simply saying that if you and I want the good life, then we must keep our mind on good things.

Many believers want the good life, but they are passively sitting around wishing that something good would happen to them. Often, they are jealous of others who are living in victory and are resentful that their own lives are so difficult.

If you desire victory over your problems, if you truly want to live the resurrection life, *you must have backbone and not just wishbone!* You must be active—not passive. Right action begins with right thinking. Don't be passive in your mind. Start today choosing right thoughts.

Chapter
15

The Mind of Christ

The Mind of Christ

I believe that you have now made a firm decision to choose right thoughts, so let's look at the types of thinking that would be considered right according to the Lord. There are certainly many types of thoughts that would have been considered unthinkable to Jesus when He was on the earth. If we want to follow in His footsteps, then we must begin to think as He did.

For who has known or understood the mind (the counsels and purposes) of the Lord so as to guide and instruct Him and give Him knowledge? But we have the mind of Christ (the Messiah) and do hold the thoughts (feelings and purposes) of His heart.

1 CORINTHIANS 2:16

Right away you're probably thinking, "That's impossible, Joyce. Jesus was perfect. I may be able to improve my thinking, but I will never be able to think as He did."

Well, the Bible tells us that we have the mind of Christ—and a new heart and spirit.

A NEW HEART AND SPIRIT

A new heart will I give you and a new spirit will I put within you, and I will take away the stony heart out of your flesh and give you a heart of flesh.

And I will put my Spirit within you and cause you to walk in My statutes, and you shall heed My ordinances and do them.

Ezekiel 36:26,27

As Christians, you and I have a new nature, which is actually the nature of God deposited in us at the New Birth.

We can see from this Scripture that God knew if we were to heed His ordinances and walk in His statutes that He would have to give us His Spirit and a new heart (and mind). Romans 8:6 speaks of the mind of the flesh and tells us that death is the result of following the mind of the flesh, and life is the result of following the mind of the Spirit.

We would make tremendous progress simply by learning how to discern life and death.

If something is ministering death to you, don't do it any longer. When certain lines of thought fill you full of death (every kind of misery), you know immediately that it is not the mind of the Spirit.

To illustrate, let's say I'm thinking about an injustice I suffered because of another person, and I begin to get angry. I start thinking about how much I dislike that individual. If I am discerning, I will notice that I am being filled with death. I am getting upset, tense, stressed out—I may even be experiencing physical discomfort. Headache, stomach pain, or undue fatigue may be the fruit of my wrong thinking. On the other hand, if I am thinking how blessed I am and how good God has been to me, I will also discern that I am being filled with life.

It is very helpful to a believer to learn to discern life and death within himself. Jesus has made arrangements for us to be filled with life by putting His own mind in us. We can choose to flow in the mind of Christ.

In the following pages of this chapter is a list of things to do in order to flow in the mind of Christ.

Step 1. Think positive thoughts.

> Do two walk together except they make an appointment and have agreed?
>
> Amos 3:3

If a person is thinking according to the mind of Christ, what will his thoughts be like? They will be positive, that's for sure. In an earlier chapter we have already discussed the absolute necessity of positive thinking. You may even want to go back to Chapter 5 at this point and refresh your memory on the importance of being positive.

I just went back and read it and got blessed myself even though I wrote it.

Enough can never be said about the power of being positive. God is positive, and if you and I want to flow with Him, we must get on the same wavelength and begin to think positively. I am not talking about exercising mind control, but simply about being an all-around, positive person.

Have a positive outlook and attitude. Maintain positive thoughts and expectations. Engage in positive conversation.

Jesus certainly displayed a positive outlook and attitude. He endured many difficulties including personal attacks—being lied about, being deserted by His disciples when He needed them most, being made fun of, being lonely, misunderstood, and a host of other discouraging things. Yet in the midst of all these negatives He remained positive. He always had an uplifting comment, an encouraging word; He always gave hope to all those He came near.

The mind of Christ in us is positive; therefore, any time we become negative, we are not operating with the mind of Christ. Millions of people suffer from what I call the "downs" in life. Discouragement, depression, and despair, but I do not think it is possible to be in a down mood without being negative—unless the cause is medical. Even in that case, being negative will only increase the problem and its symptoms. When a person is down in his mood, everything about him is down. His head hangs down, the corners of his mouth turn down, his eyes are droopy, his shoulders slump down and he usually wants to sit down or lay down.

According to Psalm 3:3, God is our glory and the lifter of our heads. He wants to lift everything: our hopes, our attitudes, our moods, our head, hands, and heart—our whole life. He is our divine Lifter!

God wants to lift us up, and the devil wants to press us down. Satan uses the negative events and situations of our life to depress us. The dictionary definition of the word *depress* is "to lower in spirits: SADDEN."[1]

According to Webster, something that is *depressed* is "sunk below the surrounding region: HOLLOW."[2] *Depress* means to sink, to press down or to hold below ground level. We regularly have the opportunity to think negative thoughts, but they will only press us down further. Being negative won't solve our problems; it will only add to them.

OVERCOME DEPRESSION

Psalm 143:3-10 gives a description of depression and how to overcome it. Let's look at this passage in detail to see the steps we can take to overcome this attack of the enemy:

1. Identify the nature and cause of the problem.

For the enemy has pursued and persecuted my soul, he has crushed my life down to the ground; he has made me to dwell in dark places as those who have been long dead.

Psalm 143:3

Dwelling "in dark places as one who is long dead," certainly sounds to me like a description of someone who is as down as he can be.

Notice that the cause or source of this depression, this attack upon the soul, is Satan.

2. Recognize that depression steals life and light.

Therefore is my spirit overwhelmed and faints within me [wrapped in gloom]; my heart within my bosom grows numb.

Psalm 143:4

Depression oppresses a person's spiritual freedom and power.

Our spirit (empowered and encouraged by God's Spirit) is powerful and free. Therefore, Satan seeks to oppress its power and liberty by filling our mind with darkness and gloom. Please realize that it is vital to resist the feeling called "depression" immediately upon sensing its arrival. The longer it is allowed to remain, the harder it becomes to resist.

3. Remember the good times.

I remember the days of old; I meditate on all Your doings; I ponder the work of Your hands.

Psalm 143:5

In this verse we see the psalmist's response to his condition. Remembering, meditating, and pondering are all functions of the mind. He obviously knows that his thoughts will affect his feelings, so he gets busy thinking about the kind of things that will help him overcome the attack upon his mind.

4. Praise the Lord in the midst of the problem.

I spread forth my hands to You; my soul thirsts after You like a thirsty land [for water]. Selah [pause, and calmly think of that]!

Psalm 143:6

The psalmist knows the importance of praise; he lifts his hands in worship. He declares what his need truly is—he needs God. Only the Lord can cause him to feel satisfied.

Far too often when people get depressed, it is because they are in need of something, and they seek it in the wrong place, which only adds to their problems.

In Jeremiah 2:13 the Lord said, "For My people have committed two evils: they have forsaken Me, the Fountain of living waters, and they have hewn for themselves cisterns, broken cisterns which cannot hold water."

God alone can water a thirsty soul. Don't be deceived into thinking that anything else can satisfy you fully and completely. Chasing after the wrong thing will always leave you disappointed, and disappointment opens the door for depression.

5. Ask for God's help.

Answer me speedily, O Lord, for my spirit fails; hide not Your face from me, lest I become like those who go down into the pit (the grave).

Psalm 143:7

The psalmist asks for help. He is basically saying, "Hurry up, God, because I am not going to be able to hold on very much longer without You."

6. Listen to the Lord.

Cause me to hear Your loving-kindness in the morning, for on You do I lean and in You do I trust. Cause me to know the way wherein I should walk, for I lift up my inner self to You.

Psalm 143:8

The psalmist knows that he needs to hear from God. He needs to be assured of God's love and kindness. He needs God's attention and direction.

7. Pray for deliverance.

Deliver me, O Lord, from my enemies; I flee to You to hide me.

Psalm 143:9

Once again the psalmist is declaring that it is only God Who can help him.

Please notice that throughout this discourse he is keeping his mind on God and not on the problem.

8. Seek God's wisdom, knowledge, and leadership.

Teach me to do Your will, for You are my God; let Your good Spirit lead me into a level country and into the land of uprightness.

Psalm 143:10

Perhaps the psalmist is indicating that he has gotten out of the will of God and thus opened the door for the attack on his soul. He wants to be in God's will for he now realizes that it is the only safe place to be.

Then he requests that God help him to be stable. I believe his phrase, "Lead me into a level country," refers to his unsettled emotions. He wants to be level—not up and down.

Use Your Weapons

For the weapons of our warfare are not physical [weapons of flesh and blood], but they are mighty before God for the overthrow and destruction of strongholds,

[Inasmuch as we] refute arguments and theories and reasonings and every proud and lofty thing that sets itself up against the [true] knowledge of God; and we lead every thought and purpose away captive into the obedience of Christ (the Messiah, the Anointed One).

2 Corinthians 10:4,5

Satan uses depression and all the other "downs" in life to drag millions into the pit of darkness and despair. Suicide is often the result of depression. A suicidal person is usually one who has become so negative that he sees absolutely no hope for the future.

Remember: *negative feelings come from negative thoughts.*

The mind is the battlefield, the place where the battle is won or lost. Choose today to be positive—casting down every negative imagination and and bringing your thoughts into the obedience of Jesus Christ (see 2 Cor. 10:5 KJV).

Step 2. Be God-minded.

You will guard him and keep him in perfect and constant peace whose mind [both its inclination and its character] is stayed on You, because he commits himself to You, leans on You, and hopes confidently in You.

Isaiah 26:3

Jesus had a continual fellowship with His heavenly Father. It is impossible to have full fellowship with anyone without having your mind on that individual. If my husband and I are in the car together, and he is talking to me, but I have my mind on something else, we are not really fellowshipping because I am not giving him my full attention. Therefore, I believe we can safely say that the thoughts of a person functioning in the mind of Christ would be on God and on all His mighty work.

Meditate on God and His Works

My whole being shall be satisfied as with marrow and fatness; and my mouth shall praise You with joyful lips

When I remember You upon my bed and meditate on You in the night watches.

Psalm 63:5,6

I will meditate also upon all Your works and consider all Your [mighty] deeds.

Psalm 77:12

I will meditate on Your precepts and have respect to Your ways [the paths of life marked out by Your law].

Psalm 119:15

I remember the days of old; I meditate on all Your doings; I ponder the work of Your hands.

Psalm 143:5

The psalmist David spoke frequently about meditating on God, His goodness and His works and ways. It is tremendously uplifting to think on the goodness of God and all the marvelous works of His hands.

I enjoy watching television shows about nature, animals, ocean life, etc., because they depict the greatness, the awesomeness of God, His infinite creativity, and how He is upholding all things by the might of His power (see Heb. 1:3).

Meditating on God and His ways and works will need to become a regular part of your thought life if you want to experience victory.

One of my favorite verses of Scripture is Psalm 17:15 in which the psalmist says of the Lord, "I shall be fully satisfied, when I awake [to find myself] beholding Your form [and having sweet communion with You]."

I spent a lot of unhappy days because I started thinking about all the wrong things the minute I awoke each morning. I can truly say that I am much more satisfied since the Holy Spirit has helped me operate out of the mind of Christ (the mind of the Spirit) that is within me. Fellowshipping with God early in the morning is one sure way to start each day right and to begin enjoying life.

FELLOWSHIP WITH THE LORD

If I do not go away, the Comforter (Counselor, Helper, Advocate, Intercessor, Strengthener, Standby) will not come to you [into close fellowship with you]; but if I go away, I will send Him to you [to be in close fellowship with you].

John 16:7

These words were spoken by Jesus just before He departed into heaven where He is seated at the right hand of the Father in glory. It is obvious from this Scripture that it is God's will that we be in close fellowship with Him.

Nothing is closer to us than our own thoughts. Therefore, if we will fill our mind with the Lord, it will bring Him into our consciousness and we will begin to enjoy a fellowship with Him that will bring joy, peace, and victory to our everyday life.

He is always with us just as He promised He would be (see Matt. 28:20; Heb. 13:5). But we will not be conscious of His Presence unless we think about Him. I can be in a room with someone and if I have my mind on lots of other things, I can leave and never even know that person was there. This is the way it is with our fellowship privileges with the Lord. He is always with us, but we need to think on Him and be aware of His presence.

Step 3. Be "God-Loves-Me"- Minded.

And we know (understand, recognize, are conscious of, by observation and by experience) and believe (adhere to and put faith in and rely on) the love God cherishes for us. God is love, and he who dwells and continues in love dwells and continues in God, and God dwells and continues in him.

1 John 4:16

169

I have learned that the same thing is true of God's love that is true of His presence. If we never meditate on His love for us, we will not experience it.

Paul prayed in Ephesians 3 that the people would experience the love of God for themselves. The Bible says that He loves us. But how many of God's children still lack a revelation concerning God's love?

I remember when I began my ministry. The first week I was to conduct a meeting, I asked the Lord what He wanted me to teach and He responded, "Tell My people that I love them."

"They know that," I said. "I want to teach them something really powerful, not a Sunday school lesson out of John 3:16."

The Lord said to me, "Very few of my people really know how much I love them. If they did, they would act differently."

As I began to study the subject of receiving God's love, I realized that I was in desperate need myself. The Lord led me in my study to 1 John 4:16 which states that we should be conscious of God's love. That means it should be something we are actively aware of.

I had an unconscious, vague sort of understanding that God loved me, but the love of God is meant to be a powerful force in our lives, one that will take us through even the most difficult trials into victory.

In Romans 8:35 the Apostle Paul exhorts us, "Who shall ever separate us from Christ's love? Shall suffering and affliction and tribulation? Or calamity and distress? Or persecution or hunger or destitution or peril or sword?" Then in verse 37 he goes on to say, "Yet amid all these things we are more than conquerors and gain a surpassing victory through Him Who loved us."

I studied in this area for a long time, and I became conscious and aware of God's love for me through thinking about His love and by confessing it out loud. I learned Scriptures about the love of God, and I meditated on them and confessed them out of my mouth. I did this over and over for months, and all the time the revelation of His unconditional love for me was becoming more and more of a reality to me.

Now, His love is so real to me that even in hard times, I am comforted by the "conscious knowing" that He loves me and that I no longer have to live in fear.

FEAR NOT

There is no fear in love; but perfect love casteth out fear.
1 John 4:18 KJV

God loves us perfectly, just as we are. Romans 5:8 tells us that "God commendeth his love toward us, in that, while we were yet sinners, Christ died for us" (KJV).

Believers operating out of the mind of Christ are not going to think about how terrible they are. They will have righteousness-based thoughts. You should have a righteousness-consciousness, meditating regularly on who you are "in Christ." We don't have right standing with God because we do everything right, but because He gives us right standing as a gift of His grace. When received by faith, the gift of righteousness will begin to produce more and more right behavior.

BE RIGHTEOUSNESS-CONSCIOUS, NOT SIN-CONSCIOUS

For our sake He made Christ [virtually] to be sin Who knew no sin, so that in and through Him we might become [endued with, viewed as being in, and examples of] the righteousness of God [what we ought to be, approved and acceptable and in right relationship with Him, by His goodness].
2 Corinthians 5:21

A large number of believers are tormented by negative thinking about themselves. Thoughts about how God must be so displeased with them because of all their weaknesses and failures.

How much time do you waste living under guilt and condemnation? Notice I said how much time do you *waste,* because that is exactly what all that kind of thinking is, a waste of time!

Don't think about how terrible you were before you came to Christ. Instead, think about how you have been made the righteousness of God in Him. Remember: *thoughts turn into actions.* If you ever want to behave any better, you have to change your thinking first. Keep thinking about how terrible you are, and you will only act worse. Every time a negative, condemning thought comes to your mind, remind yourself that God loves you, that you have been made the righteousness of God in Christ.

You are changing for the better all the time. Every day you're growing spiritually. God has a glorious plan for your life. These are the truths you must think on.

This is what you are supposed to be doing with your mind!

Think deliberately according to the Word of God; don't just think whatever falls into your head, receiving it as your own thought.

Rebuke the devil and start going forward by thinking right thoughts.

Step 4. Have an exhortative mind.

He who exhorts (encourages), to his exhortation.

Romans 12:8

The person with the mind of Christ thinks positive, uplifting, edifying thoughts about other people as well as about himself and his own circumstances.

The ministry of exhortation is greatly needed in the world today. You will never exhort anyone with your words if you have not first had kind thoughts about that individual. Remember that whatever is in your heart will come out of your mouth. Do some "love thinking" on purpose.

Send thoughts of love toward other people. Speak words of encouragement to them.

Vine's Expository Dictionary of Old and New Testament Words defines the Greek word *parakaleo,* which is translated *exhort,* as "primarily, to call to a person (*para* to the side, *kaleo,* to call)...to admonish, exhort, to urge one to pursue some course of conduct."[3] I interpret this definition to mean coming alongside a person and urging him to press forward in pursuing a course of action. The ministry gift of exhortation spoken of in Romans 12:8 can readily be seen in those who have it. They are always saying something encouraging or uplifting to everyone—something that makes others feel better and encourages them to press on.

We may not all have the ministry gift of exhortation, but anyone can learn to be encouraging. The simple rule is: if it's not good, then don't think it or say it.

Everyone has enough problems already; we don't need to add to their troubles by tearing them down. We should build up one another in love (see Eph. 4:29). Don't forget: love always believes the best of everyone (see 1 Cor. 13:7).

As you begin to think lovely thoughts about people, you will find them behaving in a more lovely manner. Thoughts and words are containers or weapons for carrying creative or destructive power. They can be used against Satan and his works or they can actually help him in his plan of destruction.

Let's say you have a child who has some behavior problems and definitely needs to change. You pray for him and ask God to work in his life, making whatever changes are necessary. Now what do you do with your thoughts and words concerning him during the waiting period? Many people never see the answer to their prayers because they negate what they have asked for with their own thoughts and words before God ever gets a chance to work in their behalf.

Do you pray for your child to change and then entertain all kinds of negative thoughts about him? Or, perhaps pray for change and then think and even say to others, "This kid will never change!"

To live in victory, you must begin by lining up your thoughts with God's Word.

We are not walking in the Word if our thoughts are opposite of what it says. We are not walking in the Word if we are not thinking in the Word.

When you pray for someone, line up your thoughts and words with what you have prayed and you will begin to see a breakthrough.

I am not suggesting that you get out of balance and refuse to acknowledge that a problem exists. If your child has a behavior problem in school, and a friend asks how he is doing, what should you do if, in reality, no change has been manifested? You can say, "Well, we have not seen the breakthrough yet, but I believe God is working and we will see change soon."

Step 5. Develop a thankful mind.

Enter into His gates with thanksgiving and a thank offering and into His courts with praise! Be thankful and say so to Him, bless and affectionately praise His name!

Psalm 100:4

A person flowing in the mind of Christ will find his thoughts filled with praise and thanksgiving

Many doors are opened to the enemy through complaining. Some people are physically ill and live weak, powerless lives due to this disease called complaining that attacks the thoughts and conversations of people.

A powerful life cannot be lived without thanksgiving. The Bible instructs us over and over in the principle of thanksgiving. Complaining in thought or word is a death principle, but being thankful and saying so is a life principle.

If a person does not have a thankful heart (mind), thanksgiving will not come out of his mouth. When we are thankful, we will say so.

Be Thankful at All Times

Through Him, therefore, let us constantly and at all times offer up to God a sacrifice of praise, which is the fruit of lips that thankfully acknowledge and confess and glorify His name.
Hebrews 13:15

When do we offer thanksgiving? At all times—in every situation, in all things—and by so doing we enter into the victorious life where the devil cannot control us.

How can he control us if we are going to be joyful and thankful no matter what our circumstances are? Admittedly, this kind of lifestyle sometimes requires a sacrifice of praise or thanksgiving, but I would rather sacrifice my thanksgiving to God than sacrifice my joy to Satan. I have learned (the hard way) that if I get grumpy and refuse to give thanks, then I will end up giving up my joy. In other words, I will lose it to the spirit of complaining.

In Psalm 34:1 the psalmist says, "I will bless the Lord at all times; His praise shall continually be in my mouth." How can we be a blessing to the Lord? By letting His praise *continually* be in our thoughts and mouths.

Be a grateful person—one filled with gratitude not only toward God, but also toward people. When someone does something nice for you, let him know that you appreciate it.

Show appreciation in your family among the various members. So often, we take for granted the things that God has blessed us with. A sure way to lose something is not to appreciate it.

I appreciate my husband; we have been married a long time but I still tell him that I appreciate him. He is a very patient man in many ways and has a lot of other really good qualities. I know that it helps build and maintain good relationships to let people know that we appreciate them, even mentioning certain things specifically that we are thankful for.

I deal with many people, and it continues to amaze me how some people are so thankful for every little thing that is done for them, while others are never satisfied no matter how much is done on their behalf. I believe pride has something to do with this problem. Some people are so full of themselves that no matter what others do for them, they think they deserve not only that, but more! They seldom express appreciation.

Expressing appreciation is not only good for the other person, but it is good for us, because it releases joy in us.

Meditate daily on all the things you have to be thankful for. Rehearse them to the Lord in prayer, and as you do you will find your heart filling up with life and light.

OFFER THANKS ALWAYS FOR EVERYTHING

And do not get drunk with wine, for that is debauchery; but ever be filled and stimulated with the [Holy] Spirit.

Speak out to one another [the *King James Version* says "speaking to yourselves"] in psalms and hymns and spiritual songs, offering praise with voices [and instruments] and making melody with all your heart to the Lord,

At all times and for everything giving thanks in the name of our Lord Jesus Christ to God the Father.

Ephesians 5:18-20

What a powerful group of Scriptures!

How can you and I stay ever filled with the Holy Spirit? By speaking to ourselves (through our thoughts) or to others (through our words) in psalms and hymns and spiritual songs. I don't think that means we have to merely quote Scripture and sing songs to one another, but it infers that we should keep our thoughts and words on, and full of, the Word of God by offering praise *at all times and for everything, giving thanks.*

Step 6. Be Word-Minded.

> And you have not His word (His thought) living in your hearts, because you do not believe and adhere to and trust in and rely on Him Whom He has sent. [That is why you do not keep His message living in you, because you do not believe in the Messenger Whom He has sent.]
>
> John 5:38

God's Word is His thoughts written down on paper for our study and consideration. His Word is how He thinks about every situation and subject.

In John 5:38 Jesus was chastising some unbelievers. We see from this translation that God's Word is a written expression of His thoughts and that people who want to believe and experience all the good results of believing must allow His Word to be a living message in their hearts. This is accomplished by meditating on the Word of God. This is how His thoughts can become our thoughts—the only way to develop the mind of Christ in us.

The Bible in John 1:14 says that Jesus was the Word made flesh. That would not have been possible had His mind not been filled with the Word of God continually.

Meditating on the Word of God is one of the most important life principles that we can learn. *Vine's Expository Dictionary of Old and New Testament Words* defines the two Greek words translated *meditate* as follows: "to care for," "to attend to, practise," to "be diligent in," "to practise [in] the prevalent sense of the word," "to ponder, imagine," "to premeditate."[4] Another resource adds "to murmur" or "to mutter" to the definition.[5]

I can't emphasize strongly enough how important this principle is. I call it a life principle because meditating on the Word of God will minister life to you and ultimately to those around you.

Many Christians have become fearful of the word *meditate* due to the meditation practices of pagan and occult religions. But I urge you to remember that Satan has really never had an original idea. He takes what belongs to the Kingdom of Light and perverts it for the kingdom of darkness. We must be wise enough to realize that if meditation produces such power for the side of evil, that it will also produce power for the cause of good. The principle of meditation comes straight out of the Word of God; let's take a look at what the Bible has to say about it.

MEDITATE AND PROSPER

This Book of the Law shall not depart out of your mouth, but you shall meditate on it day and night, that you may observe and do according to all that is written in it. For then you shall make your way prosperous, and then you shall deal wisely and have good success.

Joshua 1:8

In this verse, the Lord is telling us plainly that we will never put the Word into practice physically if we don't first practice it mentally.

Psalm 1:2,3 speaks of the godly man and says, "But his delight and desire are in the law of the Lord, and on His law (the precepts, the instructions, the teachings of God) he habitually meditates (ponders and studies) by day and by night. And he shall be like a tree firmly planted [and tended] by the streams of water, ready to bring forth its fruit in its season; its leaf also shall not fade or wither; and everything he does shall prosper [and come to maturity]."

MEDITATE AND BE HEALED

My son, attend to my words; consent and submit to my sayings. Let them not depart from your sight; keep them in the center of your heart. For they are life to those who find them, healing and health to all their flesh.

Proverbs 4:20-22

Remembering that one of the defining words for *meditate* is "to attend to," consider this passage of Scripture which says that the words of the Lord are a source of health and healing to the flesh.

Meditating (pondering, thinking about) the Word of God in our mind will actually affect our physical body. My appearance has been changed during the years I have been in relationship with Jesus. I look better because I am not worried, sad, and miserable. Misery shows on our faces, but so does joy. The happier we are, the younger we look, so even though I am aging in years, inwardly I am being renewed day by day and it shows on the outside.

HEAR AND HARVEST

And He said to them, Be careful what you are hearing. The measure [of thought and study] you give [to the truth you hear] will be the measure [of virtue and knowledge] that comes back to you—and more [besides] will be given to you who hear.

Mark 4:24

This is like the principle of sowing and reaping. The more we sow, the more we will reap at harvest time. The Lord is saying in Mark 4:24 that the greater the amount of time you and I personally put into thinking about and studying the Word we hear, the more we will get out of it.

READ AND REAP

[Things are hidden temporarily only as a means to revelation.] For there is nothing hidden except to be revealed, nor is anything [temporarily] kept secret except in order that it may be made known.

Mark 4:22

These two verses together are surely telling us that the Word has hidden in it tremendous treasures, powerful life-giving secrets that God wants to reveal to us. They are manifested to those who meditate on, ponder, study, think about, practice mentally, and mutter the Word of God.

I know personally, as a teacher of God's Word, the truth of this principle. It seems there is no end to what God can show me out of one verse of Scripture. I will study it one time and get one thing, and another time see something new that I did not even notice before.

The Lord keeps revealing His secrets to those who are diligent about the Word. Don't be the kind of person who always wants to live off of someone else's revelation. Study the Word yourself and allow the Holy Spirit to bless your life with truth.

I could go on and on about the subject of meditating on God's Word. As I have said, it is one of the most important things that you and I can learn to do. All day long, as you go about your daily affairs, ask the Holy Spirit to remind you of certain Scriptures so you can meditate on them. You will be amazed at how much power will be released into your life from this practice. The more you meditate on the Word of God, the more you will be able to readily draw upon its strength in times of trouble. Remember: *the power to do the Word comes from the practice of meditating on it.*

RECEIVE AND WELCOME THE WORD

So get rid of all uncleanness and the rampant outgrowth of wickedness, and in a humble (gentle, modest) spirit receive and welcome the Word which implanted and rooted [in your hearts] contains the power to save your souls.

James 1:21

We see from this Scripture that the Word has the power to save us from a life of sin, but only as it is received, welcomed and implanted and rooted in our hearts (minds). This implanting and rooting takes place through attending to God's Word—by having it on our mind more than anything else.

If you and I meditate on our problems all the time, we will become more deeply rooted in them. If we meditate on what is wrong with ourselves or others, we will become more deeply convinced of the problem and never see the solution. It is as if there is an ocean full of life available to us, and the instrument we are given to draw it forth is diligent study and meditation of the Word of God.

Our ministry is called Enjoying Everyday Life, and I can say from experience that we truly can enjoy life to the fullest through loving and obeying the Word of God.

CHOOSE LIFE!

Now the mind of the flesh [which is sense and reason without the Holy Spirit] is death [death that comprises all the miseries arising from sin, both here and hereafter]. But the mind of the [Holy] Spirit is life and [soul] peace [both now and forever].

Romans 8:6

Calling your attention again to Philippians 4:8 seems to be a good way to close this section of the book, "Whatever is true, whatever is worthy of reverence and is honorable and seemly, whatever is just, whatever is pure, whatever is lovely and lovable, whatever is kind and winsome and gracious, if there is any virtue and excellence, if there is anything worthy of praise, think on and weigh and take account of these things [fix your minds on them]."

The condition your mind should be in is described in this Scripture. You have the mind of Christ, begin to use it. If He wouldn't think it, you shouldn't think it either.

It is by this continual "watching over" your thoughts that you begin to take every thought captive unto the obedience of Jesus Christ (see 2 Cor. 10:5 KJV).

The Holy Spirit is quick to remind you if your mind is beginning to take you in a wrong direction, then the decision becomes yours. Will you flow in the mind of the flesh or in the mind of the Spirit? One leads to death, the other to life. The choice is yours.

Choose life!

PART III:

Wilderness Mentalities

Introduction

The people of the nation of Israel wandered around in the wilderness for forty years making what was actually an eleven-day journey. Why? Was it their enemies, their circumstances, the trials along the way, or something entirely different that prevented them from arriving at their destination?

It is [only] eleven days' journey from Horeb by the way of Mount Seir to Kadesh-barnea [on Canaan's border; yet Israel took forty years to get beyond it].

DEUTERONOMY 1:2

As I was pondering this situation, God gave me a powerful revelation that has helped me personally as well as thousands of others. The Lord said to me, "The Children of Israel spent forty years in the wilderness making an eleven-day trip because they had a 'wilderness mentality.'"

YOU HAVE STAYED HERE LONG ENOUGH

The Lord our God said to us in Horeb, You have dwelt long enough on this mountain.

Deuteronomy 1:6

We really shouldn't look at the Israelites with such astonishment because most of us do the same thing they did. We keep going around and around the same mountains instead of making progress. The result is, it takes us years to experience victory over something that could have and should have been dealt with quickly.

I think the Lord is saying the same thing to you and me today that He said to the Children of Israel in their day:

"You have dwelt long enough on the same mountain; it is time to move on."

Set Your Mind and Keep It Set

And set your minds and keep them set on what is above (the higher things), not on the things that are on the earth.

Colossians 3:2

God showed me ten "wilderness mentalities" that the Israelites had that kept them in the wilderness. A wilderness mentality is a wrong mindset.

We can have right or wrong mindsets. The right ones benefit us, and the wrong ones hurt us and hinder our progress. Colossians 3:2 teaches us to set our minds and keep them set. We need our minds set in the right direction. Wrong mindsets not only affect our circumstances, but they also affect our inner life.

Some people have a wilderness-type life, because they *are* a wilderness.

There was a time when my circumstances were not really bad, but I could not enjoy anything in my life because I was a "wilderness" inside. Dave and I had a nice home, four lovely children, good jobs, and enough money to live comfortably. I could not enjoy our blessings because I had several wilderness mentalities. My life appeared to me to be a wilderness because that is the way I saw everything.

Some people see things negatively because they have experienced unhappy circumstances all their lives and can't imagine anything getting any better. Then there are some people who see everything as bad and negative simply because that is the way they are on the inside. Whatever its cause, a negative outlook leaves a person miserable and unlikely of making any progress toward the Promised Land.

God had called the Children of Israel out of bondage in Egypt to go to the land He had promised to give them as a perpetual inheritance—a land that flowed with milk and honey and every good thing that they could imagine, a land in which there would be no shortage of anything they needed, a land of prosperity in every realm of their existence.

Most of the generation that the Lord called out of Egypt never entered into the Promised Land; instead, they died in the wilderness. To me, this is one of the saddest things that can happen to a child of God—to have so much available and yet never be able to enjoy any of it.

I was one of those people for many years of my Christian life. I was on my way to heaven, but I was not enjoying the trip. I was miserable in the wilderness. But, thank God for His mercy, a light shone in my darkness, and He led me out.

I pray that this section of the book will be a light to you and prepare you to walk out of your wilderness into the glorious light of God's marvelous Kingdom.

Chapter
16

*"My future is determined by
my past and my present."*

Wilderness Mentality #1

Wilderness Mentality #1

The Israelites had no positive vision for their lives—no dreams. They knew where they came from, but they did not know where they were going. Everything was based on what they had seen and could see. They did not know how to see with "the eye of faith."

Where there is no vision, the people perish.
PROVERBS 29:18 KJV

ANOINTED TO BRING DELIVERANCE

The Spirit of the Lord is upon me, because he hath anointed me to preach the gospel to the poor; he hath sent me to heal the brokenhearted, to preach deliverance to the captives, and recovering of sight to the blind, to set at liberty them that are bruised.

To preach the acceptable year of the Lord.

Luke 4:18,19 KJV

I come from a background of abuse; I was raised in a dysfunctional home. My childhood was filled with fear and torment. The experts say that a child's personality is formed within the first five years of his life. My personality was a mess! I lived in pretense behind walls of protection that I had built to keep people from hurting me. I was locking others out, but I was also locking myself in. I was a controller, so filled with fear that the only way I could face life was to feel that I was in control, and then no one could hurt me.

As a young adult trying to live for Christ and follow the Christian lifestyle, I knew where I had come from, but I did not know where I was going. I felt that my future would always be marred by my past. I thought, "How could anyone who has the kind of past I do ever be really all right? It's impossible!" However, Jesus said that He came to make well those who were sick, brokenhearted, wounded and bruised, those broken down by calamity.

Jesus came to open the prison doors and set the captives free. I did not make any progress until I started to believe that I could be set free. I had to have a positive vision for my life; I had to believe that my future was not determined by my past or even my present.

You may have had a miserable past, you may even be in current circumstances that are very negative and depressing. You may be facing situations that are so bad it seems you have no real reason to hope. But I say to you boldly, *your future is not determined by your past or your present!*

Get a new mindset. Believe that with God all things are possible (see Luke 18:27); with man some things may be impossible, but we serve a God Who created everything we see out of nothing (see Heb. 11:3). Give Him your nothingness and watch Him go to work. All He needs is your faith in Him. He needs for you to believe, and He will do the rest.

EYES TO SEE, EARS TO HEAR

And there shall come forth a rod out of the stem of Jesse, and a Branch shall grow out of his roots:

And the spirit of the LORD shall rest upon him, the spirit of wisdom and understanding, the spirit of counsel and might, the spirit of knowledge and of the fear of the LORD;

And shall make him of quick understanding in the fear of the LORD: and he shall not judge after the sight of his eyes, neither reprove after the hearing of his ears.

Isaiah 11:1-3 KJV

We cannot judge things accurately by the sight of our natural eyes. We must have spiritual "eyes to see" and "ears to hear." We need to hear what the Spirit says, not what the world says. Let God speak to you about your future—not everyone else.

The Israelites continually looked at and talked about the way things were. God brought them out of Egypt by the hand of Moses, talking to them through him about the Promised Land. He wanted them to keep their eyes on where they were going—and off of where they had been. Let's look at a few Scriptures that clearly depict their wrong attitude.

What Is the Problem?

All the Israelites grumbled and deplored their situation, accusing Moses and Aaron, to whom the whole congregation said, Would that we had died in Egypt! Or that we had died in this wilderness!

Why does the Lord bring us to this land to fall by the sword? Our wives and little ones will be a prey. Is it not better for us to return to Egypt?

Numbers 14:2,3

I encourage you to look over this passage carefully. Notice how negative these people were—complaining, ready to give up easily, preferring to go back to bondage rather than press through the wilderness into the Promised Land.

Actually, they did not have a problem, they were the problem!

Bad Thoughts Produce Bad Attitudes

Now there was no water for the congregation, and they assembled together against Moses and Aaron.

And the people contended with Moses, and said, Would that we had died when our brethren died [in the plague] before the Lord!

And why have you brought up the congregation of the Lord into this wilderness, that we should die here, we and our livestock?

Numbers 20:2-4

It is easy to see from their own words that the Israelites were not trusting God at all. They had a negative, failure attitude. They decided they would fail before they ever really got started, simply because every circumstance was not perfect. They displayed an attitude that came from a wrong mindset.

Bad attitudes are the fruit of bad thoughts.

A LACK OF AN ATTITUDE OF GRATITUDE

And they journeyed from Mount Hor by the way to the Red Sea, to go around the land of Edom, and the people became impatient (depressed, much discouraged), because [of the trials] of the way.

And the people spoke against God and against Moses, Why have you brought us out of Egypt to die in the wilderness? For there is no bread, neither is there any water, and we loathe this light (contemptible, unsubstantial) manna.

Numbers 21:4,5

Along with all the other bad attitudes we have already seen in the previous Scriptures, in this passage we see evidence in the Israelites of a tremendous lack of gratitude. The Children of Israel simply could not quit thinking about where they had come from and where they were long enough to get where they were going.

It would have helped them to consider their forefather Abraham. He went through some disappointing experiences in his life, but he did not allow them to negatively affect his future.

NO LIFE WITH STRIFE

And there was strife between the herdsmen of Abram's cattle and the herdsmen of Lot's cattle. And the Canaanite and the Perizzite were dwelling then in the land [making fodder more difficult to obtain].

So Abram said to Lot, Let there be no strife, I beg of you, between you and me, or between your herdsmen and my herdsmen, for we are relatives.

Is not the whole land before you? Separate yourself, I beg of you, from me. If you take the left hand, then I will go to the right; or if you choose the right hand, then I will go to the left.

And Lot looked and saw that everywhere the Jordan Valley was well watered. Before the Lord destroyed Sodom and Gomorrah, [it was all] like the garden of the Lord, like the land of Egypt, as you go to Zoar.

Then Lot chose for himself all the Jordan Valley and [he] traveled east. So they separated.

Genesis 13:7-11

Abraham knew the dangers of living in strife; therefore, he told Lot that they needed to separate. In order to walk in love, and to ensure that there would be no strife between them in the future, Abraham allowed his nephew to choose which valley he wanted first. Lot chose the best one—the Jordan Valley—and they separated.

We must remember that Lot had nothing until Abraham blessed him. Think of the attitude that Abraham could have had, but chose not to! He knew that if he acted properly God would take care of him.

LIFT UP YOUR EYES AND LOOK

The Lord said to Abram after Lot had left him, Lift up now your eyes and look from the place where you are, northward and southward and eastward and westward;

For all the land which you see I will give to you and to your posterity forever.

Genesis 13:14,15

This passage clearly reveals that even though Abraham found himself in less desirable circumstances after his separation from his nephew, God wanted him to "look up" from the place where he was to the place that He wanted to take him.

Abraham had a good attitude about his situation, and as a result the devil could not keep the blessings of God from him. God gave him even more possessions than he had enjoyed before the separation, and blessed him mightily in every way.

I encourage you to take a positive look at the possibilities of the future and begin to "calleth those things which be not as though they were" (Rom. 4:17 KJV). Think and speak about your future in a positive way, according to what God has placed in your heart, and not according to what you have seen in the past or are seeing even now in the present.

Chapter 17

*"Someone do it for me; I don't
want to take the responsibility."*

Wilderness Mentality #2

"Someone do it for me; I don't want to take the responsibility."

Wilderness Mentality #2

Responsibility is often defined as our response to God's ability. To be responsible is to respond to the opportunities that God has placed in front of us.

God gave Abram's father a responsibility, a chance to respond to His ability. He placed before him the opportunity to go to Canaan. But instead of going all the way with the Lord, he chose to stop and settle in Haran.

And Terah took Abram his son, Lot the son of Haran, his grandson, and Sarai his daughter-in-law, his son Abram's wife, and they went forth together to go from Ur of the Chaldees into the land of Canaan; but when they came to Haran, they settled there.

GENESIS 11:31

It is fairly easy to be excited when God first speaks to us and gives us an opportunity to do something. But, like Terah, many times we never finish what we start because we get into it and realize there is more involved than goose bumps and excitement.

Most new ventures are exciting simply because they are new. Excitement will carry a person along for a while, but it will not take him across the finish line.

Many believers do what the Bible says Terah did. They start out for one place and settle somewhere else along the way. They get tired or weary; they would like to finish their course, but they really don't want all the responsibility that goes with it. If someone else would do it for them, they would love to reap the benefits, but it just does not work that way.

PERSONAL RESPONSIBILITY CAN'T BE DELEGATED

The next day Moses said to the people, You have sinned a great sin. And now I will go up to the Lord; perhaps I can make atonement for your sin.

So Moses returned to the Lord, and said, Oh, these people have sinned a great sin and have made themselves gods of gold!

Yet now, if You will forgive their sin—and if not, blot me, I pray You, out of Your book which You have written!

Exodus 32:30-32

In my reading and study, I noticed that the Israelites did not want to take responsibility for anything. Moses did their praying; he sought God for them, he even did their repenting when they got themselves in trouble. (See Ex. 32:1-14.)

A baby has no responsibility at all, but as the child grows up, he is expected to take more and more responsibility. One of the main roles of a parent is to teach their children to accept responsibility. God desires to teach His children the same thing.

The Lord gave me an opportunity to be in full-time ministry—to teach His Word on international radio and television—to preach the gospel all over the United States and in other nations. But I can assure you that there is a responsibility side to that call that many know nothing of. A lot of people say they want to be in ministry because they think it is a continual spiritual event.

Many times people apply for a job in our ministry thinking that the greatest thing that could ever happen to them would be to become a part of a Christian ministry. Later, they discover that they have to work there the same as any other place; they have to get up and get there on time, come under authority, follow a daily routine, etc. When people say they want to come to work for us, we tell them that we don't float around on a cloud all day singing "The Hallelujah Chorus"—we work, and we work hard. We walk in integrity and do what we do with excellence.

Of course, it *is* a privilege to work in ministry, but we try to make the point to new applicants that when the goose bumps and excitement have subsided, they will find us expecting high levels of responsibility from them.

GO TO THE ANT!

Go to the ant, you sluggard; consider her ways and be wise!—

Which, having no chief, overseer, or ruler,

Provides her food in the summer and gathers her supplies in the harvest.

How long will you sleep, O sluggard? When will you arise out of your sleep?

Yet a little sleep, a little slumber, a little folding of the hands to lie down and sleep—

So will your poverty come like a robber or one who travels [with slowly but surely approaching steps] and your want like an armed man [making you helpless].

Proverbs 6:6-11

This lazy mindset that the Israelites had was one of the things that kept them in the wilderness forty years making an eleven-day trip.

I like to read this passage in Proverbs in which our attention is called to the ant, who without having any supervisor or taskmaster provides for herself and her family.

People who must always have someone else pushing them will never really do anything great. Those who only do what is right when someone is looking won't get very far either. We must be motivated from within, not from without. We must live our lives before God, knowing that He sees all and that our reward will come from Him if we persist in doing what He has asked us to do.

Many Called, Few Chosen

For many are called, but few chosen.

Matthew 20:16

I once heard a Bible teacher say that this verse means that many are called or given an opportunity to do something for the Lord, but very few are willing to take the responsibility to answer that call.

As I mentioned in a previous chapter, a lot of people have wishbone but no backbone. People with a "wilderness mentality" want to have everything and do nothing.

Get Up and Go!

After the death of Moses the servant of the Lord, the Lord said to Joshua son of Nun, Moses' minister,

Moses My servant is dead. So now arise [take his place], go over this Jordan, you and all this people, into the land which I am giving to them, the Israelites.

Every place upon which the sole of your foot shall tread, that have I given to you, as I promised Moses.

Joshua 1:1-3

When God told Joshua that Moses was dead and he was to take his place and lead the people across the Jordan into the Promised Land, it meant a lot of new responsibility for Joshua.

The same is true for us as we go forth to claim our spiritual inheritance. You and I will never have the privilege of being used by God if we are not willing to take our responsibility seriously.

Behold, Now Is the Favorable Time!

He who observes the wind [and waits for all conditions to be favorable] will not sow, and he who regards the clouds will not reap.

Ecclesiastes 11:4

In 1993, when God showed Dave and me that He wanted us to go on TV, He said, "I am giving you an opportunity to go on television; but if you don't take the opportunity now, it will never pass by you again." Perhaps if God had not let us know that we needed to respond immediately, we might have procrastinated. After all, we were finally in a position where we could be comfortable. If we procrastinate long enough, sometimes God has to find someone else who will respond to His call right away.

For nine years, we had been in the process of "birthing" the ministry. Now suddenly God was giving us an opportunity to reach more people, which we wanted to do with all of our heart. However, in order to do it, we would need to leave our comfortable position and take on new responsibility.

When the Lord asks His people to do something, there is a temptation to wait for "a convenient season" (Acts 24:25 KJV). There is always the tendency to hold back until it won't cost anything or be so difficult.

I encourage you to be a person who is not afraid of responsibility. In meeting resistance you will build your strength. If you only do what is easy, you will always remain weak.

God expects you and me to be responsible and to take care of everything He gives us—to do something with it that will produce good fruit. If we do not use the gifts and talents that He has given us, then we are not being responsible over what He has entrusted to us.

BE PREPARED!

Watch therefore [give strict attention and be cautious and active], for you know neither the day nor the hour when the Son of Man will come.

Matthew 25:13

Matthew 25 is a chapter in the Bible that teaches us what we are to be doing while we are waiting for the Master's return.

The first twelve verses show us ten virgins, five who were foolish and five who were wise. The foolish did not want to do anything extra to be sure they were prepared to meet Him when He returned. They did the bare minimum they could get by with; they did not want to go the extra mile so they took only the amount of oil they needed for their lamps. The wise virgins, however, went beyond what they absolutely had to do. They took extra oil to be sure they were prepared for a long wait.

When the bridegroom came, the foolish found their lamps going out and they, of course, wanted the wise virgins to give them some of their oil. This is usually the case. People who are lazy and procrastinating always want those who work hard and take responsibility to do for them what they should have been doing for themselves.

USE WHAT YOU'VE BEEN GIVEN

You wicked and lazy and idle servant!

Matthew 25:26

Matthew 25 then records a parable that Jesus told about three servants who were given talents that belonged to their master. The master then went away into a far country, expecting his servants to take good care of his goods while he was away.

The man given five talents used them. He invested them and gained five more besides. The man given two talents did the same. But the man given one talent buried it in the ground because he was full of fear. He was scared to step out and do anything. He was afraid of responsibility.

When the master returned, he commended the two servants who had taken what he had given them and had done something with it. But to the man who buried his talent and had done nothing with it, he said, "You wicked and lazy and idle servant!" He then ordered that the one talent be taken from him and given to the man with the ten talents and that the lazy, idle servant be severely punished.

I encourage you to respond to the ability that God has placed in you by doing all that you can with it, so that when the Master returns, you can not only give Him what He has given you, but more besides.

The Bible clearly shows us that it is God's will for us to bear good fruit (see John 15:16).

CASTING CARE, NOT RESPONSIBILITY

Humble yourselves therefore under the mighty hand of God, that he may exalt you in due time: Casting all your care upon him; for he careth for you.

1 Peter 5:6,7 KJV

Don't be afraid of responsibility. Learn to cast your care, but not your responsibility. Some people learn not to worry about anything; becoming experts at "casting their care," they get so comfortable that they also cast their responsibility.

Set your mind to do what is in front of you and not to run from anything just because it looks challenging.

Always remember that if God gives you whatever you ask Him for, there is a responsibility that goes along with the blessing. If you own a home or a car, God expects you to take care of it. Laziness may attack your mind and your feelings, but you have the mind of Christ. You certainly can recognize the devil's deception and press past your feelings and do what you know is right. Asking for something is easy ... being responsible for it is the part that develops character.

I recall a time when I kept trying to talk my husband into buying a lake house—a place where we could go to rest, pray, and study. A place to "get away from it all." I told him how wonderful it would be, how our children and grandchildren could enjoy it, and even how we could take our leadership there and have business meetings and glorious times in prayer together.

It all sounded good, and it felt good to my emotions, but Dave kept telling me everything we would have to do to take care of it. He reminded me of how busy we already were and that we did not have time to be responsible for another home. He told me about the lawn care, the upkeep, the payments, etc. He said we would be better off to rent a place when we needed to get away and not take on the responsibility of owning one.

I was looking at the emotional side of the issue, and he was looking at the practical side. Any time we make a decision, we should look at both sides—not just what will be enjoyable, but the responsibility it will require. A lake home is perfectly fine for those who have the time to put into it, but we really didn't. Deep down I knew that, but on and off for a year I tried to talk Dave into buying one.

I'm glad he stayed firm. If he hadn't, I am sure we would have bought the place, kept it for a while, complained a lot about having to take care of it, and probably ended up selling it because it was too much work. As it turned out, friends of ours bought a lake home and let us use it as our schedule and theirs permitted. Several years later we were in a position to own a place of our own, and it was the right time to move forward. But when I first wanted a lake house, it would have been the wrong time in our lives to buy one. Wanting something is not enough—we must also be fully prepared to take responsibility for it.

If you use wisdom, you will find God meeting your needs. Anyone operating in the mind of Christ will walk in wisdom—not emotions.

Be responsible!

Chapter
18

*"Please make everything easy;
I can't take it if things are too hard!"*

Wilderness Mentality #3

"Please make everything easy; I can't take it if things are too hard!"

Wilderness Mentality #3

This wrong mindset is similar to the one we have just discussed, but enough of a problem among God's people that I believe it is worthy of a chapter in this book.

For this commandment which I command you this day is not too difficult for you, nor is it far off.

DEUTERONOMY 30:11

It is one of the most commonly expressed excuses I hear from people who request prayer. So often, someone will come to me for advice and prayer, and when I tell them what the Word of God says, or what I think the Holy Spirit is saying, their response is, "I know that's right; God has been showing me the same thing. But Joyce, *it's just too hard.*"

God has shown me that the enemy tries to inject this phrase into people's minds to get them to give up. A few years ago when God revealed this truth to me, He instructed me to stop saying how hard everything was, assuring me that if I did, things would get easier.

Even when we are determined to press through and do something, we spend so much time thinking and talking about "how hard it is" that the project ends up being much more difficult than it would have been had we been positive instead of negative.

When I initially began to see from the Word of God how I was supposed to live and behave, and compared it to where I was, I was always saying, "I want to do things Your way, God, but it is so hard." The Lord led me to Deuteronomy 30:11 in which He says that His commandments are not too difficult or too far away.

The reason our Lord's commands are not too difficult for us is because He gives us His Spirit to work in us powerfully and to help us in all He has asked of us.

The Helper

And I will ask the Father, and He will give you another Comforter (Counselor, Helper, Intercessor, Advocate, Strengthener, and Standby), that He may remain with you forever.

John 14:16

Things get hard when we are trying to do them independently without leaning on and relying on God's grace. If everything in life were easy, we would not even need the power of the Holy Spirit to help us. The Bible refers to Him as "the Helper." He is in us and with us all the time to *help* us, to enable us to do what we cannot do—and, I might add, to do with ease what would be hard without Him.

The Easy Way and the Hard Way

When Pharaoh let the people go, God led them not by way of the land of the Philistines, although that was nearer; for God said, Lest the people change their purpose when they see war and return to Egypt.

Exodus 13:17

You can be sure that anywhere God leads you, He is able to keep you. He never allows more to come on us than we can bear (see 1 Cor. 10:13). Whatever He orders, He pays for. We do not have to live in a constant struggle if we learn to lean on Him continually for the strength we need.

If you know God has asked you to do something, don't back down just because it gets hard. When things get hard, spend more time with Him, lean more on Him and receive more grace from Him (see Heb. 4:16).

Grace is the power of God coming to you at no cost to you, to do through you what you cannot do by yourself. Beware of thoughts that say, "I can't do this; it's just too hard."

Sometimes God leads us the hard way instead of the easy way, because He is doing a work in us. How will we ever learn to lean on

Him, if everything in our lives is so easy that we can handle it by ourselves?

God led the Children of Israel the long, hard way because they were still cowards, and He had to do a work in them to prepare them for the battles they would face in the Promised Land. Even though He led them the hard way, it was not too hard for them. God never gives us more to handle than we can bear. Our way in life only becomes too hard if we think it is too hard.

Most people think that entering the Promised Land means no more battles, but that is incorrect. If you read the accounts of what took place after the Israelites crossed the Jordan River and went in to possess the land of promise, you will see that they fought one battle after another. But they won all those battles fought in God's strength and under His direction.

God led them through the wilderness the longer, harder route even though there was a shorter, easier one because He knew they were not ready for the battles they would face in possessing the land. He was concerned that when they saw the enemy, they might run back to Egypt, so He took them the harder way to teach them Who He was and that they could not depend on themselves.

When a person is going through a hard time, his mind wants to give up. Satan knows that if he can defeat us in our mind, he can defeat us in our experience. That's why it is so important that we not lose heart, grow weary and faint.

HANG TOUGH!

And let us not lose heart and grow weary and faint in acting nobly and doing right, for in due time and at the appointed season we shall reap, if we do not loosen and relax our courage and faint.
Galatians 6:9

Losing heart and fainting refer to giving up in the mind. The Holy Spirit tells us not to give up in our mind, because if we hold on, we will eventually reap.

Think about Jesus. Immediately after being baptized and filled with the Holy Ghost, He was led by the Spirit into the wilderness to be tested and tried by the devil. He did not complain and become discouraged and depressed. He did not think or speak negatively. He did not become confused trying to figure out why this had to happen! He went through each test victoriously.

In the midst of His trial and temptation, our Lord did not wander around the wilderness forty days and nights talking about how hard it was. He drew strength from His heavenly Father and came out in victory. (See Luke 4:1-13.)

Can you imagine Jesus traveling around the country with His disciples talking about how hard everything was? Can you picture Him discussing how difficult going to the cross was going to be...or how He dreaded the things ahead...or how frustrating it was to live under the conditions of their daily lives: roaming the countryside with no place to call home, no roof over their head, no bed to sleep in at night.

In my own situation as I travel from place to place all over the land preaching the gospel, I have had to learn not to talk about the hardships involved in my mobile kind of ministry. I have had to learn not to complain about how hard it is to stay in a strange hotel each time, eat out constantly, sleep in a different bed every weekend, be away from home, meet new people and grow comfortable with them just in time to move on. If I want the privilege of doing what I do, then I have to take the inconveniences that go along with it with a good attitude.

You and I have the mind of Christ, and we can handle things the way He did: by being mentally prepared through "victory thinking"—not "give-up thinking."

SUCCESS FOLLOWS SUFFERING

So, since Christ suffered in the flesh for us, for you, arm yourselves with the same thought and purpose [patiently to suffer rather than fail to please God]. For whoever has suffered in the flesh [having the mind of Christ] is done with [intentional] sin [has stopped pleasing himself and the world, and pleases God],

So that he can no longer spend the rest of his natural life living by [his] human appetites and desires, but [he lives] for what God wills.

1 Peter 4:1,2

This passage teaches us a secret concerning how to make it through difficult things and times. Here is my rendition of these two Scriptures:

Think about everything Jesus went through and how He endured suffering in His flesh, and it will help you make it through your difficulties. Arm yourselves for battle; prepare yourselves to win by thinking as Jesus did: "I will patiently suffer rather than fail to please God." For if you suffer, having the mind of Christ toward it, you will no longer be living just to please yourself, doing whatever is easy and running from all that is hard. But you will be able to live for what God wills and not by your feelings and carnal thoughts.

There is a suffering "in the flesh" that we will have to endure in order to do God's will.

My flesh is not always comfortable with the traveling ministry lifestyle, but I know it is the will of God for me to follow it. Therefore, I have to arm myself with right thinking about it; otherwise, I am defeated before I ever really get started.

There may be an individual in your life who is very difficult to be around, and yet you know that God wants you to stick with the relationship and not run away from it. Your flesh suffers, in that it is not easy to be around that person, but you can prepare yourself by thinking properly about the situation. Even though being in God's will sometimes has some difficulties attached to it, being out of His will is much more difficult.

SELF-SUFFICIENT IN CHRIST'S SUFFICIENCY

I know how to be abased and live humbly in straitened circumstances, and I know also how to enjoy plenty and live in abundance. I have learned in any and all circumstances the secret of facing every situation, whether well-fed or going hungry, having a sufficiency and enough to spare or going without and being in want.

I have strength for all things in Christ Who empowers me [I am ready for anything and equal to anything through Him Who infuses inner strength into me; I am self-sufficient in Christ's sufficiency].

Philippians 4:12,13

Right thinking "arms" us for battle. Going into battle with wrong thinking is like going to the front lines in a war without a weapon. If we do that, we won't last long.

The Israelites were "whiners," which was one reason why they wandered around forty years, making an eleven-day trip. They whined about every difficulty and complained about each new challenge—always talking about how hard everything was. Their mentality was, "Please make everything easy; I can't take it if things are too hard!"

Many believers are Sunday warriors and Monday whiners. They talk a good talk on Sunday—in church with all their friends—but on Monday, when it's time to "walk the talk" and there is nobody around to impress, they faint at the slightest test.

If you are a whiner and a complainer, get a new mindset that says, "I can do all things through Christ who strengthens me" (Phil. 4:13 NKJV).

Chapter 19

*"I can't help it; I'm just addicted
to grumbling, faultfinding,
and complaining."*

Wilderness Mentality #4

"I can't help it; I'm just addicted to grumbling, faultfinding, and complaining."

Wilderness Mentality #4

Until we learn to glorify God by our attitude during hard times, we won't get delivered. It is not suffering that glorifies God, but a godly attitude in suffering that pleases Him and brings glory to Him.

If you and I are going to receive from these verses what God wants us to have, we will have to read them slowly and digest each phrase and sentence thoroughly. I will admit that I studied them for years trying to understand why it pleased God so much to see me suffer when the Bible plainly states that Jesus bore my suffering and pains of punishment (Is. 53:3-6).

For one is regarded favorably (is approved, acceptable, and thankworthy) if, as in the sight of God, he endures the pain of unjust suffering.

[After all] what kind of glory [is there in it] if, when you do wrong and are punished for it, you take it patiently? But if you bear patiently with suffering [which results] when you do right and that is undeserved, it is acceptable and pleasing to God.

1 PETER 2:19,20

It was many years before I realized that the focal point of these verses in 1 Peter is not the suffering but the attitude one should have in suffering.

Notice the word "patiently" being used in this passage, which says that if someone treats us wrong and we handle it patiently, it is pleasing to God. The thing that pleases Him is our patient attitude— not our suffering. To encourage us in our suffering, we are exhorted to look at how Jesus handled the unjust attacks made on Him.

Jesus as Our Example

For even to this were you called [it is inseparable from your vocation]. For Christ also suffered for you, leaving you [His personal] example, so that you should follow in His footsteps.

He was guilty of no sin, neither was deceit (guile) ever found on His lips.

When He was reviled and insulted, He did not revile or offer insult in return; [when] He was abused and suffered, He made no threats [of vengeance]; but He trusted [Himself and everything] to Him Who judges fairly.

1 Peter 2:21-23

Jesus suffered gloriously! Silently, without complaint, trusting God no matter how things looked, he remained the same in every situation. He did not respond patiently when things were easy and impatiently when they were hard or unjust.

The above Scriptures let us know that Jesus is our example and that He came to show us how to live. How we handle ourselves in front of other people shows them how they should live. We teach our children more by example than by words. We are to be living epistles read of all men (see 2 Cor. 3:2,3 KJV)—lights shining out brightly in a dark world (see Phil. 2:15).

Called to Humility, Meekness and Patience

I therefore, the prisoner for the Lord, appeal to and beg you to walk (lead a life) worthy of the [divine] calling to which you have been called [with behavior that is a credit to the summons to God's service,

Living as becomes you] with complete lowliness of mind (humility) and meekness (unselfishness, gentleness, mildness), with patience, bearing with one another and making allowances because you love one another.

Ephesians 4:1,2

Some time ago in our family life there was a situation that serves as an excellent example of my point about suffering humbly, meekly, and patiently.

Our son, Daniel, had just returned from a missions trip to the Dominican Republic. He came back with a severe rash on his arms and several open sores. He had been told that it was the Dominican Republic version of poison ivy. It looked so bad we felt we needed to confirm what it was. Our family doctor was off that day so we made an appointment with the doctor taking his calls.

Our daughter, Sandra, called and made the appointment, told them how old Daniel was, and that she was his sister and would be bringing him in. We were all very busy that day, including Sandra. After a forty-five minute drive, she arrived at the doctor's office only to be told, "Oh, I'm sorry, but it is our policy not to treat minors unaccompanied by a parent."

Sandra explained that when she called, she had specifically said she would be bringing her brother in—that she frequently took him to the doctor for us because of our travels. The nurse stood firm that he had to have a parent with him.

Sandra had an opportunity to get upset. She had pushed herself to add this errand to her already overloaded schedule only to learn that her planning and efforts were all in vain. She had another forty five minute drive home facing her, and the whole thing seemed like such a waste of time.

God helped her remain calm and loving. She called her dad, who was visiting his mother, and he said he would come and take care of the situation. Dave had felt led that morning to go by our offices and pick up some of my books and recorded messages, not even really knowing what he was going to do with them. He just felt he was to go get them.

When he got to the doctor's building, the woman registering patients and helping with paperwork asked Dave if he was a minister and if he was married to Joyce Meyer. He told her he was, and she said that she had been seeing me on television and had heard enough of our family names to wonder if it might be the same person. Dave talked with her awhile and gave her one of my books on emotional healing.

My point in telling you this story is this: what if Sandra had lost her temper and been impatient? Her witness would have been damaged, if not ruined. Actually, it could have done spiritual harm to the woman who sees me on television, and then observes my family behaving badly.

Many people in the world are trying to find God, and what we show them is much more important than what we tell them. It is, of course, important that we verbally share the gospel, but to do so and negate what we have said with our own behavior is worse than to say nothing.

Sandra bore her suffering patiently in this situation, and the Word of God states that we are called to this kind of behavior and attitude.

THE PATIENT SUFFERING OF JOSEPH

He sent a man before them, even Joseph, who was sold as a servant. His feet they hurt with fetters; he was laid in chains of iron and his soul entered into the iron, until his word [to his cruel brothers] came true, until the word of the Lord tried and tested him.

Psalm 105:17-19

As an Old Testament example, think about Joseph who was unjustly mistreated by his brothers. They sold him into slavery and told his father that he had been killed by a wild animal. Meanwhile, he was purchased by a wealthy man named Potiphar, who took him into his home as a slave. God gave Joseph favor everywhere he went, and soon he had favor with his new master.

Joseph kept getting promoted, but another unjust thing happened to him. Potiphar's wife tried to entice him into having an affair, but because he was a man of integrity he would have nothing to do with her. Lying to her husband, she said that Joseph had attacked her, which caused him to be imprisoned for something he hadn't done!

Joseph tried to help others the entire time he was in prison. He never complained, and because he had a proper attitude in suffering, God eventually delivered and promoted him. He ultimately had so much authority in Egypt that no one else in the entire land was above him except Pharaoh himself.

God also vindicated Joseph concerning the situation with his brothers, in that they had to come to Joseph for food when the whole land was in a state of famine. Once again, Joseph displayed a godly attitude by not mistreating them even though they deserved it. He told them what they had meant for his harm, God had worked out for his good—that they were in God's hands, not his, and that he had no right to do anything but bless them. (See Gen. 39-50).

THE DANGERS OF COMPLAINING

We should not tempt the Lord [try His patience, become a trial to Him, critically appraise Him, and exploit His goodness] as some of them did—and were killed by poisonous serpents;

Nor discontentedly complain as some of them did—and were put out of the way entirely by the destroyer (death).

Now these things befell them by way of a figure [as an example and warning to us]; they were written to admonish and fit us for right action by good instruction, we in whose days the ages have reached their climax (their consummation and concluding period).

1 Corinthians 10:9-11

From these passages, we can quickly see the difference between Joseph and the Israelites. He did not complain at all, and all they did was complain about every little thing that did not go their way. The

Bible is very specific about the dangers of grumbling, faultfinding, and complaining.

The message is quite plain. The complaining of the Israelites opened a door for the enemy who came in and destroyed them. They should have appreciated God's goodness—but they didn't—so they paid the price.

We are told that the entire account of their suffering and death was written down to show us what will happen if we behave the way they did.

You and I do not complain with our mouth unless we have first complained in our thoughts. Complaining is definitely a wilderness mentality that will prevent us from crossing over into the Promised Land.

Jesus is our example, and we should do what He did.

The Israelites *complained and remained* in the wilderness.

Jesus *praised and was raised* from the dead.

In this contrast, we can see the power of praise and thanksgiving and also the power of complaining. Yes, complaining, grumbling, murmuring, and faultfinding have power—but it is negative power. Each time we give our minds and mouths over to any of it, we are giving Satan a power over us that God has not authorized him to have.

DON'T GRUMBLE, FIND FAULT, OR COMPLAIN

Do all things without grumbling and faultfinding and complaining [against God] and questioning and doubting [among yourselves],

That you may show yourselves to be blameless and guiltless, innocent and uncontaminated, children of God without blemish (faultless, unrebukable) in the midst of a crooked and wicked generation [spiritually perverted and perverse], among whom you are seen as bright lights (stars or beacons shining out clearly) in the [dark] world.

Philippians 2:14,15

Sometimes it seems that the whole world is complaining. There is so much grumbling and murmuring and so little gratitude and appreciation. People complain about their job and their boss when they should be thankful to have regular work and appreciate the fact that they are not living in a shelter for the homeless somewhere or standing in a soup line.

Many of those poor people would be thrilled to have that job, despite its imperfections. They would be more than willing to put up with a not-so-perfect boss in order to have a regular income, live in their own home, and cook their own food.

Maybe you do need a better paying job or perhaps you do have a boss who treats you unfairly. That is unfortunate, but the way out is not through complaining.

DON'T FRET OR WORRY—PRAY AND GIVE THANKS!

Do not fret or have any anxiety about anything, but in every circumstance and in everything, by prayer and petition (definite requests), with thanksgiving, continue to make your wants known to God.

Philippians 4:6

In this verse the Apostle Paul teaches us how to solve our problems. He instructs us to pray *with thanksgiving* in *every* circumstance.

The Lord taught the same principle to me this way: "Joyce, why should I give you anything else, if you're not thankful for what you already have? Why should I give you something else to complain about?"

If we cannot offer our current prayer requests from a foundation of a life that is currently filled with thanksgiving, we will not get a favorable response. The Word does not say pray with complaining, it says pray with thanksgiving.

Murmuring, grumbling, faultfinding, and complaining usually occur when either something or someone has not gone the way we want it to, or when we have to wait for something longer than we expected. The Word of God teaches us to be patient during these times.

I have discovered that patience is not the ability to wait, but the ability to keep a good attitude while waiting.

It is very important that this matter of complaining and all related types of negative thinking and conversation be taken very seriously. I sincerely believe that God has given me understanding of how dangerous it is to give our mind and mouth over to them.

God told the Israelites in Deuteronomy 1:6, "You have dwelt long enough on this mountain." Perhaps you have been around the same mountain many times and are now ready to press on. If so, it will be good for you to remember that you will not go forward in any positive way as long as your thoughts and conversation are filled with complaining.

I did not say it would be easy not to complain, but you do have the mind of Christ. Why not make the most of it?

Chapter
20

"Don't make me wait for anything;
I deserve everything immediately."

Wilderness Mentality #5

"Don't make me wait for anything; I deserve everything immediately."

20

Wilderness Mentality #5

*I*mpatience is the fruit of pride. A proud person cannot seem to wait for anything with the proper attitude. As we discussed in the previous chapter, patience is not the ability to wait, it is the ability to keep a good attitude while waiting.

This Scripture does not say "be patient *if* you wait," it says "be patient *as* you wait." Waiting is part of life. Many people don't "wait well," and yet, we actually spend more time in our lives waiting than we do receiving.

So be patient, brethren, [as you wait] till the coming of the Lord. See how the farmer waits expectantly for the precious harvest from the land. [See how] he keeps up his patient [vigil] over it until it receives the early and late rains.

JAMES 5:7

What I mean is this: we ask God for something in prayer, believing, and then we wait and wait for the manifestation. When it arrives, we rejoice because we have finally received what we have been waiting for.

However, because we are goal-oriented people who must always have something to press toward—something to look forward to—we go right back into the process of asking and believing God for something else, and waiting and waiting some more until that next breakthrough comes.

Thinking about this situation made me realize that I end up spending much more time in my life waiting than I do receiving. So I decided to learn to enjoy the waiting time, not just the receiving time.

We need to learn to enjoy where we are while we are on our way to where we are going!

PRIDE PREVENTS PATIENT WAITING

For by the grace (unmerited favor of God) given to me I warn everyone among you not to estimate and think of himself more highly than he ought [not to have an exaggerated opinion of his own importance], but to rate his ability with sober judgment, each according to the degree of faith apportioned by God to him.

Romans 12:3

It is impossible to enjoy waiting if you don't know how to wait patiently. Pride prevents patient waiting because the proud person thinks so highly of himself that he believes he should never be inconvenienced in any way.

Although we are not to think badly of ourselves, we are also not to think too highly of ourselves. It is dangerous to lift ourselves up to such an elevated place that it causes us to look down on others. If they are not doing things the way we want, or as quickly as we think they should be done, we behave impatiently.

A humble person will not display an impatient attitude toward God or man.

BE REALISTIC!

In the world you have tribulation and trials and distress and frustration; but be of good cheer [take courage; be confident, certain, undaunted]! For I have overcome the world. [I have deprived it of power to harm you and have conquered it for you.]

John 16:33

Another way that Satan uses our mind to lead us into impatient behavior is through thinking that is idealistic rather than realistic.

If we get the idea in our heads that everything concerning us and our circumstances and relationships should always be perfect—no inconveniences, no hindrances, no unlovely people to deal with—then we are setting ourselves up for a fall. Or, actually, I should say that Satan is setting us up for a fall through wrong thinking.

I am not suggesting that we be negative; I am a firm believer in positive attitudes and thoughts. But I am suggesting that we be realistic enough to realize ahead of time that very few things in real life are ever perfect.

In the early years of our ministry, my husband and I traveled almost every weekend to a different city to hold seminars. Many times we rented hotel ballrooms and civic or convention centers. In the beginning, I would get impatient and frustrated every time something went wrong in one of these places—things like the air-conditioning not working right (or perhaps not working at all), insufficient lighting in the conference room, chairs that were stained and ripped with the stuffing hanging out, or remains of the cake from the previous night's wedding reception still on the floor.

I felt that we had paid good money for the use of these rooms and that we had rented them in good faith expecting them to be in proper order, so I was irritated when that was not the case. We did everything we could to try to ensure that the places we rented were clean and comfortable, and yet, in about 75 percent of them something did not live up to our expectations.

There were times when we had been promised early check-in for our travel team; yet we would arrive and be told there would be no rooms available for several hours. Hotel employees often gave out wrong information concerning the times of our meetings, even though we had told them repeatedly, and had even sent printed material to them, showing the exact dates and times. Frequently, hotel and banquet employees were rude and lazy. Many times the food we had ordered for seminar luncheons was not what it was supposed to be.

I remember one time in particular when the dessert served to our Christian women (approximately eight hundred of them) was laced with rum. The kitchen got the dishes mixed up with what was being served at a wedding reception. Needless to say, we were a little embarrassed when the women started telling us the dessert tasted like it had liquor in it.

I could go on and on, but the point is simply this: occasionally, but very rarely, we ended up with a perfect place, perfect people, and a perfect seminar.

I finally realized that one of the reasons these situations left me impatient and behaving badly was because I was being idealistic and not realistic.

I don't plan for failure, but I do remember that Jesus said that in this world we will have to deal with tribulation and trials and distress and frustration. These things are part of life on this earth—for the believer as well as the unbeliever. But all the mishaps in the world cannot harm us if we will remain in the love of God, displaying the fruit of the Spirit.

UPDATE: We still travel a lot, and after twenty-five years of traveling in ministry we still have inconveniences and mishaps at most locations. During the last two conferences, when returning to our room after an evening session, our keys would not open the door. I have yet to figure out why the computer system at the hotel changes the keys while the patron is still in the room, but it happens frequently. We wait in the hallway while someone goes to the desk to get new keys and of course they always apologize.

We rarely get upset now about the imperfections of our journeys because we know that it is part of everyday life. Our job is not to control our circumstances, but to respond toward them in a godly way.

PATIENCE: POWER TO ENDURE

Clothe yourselves therefore, as God's own chosen ones (His own picked representatives), [who are] purified and holy and well-beloved [by God Himself, by putting on behavior marked by] tenderhearted pity and mercy, kind feeling, a lowly opinion of yourselves, gentle ways, [and] patience [which is tireless and long-suffering, and has the power to endure whatever comes, with good temper].

Colossians 3:12

I turn to this Scripture often to remind me of what kind of behavior I should be displaying in all situations. I remind myself that patience is not my ability to wait, but my ability to keep a good attitude while I wait.

PATIENCE IS BROUGHT OUT BY TRIALS

Consider it wholly joyful, my brethren, whenever you are enveloped in or encounter trials of any sort or fall into various temptations.

Be assured and understand that the trial and proving of your faith bring out endurance and steadfastness and patience.

But let endurance and steadfastness and patience have full play and do a thorough work, so that you may be [people] perfectly and fully developed [with no defects], lacking in nothing.

James 1:2-4

Patience is a fruit of the Spirit (see Gal. 5:22) and is deposited in the spirit of every born-again person. The display or manifestation of patience by His people is very important to the Lord. He wants other people to see His character through His children.

Chapter 1 in the book of James teaches us that when we have become perfect, we will be lacking in nothing. The devil cannot control a patient man.

James 1 also teaches us that we should rejoice when we find ourselves involved in difficult situations, knowing that the method God uses to bring out patience in us is by what the *New King James Version* calls "various trials."

I have found in my own life that "various trials" did eventually bring out patience in me, but first they brought out a lot of other things that were not godly traits: things like pride, anger, rebellion, self-pity, complaining, and many others. It seems that these other things must be faced and dealt with before patience can come forth.

Trial or Inconvenience?

And they journeyed from Mount Hor by the way to the Red Sea, to go around the land of Edom, and the people became impatient (depressed, much discouraged), because [of the trials] of the way.

Numbers 21:4

If you remember, an impatient attitude was one of the wilderness mentalities that kept the Israelites wandering in the wilderness for forty years. Were their trials that terrible, or were they simply inconveniences? I am sure some were worse than others, but quite often we murmur about things that a more mature person would pay no attention to at all.

How could these people possibly be ready to go into the Promised Land and drive off the current occupants so they could possess the land if they could not even remain patient and steadfast during a little inconvenience?

I really encourage you to work with the Holy Spirit as He develops the fruit of patience in you. The more you resist Him, the longer the process will take. Learn to respond patiently in all kinds of trials, and you will find yourself living a quality of life that is not just endured but enjoyed to the full.

The Importance of Patience and Endurance

For you have need of steadfast patience and endurance, so that you may perform and fully accomplish the will of God, and thus receive and carry away [and enjoy to the full] what is promised.

Hebrews 10:36

This Scripture tells us that without patience and endurance we will not receive the promises of God. And Hebrews 6:12 tells us that it is only through faith and patience that we inherit the promises (KJV).

The proud man runs in the strength of his own flesh and tries to make things happen in his own timing. Pride says, "I'm ready now!"

Humility says, "God knows best, and He will not be late!"

A humble man waits patiently; he actually has a "reverential fear" of moving in the strength of his own flesh. But a proud man tries one thing after another, all to no avail.

A straight Line Is Not Always the Shortest Distance to a Goal

There is a way that seems right to a man and appears straight before him, but at the end of it is the way of death.

Proverbs 16:25

We must learn that in the spiritual realm sometimes a straight line is not the shortest distance between us and where we want to be. It may just be the shortest distance to destruction!

We must learn to be patient and wait on the Lord, even if it seems that He is taking us in a roundabout way to get to our desired destination.

There are multitudes of unhappy, unfulfilled Christians in the world simply because they are busy trying to make something happen, instead of waiting patiently for God to bring things to pass in His own time and His own way.

When you are trying to wait on God, the devil will pound your mind continuously demanding that you "do something." He wants to move you in fleshly zeal and action because he knows that the flesh profits nothing (see John 6:63; Romans 13:14).

As we have seen, impatience is a sign of pride, and the only answer to pride is humility.

Humble Yourself and Wait on the Lord

Therefore humble yourselves [demote, lower yourselves in your own estimation] under the mighty hand of God, that in due time He may exalt you.

1 Peter 5:6

This phrase "lower yourself in your own estimation" does not mean to think badly of yourself. It simply means, "Don't think you can solve all your problems on your own."

Instead of pridefully taking matters into our own hands, we must learn to humble ourselves under God's mighty hand. When He knows that the time is right, He will exalt us and lift us up.

As we wait on God and refuse to move in fleshly zeal, there is a "dying to self" that takes place. We begin to die to our own ways and our own timing and to become alive to God's will and way for us.

We should always be promptly obedient to do whatever God tells us to do, but we should also have a godly fear of fleshly pride. Remember: it is pride that is at the root of impatience. The proud man says, "Please don't make me wait for anything; I deserve everything immediately."

When you are tempted to become frustrated and impatient, I recommend that you begin to say, "Lord, I want Your will in Your timing. I do not want to be ahead of You, nor do I want to be behind You. Help me, Father, to wait patiently on You!"

Chapter
21

*"My behavior may be wrong,
but it's not my fault."*

Wilderness Mentality #6

"My behavior may be wrong, but it's not my fault."

Wilderness Mentality #6

An unwillingness to take responsibility for one's own actions, blaming everything that is wrong or goes wrong on someone else, is a major cause for wilderness living.

We see the problem manifesting itself from the beginning of time. When confronted with their sin in the Garden of Eden, Adam and Eve blamed each other, God and the devil, thus evading personal responsibility for their actions.

And the man said, The woman whom You gave to be with me—she gave me [fruit] from the tree, and I ate.

...And the woman said, The serpent beguiled (cheated, outwitted, and deceived) me, and I ate.

GENESIS 3:12,13

IT'S ALL YOUR FAULT!

Now Sarai, Abram's wife, had borne him no children. And she had an Egyptian maidservant whose name was Hagar.

So Sarai said to Abram, "See now, the LORD has restrained me from bearing children. Please, go in to my maid; perhaps I shall obtain children by her." And Abram heeded the voice of Sarai. Then Sarai, Abram's wife, took Hagar her maid, the Egyptian, and gave her to her husband Abram to be his wife, after Abram had dwelt ten years in the land of Canaan.

So he went in to Hagar, and she conceived. And when she saw that she had conceived, her mistress became despised in her eyes.

Then Sarai said to Abram, "My wrong be upon you! I gave my maid into your embrace; and when she saw that she had conceived, I became despised in her eyes. The LORD judge between you and me."

So Abram said to Sarai, "Indeed your maid is in your hand; do to her as you please." And when Sarai dealt harshly with her, she fled from her presence.

Genesis 16:1-6 NKJV

The same scenario played out between Adam and Eve is seen here in the dispute between Abram and Sarai. They were tired of waiting on God to fulfill His promise of a child born to them, so they acted in the flesh and "did their own thing." When it turned out badly and started causing trouble, they began to blame each other.

In the past, I observed this same kind of scene countless times in my own home between Dave and me. It seemed that we were continually evading the real issues in life, never wanting to face reality.

I vividly remember praying for Dave to change. I had been reading my Bible and was seeing more and more of his flaws, and how much he needed to be different! As I prayed, the Lord spoke to me and said, "Joyce, Dave is not the problem...you are."

I was devastated. I cried and cried. I wept for three days because God was showing me what it was like to live in the same house with me. He showed me how I tried to control everything that went on, how I nagged and complained, how hard it was to please me, how negative I was—and on and on. It was a shocking blow to my pride, but it was also the beginning of my recovery in the Lord.

Like most people, I blamed everything on someone else or some circumstance beyond my control. I thought I was acting badly because I had been abused, but God told me, "Abuse may be the reason you act this way, but don't let it become an excuse to stay this way!"

Satan works hard on our minds—building strongholds that will prevent us from facing truth. The truth will set us free, and he knows it!

I don't think there is anything more emotionally painful than facing the truth about ourselves and our behavior. Because it is painful, most people run from it. It is fairly easy to face truth about someone else—but when it comes to facing ourselves, we find it much harder to handle.

IF . . .

And the people spoke against God and against Moses, Why have you brought us out of Egypt to die in the wilderness? For there is no bread, neither is there any water, and we loathe this light (contemptible, unsubstantial) manna.

Numbers 21:5

As you recall, the Israelites complained that all their problems were the fault of God and Moses. They successfully evaded any personal responsibility for why they were staying in the wilderness so long. God showed me this was one of the major wilderness mentalities that kept them there forty years.

It was also one of the main reasons I spent so many years going around and around the same mountains in my life. My list of excuses for why I was behaving badly was endless:

"If I hadn't been abused as a child, I wouldn't have a bad temper."

"If my children would help me more, I would act better."

"If Dave didn't play golf on Saturdays, I wouldn't get so upset with him."

"If Dave would talk to me more, I wouldn't be so lonely."

"If Dave would buy me more presents, I wouldn't be so negative."

"If I didn't have to work, I wouldn't be so tired and cranky." (So I quit work, and then it was . . .)

"If I could just get out of the house more, I wouldn't be so bored!"

"If we only had more money . . ."

"If we owned our own home..." (So we bought one and then, it was...)

"If we just didn't have so many bills..."

"If we had better neighbors or different friends..."

If! If! If! If! If! If! If! If! If! If!

BUT...

And the Lord said to Moses, Send men to explore and scout out [for yourselves] the land of Canaan, which I give to the Israelites. From each tribe of their fathers you shall send a man, every one a leader or head among them. So Moses by the command of the Lord sent scouts from the Wilderness of Paran, all of them men who were heads of the Israelites....

And they returned from scouting out the land after forty days.

They came to Moses and Aaron and to all the Israelite congregation in the Wilderness of Paran at Kadesh, and brought them word, and showed them the land's fruit.

They told Moses, We came to the land to which you sent us; surely it flows with milk and honey. This is its fruit.

But the people who dwell there are strong, and the cities are fortified and very large; moreover, there we saw the sons of Anak [of great stature and courage].

Numbers 13:1-3,25-28 (italics added)

"If" and "but" are two of the most deceptive words that Satan ever plants in our minds. The twelve spies who were sent into the Promised Land as a scouting party came back with one bunch of grapes so large it had to be carried by two people on a pole, but the report they gave to Moses and the people was negative.

It was the "but" that defeated them! They should have kept their eyes on God and not on the potential problem.

One of the reasons our problems defeat us is because we think they are bigger than God. That may also be the reason why we have such a hard time facing the truth. We are not sure God can change us, so we hide from ourselves rather than facing ourselves as we really are.

It is not as difficult now for me to face a truth about myself when God is dealing with me, because I know that He can change me. I have already seen what He can do, and I trust Him. However, in the beginning of my walk with Him it was difficult. I had spent most of my life hiding from one thing or another. I had lived in darkness for such a long time that coming out into the light was not easy.

TRUTH IN THE INNER BEING

Have mercy upon me, O God, according to Your steadfast love; according to the multitude of Your tender mercy and loving-kindness blot out my transgressions.

Wash me thoroughly [and repeatedly] from my iniquity and guilt and cleanse me and make me wholly pure from my sin!

For I am conscious of my transgressions and I acknowledge them; my sin is ever before me.

Against You, You only, have I sinned and done that which is evil in Your sight, so that You are justified in Your sentence and fault-less in Your judgment.

Behold, I was brought forth in [a state of] iniquity; my mother was sinful who conceived me [and I too am sinful].

Behold, You desire truth in the inner being; make me therefore to know wisdom in my inmost heart.

Psalm 51:1-6

In Psalm 51, King David was crying out to God for mercy and forgiveness because the Lord had been dealing with him about his sin with Bathsheba and the murder of her husband.

Believe it or not, David's sin had occurred one full year prior to the writing of this psalm, but he had never really faced it and acknowledged it. He was not facing truth, and as long as he refused to face truth, he could not truly repent. And as long as he could not truly repent, God could not forgive him.

Verse 6 of this passage is a powerful Scripture. It says that God desires truth "in the inner being." That means that if we want to receive God's blessings, we must be honest with Him about ourselves and our sins.

CONFESSION PRECEDES FORGIVENESS

If we say we have no sin [refusing to admit that we are sinners], we delude and lead ourselves astray, and the Truth [which the Gospel presents] is not in us [does not dwell in our hearts].

If we [freely] admit that we have sinned and confess our sins, He is faithful and just (true to His own nature and promises) and will forgive our sins [dismiss our lawlessness] and [continuously] cleanse us from all unrighteousness [everything not in conformity to His will in purpose, thought, and action].

If we say (claim) we have not sinned, we contradict His Word and make Him out to be false and a liar, and His Word is not in us [the divine message of the Gospel is not in our hearts].

1 John 1:8-10

God is quick to forgive us if we truly repent, but we cannot truly repent if we will not face and acknowledge the truth about what we have done.

To admit that we have done something wrong, but then make an excuse for it, is still not God's way of facing truth. Naturally we want to justify ourselves and our actions, but the Bible says that our justification is found only in Jesus Christ (see Rom. 3:20-24). You and I are made right with God after sinning only by the blood of Jesus— not by our excuses.

I remember when a neighbor called me one day and asked me to take her to the bank right away, before it closed, because her car would not start. I was busy doing "my thing" and did not want to stop, so I was rude and impatient with her. As soon as I hung up the phone, I knew how terrible I had acted and that I needed to call her, apologize, and take her to the bank. My mind was full of all the excuses I would give her for why I had reacted so badly: "I did not feel good..." "I was busy..." "I was having a rough day myself..."

But deep in my spirit, I could sense the Holy Spirit telling me not to make any excuse!

"Just call her and tell her you were wrong, period! Say no more than 'I was wrong, and there is no excuse for the way I behaved. Please forgive me and allow me to take you to the bank.'"

I can tell you it was hard to do. My flesh was having a fit! I could feel this little thing running around in my soul desperately trying to find a place to hide. But there is no hiding from the truth, because truth is light.

TRUTH IS LIGHT

In the beginning [before all time] was the Word (Christ), and the Word was with God, and the Word was God Himself.

He was present originally with God.

All things were made and came into existence through Him; and without Him was not even one thing made that has come into being.

In Him was Life, and the Life was the Light of men.

And the Light shines on in the darkness, for the darkness has never overpowered it [put it out or absorbed it or appropriated it, and is unreceptive to it].

John 1:1-5

Truth is one of the most powerful weapons against the kingdom of darkness. Truth is light, and the Bible says that the darkness has never overpowered the light, and it never will.

Satan wants to keep things hidden in darkness, but the Holy Spirit wants to bring them into the light and deal with them, so you and I can be truly and genuinely free.

Jesus said it was truth that would set us free (see John 8:32). That truth is revealed by the Spirit of Truth.

THE SPIRIT OF TRUTH

I have still many things to say to you, but you are not able to bear them or to take them upon you or to grasp them now.

But when He, the Spirit of Truth (the Truth-giving Spirit) comes, He will guide you into all the Truth (the whole, full Truth).

John 16:12,13

Jesus could have showed His disciples all the truth, but He knew they were not ready for it. He told them that they would have to wait until the Holy Spirit came down from heaven to abide with them and to dwell in them.

After Jesus had ascended into heaven, He sent the Holy Spirit to work with us, preparing us continually for God's glory (excellence) to be manifested through us in varying degrees.

How can we have the Holy Spirit working in our lives if we will not face truth? He is called "The Spirit of Truth." A major facet of His ministry to you and me is to help us face truth—to bring us to a place of truth, because only the truth will set us free.

Something in your past—a person, event or circumstance that hurt you—may be the source of your wrong attitude and behavior, but don't allow it to become an excuse to stay that way.

Many of my behavior problems were definitely caused from being sexually, verbally, and emotionally abused for many years—but I was trapped in the wrong behavior patterns as long as I used the abuse as an excuse for them. That is like defending your enemy by saying, "I hate this thing, but this is why I keep it."

You can definitely experience glorious freedom from every bondage. You don't have to spend forty years wandering in the wilderness. Or if you have already spent forty years or more out there because you didn't know that "wilderness mentalities" were keeping you there, today can be your day of decision.

Ask God to start showing you the truth about yourself. When He does, hang on! It won't be easy, but remember, He has promised, "I will never leave you nor forsake you" (Heb. 13:5 NKJV).

You are on your way out of the wilderness; enjoy the Promised Land!

Chapter
22

"My life is so miserable;
I feel sorry for myself because
my life is so wretched!"

Wilderness Mentality #7

"My life is so miserable; I feel sorry for myself because my life is so wretched!"

Wilderness Mentality #7

The Israelites felt exceedingly sorry for themselves. Every inconvenience became a new excuse to engage in self-pity.

And all the congregation cried out with a loud voice, and [they] wept that night. All the Israelites grumbled and deplored their situation.
NUMBERS 14:1,2

I remember when the Lord spoke to me during one of my "pity parties." He said, "Joyce, you can be pitiful or powerful, but you cannot be both."

This is a chapter that I don't want to skim over too quickly. It is *vitally* important to understand that *we cannot entertain the sin of self-pity and also walk in the power of God!*

ENCOURAGE AND EDIFY ONE ANOTHER

Therefore encourage (admonish, exhort) one another and edify (strengthen and build up) one another, just as you are doing.
1 Thessalonians 5:11

Pity was hard for me to give up; I had used it for years to comfort myself when I was hurting.

The minute someone hurts us, the moment we experience disappointment, the devil begins to whisper lies to us about how cruelly and unjustly we have been mistreated.

All you need to do is listen to the thoughts rushing into your mind during such times and you will quickly realize how the enemy uses self-pity to keep us in bondage.

The Bible, however, gives us no liberty to feel sorry for ourselves. Instead, we are to encourage and edify one another in the Lord.

There is a true gift of compassion, which is having godly pity toward others who are hurting, and spending our life relieving their suffering. But self-pity is perverted, because it is taking something that God intended to be given to others and turning it in on ourselves.

Love is the same way. Romans 5:5 says that the love of God has been shed abroad in our hearts by the Holy Ghost (KJV). He has done this so we might know how much God loves us and that we may be able to love others.

When we take the love God meant to be given away and turn it in toward ourselves, it becomes selfishness and self-centeredness, which actually destroys us. We certainly should love ourselves in a balanced way, appreciating what God has made and having self-respect, but excessive self-love is a huge problem. Self-pity is idolatry—turning in on ourselves, concentrating on us and our feelings. It makes us only aware of our own selves and our own needs and concerns—and that is certainly a narrow-minded way to live.

THINK OF OTHERS

Let each of you esteem and look upon and be concerned for not [merely] his own interests, but also each for the interests of others.

Philippians 2:4

Recently one of our speaking engagements was unexpectedly canceled. It was one I had been looking forward to, and initially, I was a bit disappointed. There was a time when an incident like that would have thrown me into a fit of self-pity, criticism, judgment of the other party, and all kinds of negative thoughts and actions. I have since learned in that kind of situation just to be quiet; it is better to say nothing than to say the wrong thing.

As I sat quietly, God began to show me the situation from the viewpoint of the other people involved. They had been unable to locate a building in which to hold the meeting, and God showed me how disappointing it was to them. They were counting on the meeting, looking forward to it with great expectation, and now they could not have it.

It is amazing how easy it is to stay out of self-pity if we look at the other person's side and not just at our own. Self-pity is supported by thinking only of us and no one else.

We literally exhaust ourselves sometimes trying to gain sympathy. Yes, self-pity is a major trap and one of Satan's favorite tools to keep us in the wilderness. If we are not careful, we can actually become addicted to it.

An addiction is something done as an automatic response to some stimulus—a learned behavior pattern that has become habitual.

How much time do you spend in self-pity? How do you respond to disappointments?

A Christian has a rare privilege, because when he experiences disappointment—he can be re-appointed. With God there is always a new beginning available. Self-pity however, keeps us trapped in the past.

LET GO AND LET GOD!

Do not [earnestly] remember the former things; neither consider the things of old.

Behold, I am doing a new thing! Now it springs forth; do you not perceive and know it and will you not give heed to it? I will even make a way in the wilderness and rivers in the desert.

Isaiah 43:18,19

I wasted many years of my life feeling sorry for myself. I was one of those cases of addiction. My automatic response to any kind of disappointment was self-pity. Satan would immediately fill my mind with wrong thoughts, and not knowing how to "think about what I was thinking about," I simply thought on whatever fell into my head. The more I thought, the more pitiful I felt.

I often tell stories about the early years of our marriage. Every Sunday afternoon during football season, Dave wanted to watch the games on television. If it was not football season, it was some other "ball season." Dave enjoyed it all, and I did not enjoy any of it. He liked anything that involved a bouncing ball and could easily get so caught up in some sports event that he didn't even know I existed.

One time I stood right in front of him and said very clearly, "Dave I don't feel well at all; I feel like I'm going to die."

Without raising his eyes from the television screen, he said, "Uh huh, that's nice, dear."

I spent many Sunday afternoons angry and in self-pity. I always cleaned house when I got mad at Dave. I know now that I was trying to make him feel guilty for enjoying himself while I was being so miserable. I would storm around the house for hours, slamming doors and drawers, marching back and forth through the room where he was, vacuum sweeper in hand, making a loud display of how hard I was working.

I was, of course, trying to get his attention, but he hardly noticed me at all. I would give up, go to the back of the house, sit on the bathroom floor, and cry. The more I cried, the more pitiful I felt. God gave me insight in later years about why a woman goes to the bathroom to cry. He said it is because there is a big mirror in there, and after she has cried a long time, she can then stand up and take a long look at herself and see how truly pitiful she looks.

I looked so bad sometimes that when I saw my reflection in the mirror I'd start crying all over again. Finally, I would make my sorrowful last stroll through the family room where Dave was, walking slowly, and ever so pitifully. He would occasionally look up long enough to ask me to bring him some iced tea if I was going to the kitchen.

The bottom line is, it didn't work! I exhausted myself emotionally—often ending up feeling physically sick due to all the wrong emotions I had experienced all day.

God will not deliver you by your own hand, but by His. Only God can change people! Nobody but the Almighty could have discouraged Dave from wanting to watch as many sports as he did. As I learned to trust the Lord and to stop wallowing in self-pity when I did not get my way, Dave did come into more balance concerning watching every sporting event.

He still enjoys them, and now it really does not bother me. I just use the time to do things I enjoy. If I really do want or need to do something else, I ask Dave sweetly (not angrily) and most of the time he is willing to alter his plans. There are those times though—and there always will be—when I don't get my way. As soon as I feel my emotions starting to rise, I pray, "Oh God, help me pass this test. I don't want to go around this mountain even one more time!"

Chapter
23

*"I don't deserve God's blessings
because I am not worthy."*

Wilderness Mentality #8

"I don't deserve God's blessings because I am not worthy."

23

Wilderness Mentality #8

After Joshua had led the Israelites across the Jordan River into the Promised Land, there was something God needed to do before they would be ready to conquer and occupy their first town, which was to be Jericho.

And the Lord said to Joshua, This day have I rolled away the reproach of Egypt from you. So the name of the place is called Gilgal [rolling] to this day.

JOSHUA 5:9

The Lord ordered that all the Israelite males be circumcised, since this had not been done during the entire forty years they had wandered in the Wilderness. This required obedience and was to be a sign of their willingness to turn away from fleshly, worldly ways and embark upon a new way of living for God.

After this was done, the Lord told Joshua that He had "rolled away" the reproach of Egypt from His people.

A few verses later in Chapter 6, the account begins of how God led the Children of Israel to overcome and capture Jericho. Why did the reproach have to be lifted off of them first? What is a reproach?

REPROACH DEFINED

The word *reproach* means "blame...disgrace: shame."[1] When God said that He would "roll away" the reproach of Egypt from the Israelites, He was making a point. Egypt represents the world. After a few years of being in the world and becoming worldly, we all need the reproach of it rolled away.

Because of the things I had done and what had been done to me, I had a shame-based nature. I blamed myself for what had happened to me (even though much of it had taken place in my childhood, and there was nothing I could have done to stop it).

We have said that grace is the power of God coming to us, as a free gift from Him, to help us do with ease what we cannot do ourselves. God wants to give us grace, and Satan wants to give us disgrace, which is another word for reproach.

Disgrace told me that I was no good—not worthy of God's love or help. Shame had poisoned my inner man. I was not only ashamed of what had been done to me, but I was ashamed of myself. Deep down inside, I did not like myself.

God's rolling away the reproach from us means that each of us must receive for ourselves the forgiveness He is offering for all our past sins.

You must realize that you can never deserve God's blessings— you can never be worthy of them. You can only humbly accept and appreciate them, and be in awe of how good He is and how much He loves you.

Self-hatred, self-rejection, refusal to accept God's forgiveness (by forgiving yourself), not understanding righteousness through the blood of Jesus and all related problems will definitely keep you wandering in the wilderness. Your mind must be renewed concerning right standing with God through Jesus—and not through your own works.

I am convinced, after many years in ministry, that about 85 percent of our problems stem from the way we feel about ourselves. Any person you know who is walking in victory is also walking in righteousness.

I know I don't deserve God's blessings, but I receive them anyway because I am a joint-heir with Christ (see Rom. 8:17 KJV). He earned them, and I get them by placing my faith in Him.

Heir or Laborer?

Therefore, you are no longer a slave (bond servant) but a son; and
if a son, then [it follows that you are] an heir by the aid of God,
through Christ.

Galatians 4:7

Are you a son or a slave—an heir or a bond servant? An heir is
one who receives something other than by merit, as when property is
passed down from one person to another through a will. A bond servant or laborer, in the biblical sense, is one who is weary from trying
to follow the Law. The term denotes burdensome toil and trouble.

I wandered around in the wilderness for years as a laborer, trying to be good enough to deserve what God wanted to give me freely
by His grace. I had a wrong mindset.

First, I thought that everything must be earned and deserved:
"Nobody does anything for you for nothing." I had been taught that
principle for years. Over and over I had heard that statement while
growing up. I was told that anyone who acted like he wanted to
do something for me was lying and would take advantage of me in
the end.

Experience with the world teaches us that we must deserve
everything we get. If we want friends, we are told, we must keep them
happy all the time or they will reject us. If we want a promotion on
our job, everyone says, we must know the right people, treat them a
certain way, and maybe one day we will get a chance to go forward. By
the time we are weary with the world and all of its ways, the reproach
of it lies heavy upon us and definitely needs to be rolled away.

How Do You See Yourself?

There we saw the Nephilim [or giants], the sons of Anak, who
come from the giants; and we were in our own sight as grasshoppers, and so we were in their sight.

Numbers 13:33

The Israelites had that reproach on them. The fact that they had a negative opinion of themselves is seen in this verse. Ten of the twelve spies who were sent in to scout out the Promised Land before the entire nation crossed over the Jordan came back saying that the land was inhabited by giants who saw them as grasshoppers—and so they were in their own eyes.

This plainly lets us know what these people thought of themselves.

Please be aware that Satan will fill your mind (if he is allowed to) with all types of negative thinking about yourself. He began early building strongholds in your mind, many of them negative things about you and about how other people feel about you. He always arranges for a few situations in which you experience rejection, so he can bring the pain of it back to your remembrance during a time when you are trying to make some progress.

Fear of failure and rejection keep many people in the wilderness. Being slaves in Egypt for so many years and living under severe mistreatment had left a reproach on the Israelites. It is interesting to note that almost none of the generation that originally came out with Moses entered the Promised Land. It was their children who went in. Yet God told them He had to roll away the reproach from them.

Most of them had been born in the wilderness after their parents had left Egypt. How could they have the reproach of Egypt upon them when they did not even live there?

Things that were on your parents can be passed on to you. Attitudes, thoughts and behavior patterns can be inherited. A wrong mindset that your parents had can become your mindset. The way you think about a certain subject can be passed down to you, and you won't even know why you think that way.

A parent who has a poor self-image, an attitude of unworthiness and an "I-don't-deserve-God's-blessings" mindset can definitely pass that mindset on to his children.

Even though I talked about this earlier in the book, because it is such an important area let me mention again that you need to be aware of what goes on in your mind in regard to yourself. God is willing to give you mercy for your failures if you are willing to receive it. He does not reward the perfect who have no flaws and never make mistakes, but those who put their faith and trust in Him.

Your Faith in God Pleases Him

But without faith it is impossible to please and be satisfactory to Him. For whoever would come near to God must [necessarily] believe that God exists and that He is the rewarder of those who earnestly and diligently seek Him [out].

Hebrews 11:6

Please notice that without faith you cannot please God; therefore, no matter how many "good works" you offer, it will not please Him if they were done to "earn" His favor.

Whatever we do for God should be because we love Him, not because we are trying to get something from Him.

This powerful Scripture says that God is a rewarder of those who diligently seek Him. I rejoiced when I finally saw this! I know I have made many mistakes in the past, but I also know that I have diligently sought the Lord with all my heart. That means that I qualify for rewards. I decided a long time ago that I would receive any blessing that God wanted to give me.

The Lord wanted to take the Israelites into the Promised Land and bless them beyond their wildest imaginations, but first He had to roll the reproach off of them. They could not have received from Him properly as long as they were burdened down with shame, blame and disgrace.

Above Reproach

Even as [in His love] He chose us [actually picked us out for Himself as His own] in Christ before the foundation of the world, that we should be holy (consecrated and set apart for Him) and blameless in His sight, even above reproach, before Him in love.

Ephesians 1:4

This is a wonderful Scripture! In it the Lord tells us that we are His and sets forth what He wants for us—that we should know that we are loved, special, valuable and that we should be holy, blameless, and above reproach.

Naturally, we should do what we can to live holy lives. But thank God, when we do make mistakes, we can be forgiven and restored to holiness, made once again blameless and above reproach—all "in Him."

Without Reproaching or Faultfinding

If any of you is deficient in wisdom, let him ask of the giving God [Who gives] to everyone liberally and ungrudgingly, without reproaching or faultfinding, and it will be given him.

James 1:5

This is another great Scripture that teaches us to receive from God without reproach.

James had been previously speaking to people who were having trials, and now he is telling them that if they need wisdom in their situation, they should ask God. He assures them that He won't reproach or find fault with them—He will just help them.

You will never make it through the wilderness without a great deal of help from God. But, if you have a negative attitude about yourself, even when He does try to help you, you won't receive it.

If you desire to have a victorious, powerful, positive life, you cannot be negative about yourself. Don't look only at how far you have to go, but at how far you have come. Consider your progress and remember Philippians 1:6: "I am convinced and sure of this very thing, that He Who began a good work in you will continue until the day of Jesus Christ [right up to the time of His return], developing [that good work] and perfecting and bringing it to full completion in you."

Think and speak positively about yourself!

UPDATE: Although this book was written many years ago, I am more convinced than ever that how we feel about ourselves affects every area of our life. I strongly urge you to come to a place of peace with yourself. You may not like everything you do, but you can and should like yourself. I finally decided that since Jesus loved me enough to die for me, that the least I could do was like myself. Why not give yourself a big hug right now, and say out loud, "Because of what Jesus has done, I love and accept myself. He has given me a new nature, and I am ready for the new life He wants me live."

Chapter
24

*"Why shouldn't I be jealous
and envious when everybody
else is better off than I am?"*

Wilderness Mentality #9

"Why shouldn't I be jealous and envious when everybody else is better off than I am?"

Wilderness Mentality #9

In John 21 Jesus was conversing with Peter regarding the hardships that he would have to endure in order to serve and glorify Him. As soon as Jesus had said these things to him, Peter turned, saw John, and immediately asked Jesus what His will was for him. Peter wanted to make sure that if he were going to have to go through rough times ahead, so would John.

When Peter saw him [John], he said to Jesus, Lord, what about this man?

Jesus said to him, If I want him to stay (survive, live) till I come, what is that to you? [What concern is it of yours?] You follow Me!

JOHN 21:21,22

In answer, Jesus politely told Peter to mind his own business.

Minding (having our mind set on) other people's business, will keep us in the wilderness. Jealousy, envy, and mentally comparing ourselves and our circumstances with others is a wilderness mentality.

BEWARE OF JEALOUSY AND ENVY

A calm and undisturbed mind and heart are the life and health of the body, but envy, jealousy, and wrath are like rottenness of the bones.

Proverbs 14:30

Envy will cause a person to behave in a way that is callous and crude—even animalistic at times. Envy caused Joseph's brothers to sell him into slavery. They hated him because their father loved him so much.

If there is someone in your family who seems to have more favor than you, don't hate that individual. Trust God! Do what He asks you to do—believe Him for favor—and you will end up like Joseph—extremely blessed.

Vine's Expository Dictionary of Old and New Testament Words defines the Greek word translated *envy* as "the feeling of displeasure produced by witnessing the prosperity of others."[1] *Jealousy* is defined by Webster as "feelings of envy, apprehension, or bitterness."[2] I interpret this definition as being fearful of losing what you have to another, resentment of another's success, arising from feelings of envy.

Don't Compare and Compete

Now an eager contention arose among them [as to] which of them was considered and reputed to be the greatest.

But Jesus said to them, The kings of the Gentiles are deified by them and exercise lordship [ruling as emperor-gods] over them; and those in authority over them are called benefactors and well-doers.

But this is not to be so with you; on the contrary, let him who is greatest among you become like the youngest, and him who is the chief and leader like one who serves.

Luke 22:24-26

In my early life, I had an abundance of struggles with jealousy, envy, and comparison. This is a common trait of the insecure. If we are not secure concerning our own worth and value as a unique individual, we will naturally find ourselves competing with anyone who appears to be successful and doing well.

Learning that I was an individual (that God has a unique, personal plan for my life) has indeed been one of the most valuable and precious freedoms the Lord has granted me. I am assured that I need not compare myself (or my ministry) with anyone.

I am always encouraged that there is hope for me when I look at Jesus' disciples and realize that they struggled with many of the same things I do. In Luke 22 we find the disciples arguing over which of them was the greatest. Jesus responded to them by saying that the greatest was actually the one who was willing to be considered the least or the one who was willing to be a servant. Our Lord spent a great deal of His time trying to teach His disciples that life in the Kingdom of God is usually the direct opposite of the way of the world or the flesh.

Jesus taught them things like, "Many who are first will be last, and the last will be first" (see Mark 10:31), "Rejoice with those who are blessed" (see Luke 15:6,9 KJV), "Pray for your enemies, and bless those who mistreat you" (see Matt. 5:44). The world would say that this is foolishness—but Jesus says it is true power.

AVOID WORLDLY COMPETITION

Let us not become vainglorious and self-conceited, competitive and challenging and provoking and irritating to one another, envying and being jealous of one another.

Galatians 5:26

According to the world's system, the best place to be is ahead of everyone else. Popular thinking would say that we should try to get to the top no matter whom we have to hurt on the way up. But the Bible teaches us that there is no such thing as real peace until we are delivered from the need to compete with others.

Even in what is supposed to be considered "fun games," we often see competition get so out of balance that people end up arguing and hating one another, rather than simply relaxing and having a good time together. Naturally, human beings don't play games to lose; everyone is going to do his best. But when a person cannot enjoy a game unless he is winning, he definitely has a problem—possibly a deep-rooted one that is causing other problems in many areas of his life.

We should definitely do our best on the job; there is nothing wrong with wanting to do well and advance in our chosen profession. But I encourage you to remember that promotion for the believer comes from God and not from man. You and I don't need to play worldly games to get ahead. God will give us favor with Him and with others if we will do things His way (see Prov. 3:3,4 KJV).

Jealousy and envy are torments from hell. I spent many years being jealous and envious of anyone who looked better than I did or had talents I didn't have. I secretly lived in competition with others in ministry. It was very important to me that "my" ministry be bigger in size, better attended, more prosperous, etc., than anyone else's. If another person's ministry surpassed mine in any way, I wanted to be happy for that individual because I knew it was God's will and way, but something in my soul just would not allow it.

I found as I grew in the knowledge of who I was in Christ, and not in my works, that I gained freedom in not having to compare myself or anything I did with anyone else. The more I learned to trust God, the more freedom I enjoyed in these areas. I learned that my heavenly Father loves me and will do for me whatever is best— for *me*.

What God does for you or for me may not be what He does for someone else, but we must remember what Jesus said to Peter, "Don't be concerned about what I choose to do with someone else—you follow Me!"

A friend of mine was once given something as a gift from the Lord that I was believing for and had wanted a long time. Now, I did not consider this friend to be nearly as "spiritual" as I, and so I became very jealous and envious when she excitedly came to my front door sharing with me what God had done for her. Of course, in her presence, I pretended to be happy for her, but in my heart I wasn't.

When she left, attitudes rolled out of me that I never would have thought were in me! I actually resented God's blessing her because *I* did not think she deserved it. After all, *I* stayed home, fasted and prayed while *she* ran around with her friends and had a good time. You see, I was a "Pharisee," a religious snob, and did not even know it.

God arranges events quite often in a way that we would not choose because He knows what we really need. I needed to get rid of my bad attitudes much more than I needed whatever it was that I was believing for. It is important for God to arrange our circumstances in such a way that we have to eventually face ourselves. Otherwise, we never experience freedom.

As long as the enemy can hide in our soul, he will always have a certain amount of control over us. But when God exposes him, we are on our way to freedom, *if* we will put ourselves in God's hands and permit Him to do quickly what He desires to do.

God had, in fact, already purposed for my life that the ministry He would make me steward over was to be quite large and reach millions of people by radio and television, Internet, seminars, books, and all forms of recorded messages. But He would not bring me into the fullness of it, except to the degree that I "grew up" in Him.

GET A NEW MINDSET!

Beloved, I wish above all things that thou mayest prosper and be in health, even as thy soul prospereth.

3 John 2 KJV

Consider this Scripture carefully. *God desires to bless us even more than we desire to be blessed.* But He also loves us enough not to bless us beyond our capacity to handle the blessings properly and to continue giving Him glory.

Jealousy, envy, and comparing oneself with others are childish. They belong entirely to the flesh and have nothing to do with spiritual things. But jealousy is one of the major causes for wilderness living.

Take account of your thoughts in this area. When you recognize wrong thought patterns beginning to flow into your mind, talk to yourself a little. Say to yourself, "What good will it do me to be jealous of others? It won't get me blessed. God has an individual plan for each of us, and I am going to trust Him to do the best thing for me. It isn't any of my business what He chooses to do for other people." Then deliberately and purposely pray for them to be blessed more.

Don't be afraid to be honest with God about your feelings. He knows how you feel anyway, so you may as well talk to Him about it.

I have said things to the Lord like this, "God, I pray for _____ to be blessed even more. Cause her to prosper; bless her in every way. Lord, I am praying this by faith. In my spirit, I feel jealous of her and inferior to her, but I *choose* to do this Your way whether I feel like it or not."

Recently I heard someone say that no matter how well we can do something, there will always arise someone who can do it better. This statement had an impact on me because I know it to be true. And if this is true, then what is the purpose of struggling all our lives to get ahead of everyone else? As soon as we become number one, someone will be competing with us and, sooner or later, that one person will appear who can do whatever we're doing a little better then we can.

Think of sports; it seems that no matter what record some athlete sets, eventually another athlete comes along and breaks it. What about the entertainment field? The current star is only tops for a certain period of time and then someone new comes along to take his place. What a terrible deception it is to think that we must always struggle to get ahead of everyone else—and then fight to stay there. Our value is not rooted in what we do, but in the fact that God loves us and sent His only son to die for us.

God told me a long time ago to remember that "shooting stars" rise quickly and get a lot of attention, but usually they are around for only a short period of time. Most of the time they fall as quickly as they arise. He told me that it is much better to be around for the long haul—hanging in there—and doing what He has asked me to do to the best of my ability. He has assured me that He will take care of my reputation. For my part, I have decided that whatever He wants me to do and be is all right with me. Why? Because He knows what I can handle better than I do.

Perhaps you have had a mental stronghold for a long time in this area. Each time you come across someone who appears to be a little ahead of you, you feel jealousy, envy, or a desire to enter into competition with that person. If so, I exhort you to get a new mindset. Always remember that getting ahead of someone else does not make you more valuable to God than you already are.

Set your mind to be happy for others and trust God with yourself. It will take some time and persistence, but when that old mental stronghold has been torn down and replaced by the Word of God, you will be on your way out of the wilderness and into the Promised Land.

Chapter
25

"I'm going to do it my way,
or not at all."

Wilderness Mentality #10

"I'm going to do it my way, or not at all."

Chapter

25

Wilderness Mentality #10

The Israelites displayed much stubbornness and rebellion during their years in the wilderness. That is precisely what caused them to die out there. They just would not do what God told them to do! They would cry out to God to get them out of trouble when they got into a mess. They would even respond to His instructions with obedience—until circumstances improved. Then, repeatedly, they would go right back into rebellion.

That they might set their hope in God and not forget the works of God, but might keep His commandments.

And might not be as their fathers—a stubborn and rebellious generation, a generation that set not their hearts aright nor prepared their hearts to know God, and whose spirits were not steadfast and faithful to God.
PSALM 78:7,8

This same cycle is repeated and recorded so many times in the Old Testament that it is almost unbelievable. And yet, if we are not walking in wisdom, we will spend our lives doing the same thing.

I suppose some of us are just by nature a little more stubborn and rebellious than others. And then, of course, we must consider our roots and how we got started in life, because that affects us also.

I was born with a strong personality and probably would have spent many years trying to "do it my way" no matter what. But the years I spent being abused and controlled—added to an already strong personality—combined together to develop in me the mindset that nobody was going to tell me what to do.

Obviously, God had to deal with this bad attitude before He could use me.

The Lord demands that we learn to give up our own way and be pliable and moldable in His hands. As long as we are stubborn and rebellious, He can't use us.

I describe *stubborn* as obstinate; difficult to handle or work with, and *rebellious* as resisting control; resisting correction, unruly; refusing to follow ordinary guidelines. Both of these definitions describe me, as I was!

The abuse I had suffered in my early life caused a lot of my out-of-balance attitudes toward authority. But as I said earlier in the book, I could not allow my past to become an excuse to stay trapped in rebellion or anything else. Victorious living demands prompt, exact obedience to the Lord. We grow in our ability and willingness to lay aside our will and do His. It is vital that we continue to make progress in this area.

It is not enough to reach a certain plateau and think, "I've gone as far as I'm going to go." We must be obedient in all things—not holding back anything or keeping any doors in our lives closed to the Lord. We all have these "certain" areas that we hang onto as long as possible, but I exhort you to remember that a little leaven leavens the entire lump (see 1 Cor. 5:6 KJV).

GOD WANTS OBEDIENCE, NOT SACRIFICE

Samuel said [to King Saul], Has the Lord as great a delight in burnt offerings and sacrifices as in obeying the voice of the Lord? Behold, to obey is better than sacrifice, and to hearken than the fat of rams.

For rebellion is as the sin of witchcraft, and stubbornness is as idolatry and teraphim (household good luck images). Because you have rejected the word of the Lord, He also has rejected you from being king.

1 Samuel 15:22,23

An examination of Saul's life shows us vividly that he was given an opportunity to be king. He did not maintain the position for long because of stubbornness and rebellion. He had his own idea about things.

One time when Samuel the prophet was correcting Saul for not doing what he had been instructed to do, Saul's reply was, "I thought." He then proceeded to express his idea of how he thought things should have been done. (See 1 Samuel 10:6-8; 13:8-14.) Samuel's answer to King Saul was that God desires obedience, not sacrifice. If we "think" too much, we can reason our way out of God's will.

Often, we don't want to do what God asks, and then we attempt to do something to compensate for our disobedience.

How many of God's children fail to "reign as kings in life" (Rom. 5:17; see Rev. 1:6 KJV) because of their stubbornness and rebellion?

The introduction to the book of Ecclesiastes in *The Amplified Bible* says this: "The purpose of this book is to investigate life as a whole and to teach that in the final analysis life is meaningless without proper respect and reverence for God."

We must understand that without obedience, there is no proper respect and reverence. The rebellion shown by many children today is caused by a lack of proper respect and reverence for their parents. This is often the fault of the parents because they have not lived in front of their children a life that would evoke respect and reverence.

Most scholars agree that the book of Ecclesiastes was written by King Solomon, who was given more wisdom from God than any other man. If Solomon had so much wisdom, how could he have made so many sad mistakes in his life? The answer is simple: it is possible to have something and not use it. We have the mind of Christ, but do we always use it? Jesus has been made unto us wisdom from God, but do we always use wisdom?

Solomon wanted to go his own way and do his own thing. He spent his life trying first one thing and then another. He had anything and everything that money could buy—the best of every worldly pleasure—and yet this is what he said at the conclusion of the book:

> All has been heard; the end of the matter is: Fear God [revere and worship Him, knowing that He is] and keep His commandments, for this is the whole of man [the full, original purpose of his creation, the object of God's providence, the root of character, the foundation of all happiness, the adjustment to all inharmonious circumstances and conditions under the sun] and the whole [duty] for every man.
>
> Ecclesiastes 12:13

Let me put into my own words what I receive from this Scripture:

The whole purpose of man's creation is that he reverence and worship God by obeying Him. All godly character must be rooted in obedience—it is the foundation of all happiness. No one can ever be truly happy without being obedient to God. Anything in our lives that is out of order will be brought into adjustment by obedience. Obedience is the whole duty of man.

As far as I am concerned, this is one awesome Scripture, and I encourage you to continue studying it on your own.

OBEDIENCE AND DISOBEDIENCE:

BOTH HAVE CONSEQUENCES

> For as by one man's disobedience many were made sinners, so by the obedience of one shall many be made righteous.
>
> Romans 5:19 KJV

Our choice to obey or not to obey not only affects us, but multitudes of others. Just think of it: if the Israelites had promptly obeyed God, how much greater their lives would have been. Many of them and their children died in the wilderness because they would not submit to God's ways. Their children were affected by their decisions, and so are ours.

Recently, my oldest son said, "Mom, I have something to tell you, and I may cry, but hear me out." He then went on to say, "I have been thinking about you and Dad and the years you have put into this ministry, and all the times you chose to obey God and how it has not always been easy for you. I realize, Mom, that you and Dad have gone through things that nobody knows about, and I want you to know that this morning God made me aware that I am benefitting greatly from your obedience, and I appreciate it."

What he said meant a lot to me, and it reminded me of Romans 5:19.

Your decision to obey God affects other people, and when you decide to disobey God, that also affects others. You may disobey God and choose to stay in the wilderness, but please keep in mind that if you now have or ever have children, your decision will keep them in the wilderness with you. They may manage to get themselves out when they are grown, but I can assure you they will pay a price for your disobedience.

Your life might be in better shape now if someone in your past had obeyed God.

Obedience is a far-reaching thing; it closes the gates of hell and opens the windows of heaven.

I could write an entire book on obedience, but for now I simply want to make the point that a life of disobedience is the fruit of wrong thinking that leads to wrong choices.

BRING EVERY THOUGHT INTO CAPTIVITY TO CHRIST

For the weapons of our warfare are not physical [weapons of flesh and blood], but they are mighty before God for the overthrow and destruction of strongholds,

[Inasmuch as we] refute arguments and theories and reasonings and every proud and lofty thing that sets itself up against the [true] knowledge of God; and we lead every thought and purpose away captive into the obedience of Christ (the Messiah, the Anointed One).

2 Corinthians 10:4,5

Our thoughts are what get us into trouble quite often.

In Isaiah 55:8 the Lord says, "For My thoughts are not your thoughts, neither are your ways My ways." No matter what you or I may think, God has written His thoughts down for us in His book called the Bible. We must choose to examine our thoughts in light of the Word of God, always being willing to submit our thoughts to His thoughts, knowing that His are best.

This is exactly the point made in 2 Corinthians 10:4,5. Examine what is in your mind. If it does not agree with God's thoughts (the Bible), then cast down your own thoughts and think on His.

People living in the vanity of their own mind not only destroy themselves, but far too often, they bring destruction to others around them.

The mind is the battlefield!

It is on this ground of the mind that you will either win or lose the war that Satan has launched. It is my most heartfelt prayer that this book will assist you in casting down imaginations, and every high and lofty thing that exalts itself against the knowledge of God, bringing every thought into captivity, into obedience to Jesus Christ.

Endnotes

Endnotes

Chapter 7. Think About What You're Thinking About

1. W. E. Vine, Merrill F. Unger, William White, *An Expository Dictionary of Biblical Words* (Nashville: Thomas Nelson, Inc., 1985), p. 662.

2. James Strong, *The New Strong's Exhaustive Concordance of the Bible* (Nashville: Thomas Nelson Inc., 1984), "Greek Dictionary of the New Testament," p. 24.

3. *Websters II New Riverside University Dictionary*, (Boston: Houghton Mifflin Company, 1984), s.v. "meditate."

4. Vine, p. 400.

Chapter 9. A Wandering, Wondering Mind

1　*Webster's II*, s.v. "wander."

2. *Webster's II*, s.v. "wonder."

Chapter 10. A Confused Mind

1. *Webster's II*, s.v. "reason."

Chapter 11. A Doubtful and Unbelieving Mind

1. W.E. Vine, *Vine's Expository Dictionary of Old and New Testament Words*, (Old Tappan, N.J.: Fleming H. Revell, 1981), Vol. 1: A-Dys, p. 335.

2. Vine, Vol. 4: Set-Z, p. 165.

Chapter 12. An Anxious and Worried Mind

1. *Webster's II*, s.v. "worry."

2. *The Random House Unabridged Dictionary*, 2nd ed. (New York: Random House, 1993), s.v. "worry."

Chapter 13. A Judgmental, Critical, and Suspicious Mind

1. Vine, Vol. 2: E-Li, p. 281.
2. Vine, Vol. 2: E-Li, p. 280.

Chapter 15. The Mind of Christ

1. *Webster's II*, s.v. "depress."
2. *Webster's II*, s.v. "depressed."
3. Vine, Vol. 2: E-Li, p. 60.
4. Vine, Vol. 3: Lo-Ser, p. 55.
5. Strong, James, *The New Strong's Exhaustive Concordance of the Bible*, (Nashville: Thomas Nelson Publishers, 1984), "Hebrew and Chaldee Dictionary," p. 32.

Chapter 23. "I don't deserve God's blessings because I am not worthy."

1. *Webster's II*, s.v. "reproach."

Chapter 24. "Why shouldn't I be jealous and envious when everybody else is better off than I am?"

1. Vine, Vol. 2: E-Li, p. 37.
2. *Webster's II*, s.v. "jealousy."

Bibliography

The Random House Unabridged Dictionary, 2nd ed. New York: Random House, 1993.

Strong, James. *The New Strong's Exhaustive Concordance of the Bible*. Nashville: Thomas Nelson, Inc., 1984.

Vine, W. E. *Vine's Expository Dictionary of Old and New Testament Words*. Old Tappan, N.J.: Fleming H. Revell Company, 1981.

Vine, W. E.; Unger, Merrill F.; White, William, eds. *An Expository Dictionary of Biblical Words*. Nashville: Thomas Nelson, Inc., 1985.

Webster's II New Riverside University Dictionary. Boston: Houghton Mifflin Company, 1984.

Battlefield of the Mind
Study Guide

Contents

PART 1

The Importance of the Mind

Introduction

The Bible makes it clear that the mind is the leader or forerunner of all actions. Proverbs 23:7 tells us: "For as he" [a person] "thinks in his heart, so is he...." (Also see Romans 8:5.)

If we renew our mind according to God's Word, we will, as Romans 12:2 promises, prove for ourselves "what is the good and acceptable and perfect will of God" for our lives. If we think and dwell on negative thoughts, we will have a negative life.

God wants us to experience the fullness of life He sent Jesus to provide for all those who believe in Him and receive it; Satan wants to stop us from receiving all that God has for us. Because our actions are a direct result of our thoughts, Satan's strategy is to wage war against us in our minds by bombarding us with thoughts contrary to the truth of God's Word. He wants to deceive us into believing damaging patterns of untrue thoughts, or strongholds, that we will allow to influence our lives and hold us in bondage.

The battlefield is the mind, and 2 Corinthians 10:4,5 describes the weapons of warfare God has given us "for the overthrow and destruction of strongholds." This study guide describes how to use those weapons.

USING THIS STUDY GUIDE

The purpose of this workbook is to reinforce the principles taught in my book, *Battlefield of the Mind*. You will need a copy of *Battlefield of the Mind* to work through this book.

This study guide is written in a question and answer format. By reading a chapter in *Battlefield of the Mind,* the designated Scripture verses, then answering the questions in the corresponding chapter of the study guide, you will gain a deeper understanding of the principles and learn more easily how to incorporate them into your daily life.

To use this workbook, look up the corresponding chapter in *Battlefield of the Mind* and read it. Next look up in your Bible the Scriptures designated in the study guide and read them. This is an important step because those Scriptures are the basis of the teaching in that particular chapter and are taken directly from that chapter.

Answer the questions in the study guide by referring to the appropriate chapter in *Battlefield of the Mind.* Once you have finished answering the questions in each chapter, turn to the answer key in the back of this book to check your answers.

1. Work at a comfortable pace. Don't rush to finish quickly. Stay in each chapter until you have a thorough understanding of the material and how it pertains to your life.

2. Follow these steps with each chapter in this study guide.

3. Use this study guide for individual study or group discussion. When using it in a group, discuss your answers and learn how to apply the principles in a way that may not have occurred to you until you heard the experiences of others.

Consistently and steadily working through this book will help you renew your mind to God's Word. You will find that your pattern of thinking is gradually transforming from wrong, negative thoughts into God-like thoughts. Changing your way of thinking will enable you to change things in your life that you thought you would have to live with forever.

WALK IN GOD'S GOOD PLAN FOR YOU

Lining up our thoughts with God's thoughts is vital to overcoming negative thoughts from Satan and brings freedom and peace. We must know God's Word well enough to be able to compare what is in our mind with what is in the mind of God; any thought that attempts to exalt itself above the Word of God we are to cast down and bring into captivity to Jesus Christ. This process takes time.

I believe the God-directed, God-empowered principles in this study guide are important tools that will help you to achieve this goal. I want to encourage you to study and meditate on them; then apply what you learn to your life and allow the Holy Spirit to enlighten the eyes of your spirit (which is your heart) with God's wisdom and revelation. As you do, I believe you will see great results in winning the war that Satan has launched and ensure your victory in the battlefield of the mind.

If you are one of millions of people who suffer from worry, doubt, confusion, depression, anger or condemnation, you are experiencing an attack in your mind. But you don't have to live your whole life like this! Satan offers wrong thinking to everyone, but you do not have to accept his offer.

I pray that working through this study guide, along with the book, *Battlefield of the Mind*, will help firmly establish in your heart forever that you need to begin to think about what you are thinking about, so that you line up your thoughts with God's thoughts. This renewal of the mind is a process that requires time, but it is well worth the effort. For when you begin to see God's good plan for you in your thinking, you will begin to walk in it.

1. Read 2 Corinthians 10:4,5; Proverbs 23:7 KJV

    Why are our thoughts important? _____

    _____.

2. Read Romans 8:5

    How do our actions relate to our thoughts? _____

    _____

    _____.

3. Read Romans 12:2

    How will our lives be changed if we renew our minds according to God's Word? _____

    _____

    _____

    _____.

4. Review 2 Corinthians 10:4,5

    How will we know the difference between what is in our mind and what is the mind of God? _____

    _____

    _____

    _____.

The Mind Is the Battlefield

*I*n the original book, *Battlefield of the Mind,* read Chapter 1, then read in your Bible the Scriptures designated below and answer the questions that follow. When you finish, check your answers in the answer key provided at the end of this book.

As you continue to follow this procedure throughout this workbook, you can be assured that you will gain insight through understanding that will help you integrate these godly principles into your daily life and win the battle in your mind!

1. Read Ephesians 6:12; John 8:44

   a. How does Satan attempt to defeat us? _____
      _____
      _____ .

   b. What did Jesus call the devil? _____
      _____ .

   c. In what way does Satan try to bombard our minds to defeat us?
      _____
      _____ .

   d. Explain the phrase: "One of the devil's strong points is patience."
      _____
      _____ .

2. Read 2 Corinthians 10:4,5

   a. What are "strongholds," and how does Satan attempt to set them up in our mind? _____

_____

_____ .

b. Read the examples of strongholds Mary and John encountered in the text and give an example of a stronghold you have struggled with in your life. _____

_____

_____ .

c. How might this stronghold have come about? _____

_____

_____

_____ .

3. Read John 8:31,32; Mark 4:24

a. How can we overcome strongholds? _____

_____

_____

_____ .

b. How are we to use the weapon of the Word of God to overcome strongholds? _____

_____

_____ .

c. Why are prayer and praise effective weapons in overcoming strongholds? _____

_____

_____

_____ .

God never loses a battle. He has a definite battle plan — and when we follow it, we always win! Praise and worship are really a battle position! They confuse the enemy. When we take our position, we will see the enemy's defeat!

4. Read Luke 4:18,19

    a. According to this passage, what has God promised concerning the poor, the captives, the blind, the oppressed and others? _____
_____
_____
_____ .

    b. What can John and Mary (in the text) do that will set them free from their conflicting problems? _____
_____
_____ .

5. Read 1 Corinthians 10:13

    What does this verse say about God and the temptations and trials we encounter while tearing down strongholds? _____
_____
_____ .

Chapter
2

A Vital Necessity

As with the previous chapter, before answering the questions below, first read the corresponding chapter in *Battlefield of the Mind* then the Scriptures designated below. After you complete the chapter, check the answer key in the back of this book.

To gain the greatest benefit from this workbook, continue using this method throughout.

1. Read Proverbs 23:7

   This Scripture shows us how very important it is that we think properly. The first paragraph of *Battlefield of the Mind*, Chapter 2, tells us thoughts are _____, and according to the writer of the book of Proverbs, they have _____.
   Explain what this statement means: _____
   _____
   _____.

2. Read Romans 8:5

   a. To have a successful Christian life, what alternative to fleshly, wrong and negative thoughts is a vital necessity? _____
   _____
   _____.

   b. If your life is in a state of chaos because of years of wrong thinking, what can you do to straighten it out? _____
   _____
   _____.

3. Read Zechariah 4:6

    a. Since determination is not enough to be set free from strong-holds, what else is needed? _____
_____
_____ .

    b. In what way is right thinking compared to a heartbeat or blood pressure? _____
_____
_____ .

4. Read Matthew 12:33

    a. Explain how the phrase "a tree is known by its fruit" pertains to our lives. _____
_____
_____ .

    b. Can a person's thought life be discerned by looking at his attitude toward life in general? Explain. _____
_____
_____ .

Chapter

3

Don't Give Up!

1. Read Galatians 6:9

   How can you regain territory you have lost to the devil?_____
   _____
   _____ .

2. Read Isaiah 43:2

   a. What does God promise us regarding difficulties we experience?
      _____
      _____ .

   b. Quitting is easy. How can we overcome difficulties?_____
      _____
      _____ .

3. Read Deuteronomy 30:19; Proverbs 18:21

   a. How can we decide what is right or wrong for us on a daily basis?
      _____
      _____ .

   b. How can we avoid choosing death? _____
      _____
      _____ .

4. Read Deuteronomy 1:2,6-8

   a. Why did it take the Israelites forty years to make an eleven-day
      journey? How does their problem relate to us today in our spiri-
      tual journey? _____

_____
_____ .

b. When God told the Israelites, "You have dwelt long enough on this mountain," what was He really saying? What is He saying to us today?_____

_____
_____
_____ .

As we renew our minds with the Word of God, we will begin to see positive changes in our thoughts and in all other areas of life!

Chapter 4

Little by Little

1. Read Deuteronomy 7:22

   a. The process of renewing our minds takes place _____ .

   b. Why did God tell the Israelites He would clear out their enemies this way? _____
   _____
   _____ .

   c. What is the "beast" that will consume us if we receive too much freedom too quickly? _____
   _____
   _____ .

2. Read 1 Peter 5:10

   Why do we need to suffer "a little while"? _____
   _____
   _____ .

3. Read Romans 8:1

   a. What can we learn from watching a baby's attempts to walk? ___
   _____
   _____
   _____ .

   b. How does the devil try to stop you from renewing your mind? What can you do to stop his attempts? _____
   _____

_____
_____ .

c. Walking after the flesh is _____
_____ .

d. Walking after the Spirit is _____
_____ .

e. When you fail, that doesn't mean you are a failure. What does it mean? _____
_____
_____ .

4. Read Psalm 42:5; James 1:4 KJV; Philippians 1:6; 2:13

a. What happens to hope and victory when we become discouraged? _____
_____
_____ .

b. What should you do to overcome condemnation and discouragement? _____
_____
_____
_____ .

1. Read Matthew 8:13

    Explain the effect of positive and negative thoughts on the lives of people. _____

    _____

    _____ .

2. Read Romans 8:28; 12:16

    a. Does the Bible say that all things are good? _____

        _____

        _____ .

    b. How are we to react when our plans don't work out? _____

        _____

        _____ .

3. Read 2 Corinthians 5:17

    Many of us have had bad things happen to us, things which cause us to be negative about the future. According to this verse, how should we react to such situations? _____

    _____

    _____

    _____ .

4. Read John 16:7,8; Philippians 1:6

    a. Why did Jesus say it was "profitable" for us that He go away? ____

        _____

        _____ .

b. What does Jesus teach us that the Holy Spirit will do for us? __

_____

_____ .

c. What does the Bible say about the work God has begun in us?

_____

_____ .

You may not be able to resist the sin of speaking negatively, but when you do, ask God to help you. Speaking negatively about yourself will hinder the good things God has for you.

5. Read Acts 17:11 KJV

How can we achieve balance in our thinking? _____

_____

_____ .

6. Read Romans 4:18-20; Hebrews 6:19

a. Being positive does not mean that we are to ignore the obvious. How do we deal with impossible situations without losing hope?

_____

_____ .

b. What is the anchor of the soul? How does it help us? _____

_____

_____ .

7. Read Isaiah 30:18; Proverbs 15:15

a. What is God's desire toward us as reflected in these passages? What do we need to do to receive His will for us? _____

_____

_____ .

   b. What are "evil forebodings"? How are we to deal with them? __

_____

_____ .

8. Read 1 Peter 3:10

What does this verse say we must do if we want to enjoy life and see good days? _____

_____

_____

_____ .

Mind-Binding Spirits

1. Read Philippians 4:6,7 KJV

   How can we experience the peace of God? _____

   _____

   _____

   _____

   _____ .

2. Read John 8:31,32; Psalm 107:20

   How can we overcome "mind-binding spirits"? _____

   _____

   _____ .

3. Read Romans 8:26; James 1:2-8

   a. As Christians, why must we decide to believe? How can we believe during times when our minds don't understand everything? _____

      _____ .

   b. What should we do when we are going through trials? _____

      _____

      _____

      _____ .

Think About What You're
Thinking About

1. Read Psalm 119:15; Psalm 1:3

    What are we to spend our time thinking about or meditating on?
    How will this benefit us?_____

    _____

    _____.

2. Read Mark 4:24

    a. What does this statement tell us: "The more time we spend
        thinking about the Word we read and hear, the more power and
        ability we will have to do it — the more revelation knowledge we
        will have about what we have read or heard"? _____

        _____

        _____.

    b. Why aren't most Christians living victorious lives? _____

        _____

        _____.

3. Read Psalm 1:1,2; Proverbs 4:20

    a. How do we attend to God's Word? _____

        _____

        _____.

    b. How does the old saying "practice makes perfect" pertain to
        Christianity?_____

        _____

_____

_____ .

4. Read Joshua 1:8

   a. If you want to be successful and prosper in all your dealings, the Bible says you must _____

_____

_____ .

   b. How does the devil control people's lives?_____

_____ .

5. Read Ephesians 2:3

   a. The Apostle Paul warns us that we are not to be governed by _____ or to obey _____

_____ .

   b. Why must we think about what we are thinking about? _____

_____ .

6. Read Psalm 48:9; Psalm 143:4,5

   a. What was King David's response to his feelings of depression and gloom? _____

_____

_____

_____ .

   b. What role does our mind play in our victory? _____

_____

_____

_____

_____ .

7. Read Romans 12:2

   a. Why is renewing our minds so vital? _____

   _____ .

   b. To what should our minds be renewed? _____

   _____ .

8. Read Philippians 4:8

   a. Why are we instructed to think on good things? _____

   _____ .

   b. How does Satan deceive people as to the source of their misery?

   _____

   _____

   _____ .

   c. How can thinking about what you are thinking about help you?

   _____

   _____ .

PART 2

Conditions of the Mind

Introduction

*H*ave you noticed that the condition of your mind changes? One time you may be calm and peaceful, and another time anxious and worried. Or you may make a decision and be sure about it, then later find your mind in a confused condition concerning the very thing you were previously so clear and certain about.

Because it seems that the mind can be in so many different conditions, it is helpful to know when our minds are normal. That way we can learn to deal with abnormal thinking patterns immediately upon their arrival.

Our minds are not born again with the New Birth experience — they have to be renewed. (Romans 12:2.) Satan will aggressively fight against the renewal of our minds, but it is vital that we press on and continue to pray and study in this area until we gain measurable victory. I believe this next section of the guidebook will open your eyes to normal and abnormal mindsets for the believer who has determined to walk in victory.

1. Read 1 Corinthians 2:16

    a. According to this Scripture, what do we as believers "hold" when we have "the mind of Christ"? _____
    _____ .

    b. Give an example of the kind of mind that should be considered abnormal for a believer. _____
    _____
    _____ .

2. Read Romans 12:2

   Are our minds reborn with the New Birth experience? Why or why not? _____

   _____ .

3. Read 1 Peter 5:7

   Are our minds supposed to wander or be upset, confused, full of doubt and unbelief, or anxious, worried and tormented by fear? Why or why not? _____

   _____

   _____ .

When Is My Mind Normal?

1. Read Ephesians 1:17,18

   a. What does the phrase "the eyes of the heart" describe? _____
   _____ .

   b. Explain the principle of "the mind aiding the spirit."_____
   _____ .

2. Read 1 Corinthians 2:11

   a. What comparison can be made between a person's own spirit and
   the Holy Spirit? _____
   _____
   _____
   _____ .

   b. What is one of the purposes of the Holy Spirit? _____
   _____ .

   c. How is this purpose of the Holy Spirit accomplished? _____
   _____
   _____ .

   d. Why does the Holy Spirit function this way? _____
   _____
   _____ .

   e. Why is it important that our minds be enlightened concerning
   what is going on in our spirits? _____
   _____ .

3. Read 1 Kings 19:11,12 KJV

   How does God speak to us most of the time? _____
   _____ .

4. Read 1 Corinthians 14:15

   How did Paul say he prayed? _____
   _____ .

5. Read 1 Corinthians 14:13,14

   How does praying in the spirit and interpretation of tongues illustrate the principle of "mind aiding spirit"? _____
   _____
   _____ .

6. Read Isaiah 26:3

   a. Why does the devil want to overload and overwork your mind by
      filling it with every kind of wrong thought? _____
      _____
      _____ .

   b. What condition should the mind be in? _____
      _____ .

Chapter
9

A Wandering, Wondering Mind

1. Read 1 Peter 1:13 KJV

   a. What does an inability to concentrate indicate? _____
   _____ .

   b. What are some of the causes of an inability to concentrate? ___
   _____ .

   c. What is the difference between a lack of comprehension and a lack of concentration? _____
   _____
   _____
   _____ .

2. Read Ecclesiastes 5:1

   a. What does the expression "keep your foot" mean? What is it a warning against? _____
   _____
   _____ .

   b. Give an example from your own life of a wandering mind. _____
   _____
   _____
   _____
   _____ .

   c. How do you correct a wandering mind? _____
   _____ .

3. Mark 11:23,24

   a. What is wrong with wondering?_____

      _____

      _____

      _____ .

   b. As Christians, we are to _____ — not doubt or wonder.

A Confused Mind

1. Read James 1:5-8

   Why are wondering, doubt and confusion undesirable activities for us as Christians? _____

   _____

   _____ .

2. Read Matthew 16:8 KJV

   a. Why are a large percentage of God's people admittedly confused?

      _____

      _____ .

   b. What is "reasoning"? _____

      _____ .

   c. Why shouldn't we rely on reasoning when God directs us to do something? _____

      _____

      _____

      _____ .

3. Read 1 Corinthians 2:14 KJV

   a. What is the Christian alternative to reasoning in the mind? ___

      _____

      _____ .

   b. Give an example from your own life of a struggle between the carnal mind and the spiritual man. _____

      _____

_____

_____ .

4. Read James 1:22

   What are we to do when God speaks to us? _____

   _____ .

5. Read Proverbs 3:5; Romans 9:1

   a. Why is excessive reasoning dangerous? _____

      _____

      _____ .

   b. What three things does the human mind like? What is wrong
      with this? _____

      _____

      _____

      _____ .

   c. How did Paul know he was doing the right thing and not rely-
      ing on his own reasoning? _____

      _____ .

6. Read 1 Corinthians 2:1,2

   a. What was Paul's approach to reasoning? _____

      _____

      _____ .

   b. Why is this a good example for us today? _____

      _____

      _____ .

A Doubtful and Unbelieving Mind

1. Read Matthew 14:31; Mark 6:6

    What is the difference between the effects of doubt and unbelief? ___

    _____

    _____ .

2. Read 1 Kings 18:21; Romans 12:3 KJV

    a. How does the devil try to negate our faith?_____

        _____ .

    b. Why is it so important for us to know the Word of God? _____

        _____

        _____ .

3. Read Romans 4:18-21

    a. How did Abraham overcome the attack of Satan?_____

        _____

        _____ .

    b. What tools does Satan use to try to get us to "abort" our dreams? What do they both work against?_____

        _____ .

    c. Why does Satan attack us with doubt and unbelief? _____

        _____ .

    d. Why does the devil not want us to get our mind in agreement with our spirit?_____

        _____

_____
_____
_____ .

4. Read Matthew 14:24-32; Romans 4:18-21; Ephesians 6:14

   a. How were Peter and Abraham alike in their faith? How were they different?_____
   _____
   _____
   _____ .

   b. What are we to do in times of spiritual warfare?_____
   _____ .

   c. Why does Satan bring storms into your life?_____
   _____ .

   d. How do you resist him?_____
   _____
   _____ .

5. Read James 1:5-7

   Describe a time in your life when you were led by your heart rather than your head. _____
   _____
   _____
   _____ .

6. Read Matthew 21:18-22; John 14:12; Romans 12:3

   Faith is a gift from God; doubt is a _____ .
   Explain._____

   _____

   _____ .

7. Read Matthew 17:14-20 KJV; 11:28,29 KJV

   How does unbelief affect us?_____

   _____ .

8. Read Hebrews 4:11

   a. According to this Scripture, we as believers can enter _____ .

   b. The entire fourth chapter of the book of Hebrews speaks about
      _____ that is available to God's people.

   c. How does the Sabbath under the New Covenant differ from the
      Sabbath under the Old Covenant? _____

      _____

      _____ .

   d. How do we enter spiritual rest? _____

      _____ .

   e. How do we forfeit it?_____

      _____ .

9. Read Romans 1:17 KJV; Romans 15:13; James 1:7,8 KJV;
   2 Corinthians 10:5

a. How are the just (the righteous) supposed to live?_____
    _____ .

b. It is impossible to have joy and peace while living in _____ .

c. According to James 1:7,8 (KJV), what should we avoid doing in
   order to live the great life God has planned for us? _____
   _____ .

d. According to 2 Corinthians 10:5, what should we do instead? ___
   _____
   _____
   _____ .

An Anxious and Worried Mind

1. Read Psalm 37:8 KJV; Galatians 5:22; John 15:4 KJV; Matthew 6:25-34; Philippians 4:6; 1 Peter 5:7

   a. What are anxiety and worry? _____

   _____

   _____ .

   b. What is peace? _____ .

   c. How do we get the peace of God? _____ .

   Jesus said, "I am the Vine; you are the branches..." (John 15:5.) How long can a branch survive if it is broken off the vine? When we abide in Him, we enter the protection and rest of God. The life of abiding is a peaceful, restful and fruitful life. Enter in and enjoy your life while God works on your problems!

2. Read Matthew 6:25; John 10:10

   a. According to these verses, how is life intended to be? _____

   _____ .

   b. Why does Satan attack us with worry?_____ .

3. Read Matthew 6:25-30

   What does this passage of Scripture teach us about worry?_____

   _____

   _____ .

4. Read Matthew 6:31; 12:34 KJV

   The enemy knows that if he can get enough of the wrong things going on in our mind, what will eventually happen? _____

   _____ .

5. Read Matthew 6:32,33

   The world seeks after "things." What are we to seek?_____ .

6. Read Matthew 6:34

   Why shouldn't we spend today worrying about tomorrow?_____

   _____ .

7. Read Philippians 4:6; Hebrews 4:12; Ephesians 6:17 KJV

   The Word of God is our sword. Why must it be wielded against the enemy? _____

   _____

   _____ .

8. Read 2 Corinthians 10:5

   What is the single most effective weapon that can be used to win the war against worry and anxiety? _____

   _____ .

9. Read 1 Peter 5:6,7

   a. Why is a person who worries not a humble person? _____

      _____

      _____ .

b. What should our first response be in every situation? _____
_____.

10. Read 2 Chronicles 20:12,15,17; John 14:27; Matthew 11:29; 6:34

   a. What should our position be in adversity? _____
_____.

   b. There is no such thing as peace without opposition. Explain.__
_____
_____.

   c. How does being at peace, enjoying the rest of God in the midst
of the storm, give glory to God?_____ .

11. Read Hebrews 13:5; Psalm 37:3

   a. What is God letting us know in Hebrews 13:5? What has He
promised in it? _____
_____
_____.

   b. What does Psalm 37:3 tell us about worry and how to handle it?
_____
_____.

Chapter
13

A Judgmental, Critical and Suspicious Mind

1. Read Matthew 7:1 KJV

   a. What does it mean to judge others? _____
   _____ .

   b. Why is judging others wrong? _____
   _____
   _____ .

2. Read Romans 12:3

   a. Judgment and criticism are evidence of what deeper problem?
   _____ .

   b. What is the only reason we are able to excel in an area? _____
   _____ .

3. Read Galatians 6:1-3

   According to this Scripture, what mental attitude are we to maintain
   within ourselves? _____
   _____
   _____ .

4. Read Romans 14:4

   a. How can God help us with our weaknesses? _____
   _____ .

   b. Is it wrong to have a mental opinion of people? _____
   _____
   _____ .

   c. Why is it a major problem when we ponder over our opinion?

   _____

   _____ .

   d. How can the action of judging and criticizing be changed?____

   _____ .

5. Read Matthew 7:1,2; Galatians 6:7

How does the principle of sowing and reaping apply to the mental realm? _____

_____

_____ .

6. Read Matthew 7:3-5

   a. Why does the devil love to keep us busy, mentally judging the faults of others? _____

   _____ .

   b. Can we change others or ourselves? Why or why not? _____

   _____

   _____ .

7. Read Matthew 7:6

How does this verse apply to judgment and criticism?_____

_____

_____ .

8. Read Romans 2:1

   a. How do we look at ourselves through rose-colored glasses but look at everyone else through a magnifying glass? _____

_____

_____.

   b. How is a judgmental mind an offshoot of a negative mind? _____

_____.

  9. Read Proverbs 4:23

Name two things that are "unthinkable" for a believer. _____

_____.

10. Read 1 Corinthians 13:7

   a. What is the answer for a judgmental, critical, suspicious mind?

_____.

   b. What does it mean to have a "balanced attitude"? _____

_____

_____.

11. Read John 2:23-25; 1 Peter 5:8; 1 Corinthians 12:10 KJV

   a. What was Jesus' attitude toward His relationship with others?

_____

_____

_____.

   b. Why do we need balance in human relationships? _____

_____.

   c. What happens when we put our ultimate trust in God? _____

_____

_____.

d. What is the difference between suspicion and discernment? _____

_____

_____ .

e. What does true spiritual discernment provoke? _____

_____ .

12. Read Proverbs 16:23,24; John 10:10

a. What effect do our unspoken thoughts have on us?_____

_____

_____ .

b. What will happen to us when we begin to operate in the mind of Christ? _____

_____

_____ .

Chapter
14

A Passive Mind

1. Read Hosea 4:6; 1 Peter 5:8; 2 Timothy 1:6

   a. What is "passivity" and why is it a dangerous problem? _____

   _____

   _____ .

   b. Why does the devil use passivity? _____

   _____ .

   c. How can a believer guarantee that the enemy will not win the war?_____

   _____

   _____ .

2. Read Ephesians 4:27 KJV; Luke 11:24-26

   a. Why is it dangerous to give Satan the "empty space" of our mind?

   _____

   _____ .

   b. Why doesn't casting down imaginations always work? _____

   _____

   _____ .

3. Read Romans 12:2; John 15:4,10 KJV; Matthew 5:27,28

   a. Explain this dynamic principle shown throughout God's Word: "right action follows right thinking." _____

   _____

   _____

   _____ .

b. Fruit comes as the result of what? _____
_____ .

c. What does this involve? _____
_____ .

d. What must a person do to get from wrong behavior to right behavior? _____
_____
_____
_____ .

e. Why is it dangerous to "play around with sin" in the mind?___
_____
_____ .

4. Read Colossians 3:1,2

Explain the phrase, "You must have backbone and not just wishbone!" _____
_____
_____
_____ .

Chapter
15

The Mind of Christ

1. Read 1 Corinthians 2:16

   According to this Scripture, why is it possible for us to think as Jesus did? _____

   _____ .

2. Read Ezekiel 36:26,27; Romans 8:6; Amos 3:3

   a. Why did God give us His Spirit — a new nature, a new heart and mind — with the New Birth? _____

   _____ .

   b. What is the result of following the mind of the flesh? What is the result of following the mind of the Spirit? _____

   _____ .

   c. What is the first thing we must do in order to flow in the mind of Christ? _____

   _____

   _____ .

   d. What type of outlook and attitude did Jesus display?_____

   _____ .

   e. The mind of Christ in us is positive; therefore, any time we get negative, we are _____

   _____ .

   f. What is the dictionary definition of the word "depress"? How does this word apply to us?_____

   _____ .

3. Read Psalm 143:3-10

   a. What are the eight steps we can take to overcome depression?

   _____

   _____

   _____

   _____

   _____

   _____

   _____

   _____ .

   b. Give a description of someone who is depressed. _____

   _____ .

4. Read 2 Corinthians 10:4,5; Isaiah 26:3

   a. Why does Satan use depression? _____

   _____ .

   b. Where do negative feelings come from?_____

   _____ .

   c. What is the second thing we must do in order to flow in the
      mind of Christ? _____

   _____

   _____ .

5. Psalm 63:5,6; 77:12; 119:15; 143:5; 17:15

   a. If you want to experience victory, what will need to be a regular
      part of your thought life? _____

   _____ .

b. What is the advantage of fellowshipping with God early each morning? _____
_____
_____ .

6. Read John 16:7; Matthew 28:20; Hebrews 13:5; 1 John 4:16

a. Nothing is closer to us than _____ .

b. Since God is always with us, how do we become conscious of His presence? _____
_____
_____ .

c. What is the third thing we must do in order to flow in the mind of Christ? _____
_____
_____ .

7. Review 1 John 4:16, and read Romans 8:35,37

a. How can we experience God's love for us? _____
_____ .

b. What is the result of meditating on and confessing Romans 8:35,37? _____
_____
_____ .

8. Read 1 John 4:18 KJV; Romans 5:8 KJV

What is the result of righteousness-based thoughts? _____
_____ .

9. Read 2 Corinthians 5:21; Romans 12:8

   a. Why should thinking about guilt and condemnation be avoided?

      _____

      _____ .

   b. What must we do instead of feeling guilt and condemnation?

      _____

      _____ .

   c. What is the fourth thing we must do in order to flow in the mind of Christ? _____

      _____ .

10. Review Romans 12:8, and read Ephesians 4:29; 1 Corinthians 13:7; Psalm 100:4

   a. Based on the ministry gift of exhortation spoken of in Romans 12:8, what is exhortation?_____

      _____

      _____ .

   b. What happens when you begin thinking loving thoughts about others? _____

      _____

      _____ .

   c. Why do many people never see the answer to their prayers? ____

      _____

      _____

      _____ .

d. What is the fifth thing we must do in order to flow in the mind of Christ? _____

_____

_____ .

11. Review Psalm 100:4

What is a sign that a person is flowing in the mind of Christ? ____

_____

_____ .

12. Read Hebrews 13:15; Psalm 34:1

a. How can we be a blessing to the Lord? _____

_____ .

b. Why is expressing appreciation so beneficial?_____

_____

_____ .

13. Read Ephesians 5:18-20; John 5:38

a. How can we let the Holy Spirit ever fill and stimulate us?_____

_____

_____

_____

_____ .

b. What is the sixth thing we must do in order to flow in the mind of Christ? _____

_____

_____ .

14. Review John 5:38

    a. According to this verse, what is God's Word? _____

        _____

        _____ .

    b. Why was it given? _____

        _____ .

    c. How is this accomplished? _____

        _____ .

15. Read Joshua 1:8; Psalm 1:2,3

    How do we put the Word of God into practice physically? _____

    _____ .

16. Read Proverbs 4:20-22

    The words of the Lord are a source of _____ and
    _____ to the flesh.

17. Read Mark 4:24

    How does the principle of sowing and reaping apply to this verse?

    _____

    _____

    _____

    _____ .

18. Read Mark 4:22

    Where does the power to do the Word of God come from? _____

    _____ .

19. Read James 1:21

    How does the implanting and rooting of the Word of God take place in our hearts? _____

    _____

    _____ .

20. Read Romans 8:6; Philippians 4:8; 2 Corinthians 10:5 KJV

    What do you achieve by continually "watching over" your thoughts?

    _____

    _____

    _____

    _____ .

PART 3

Wilderness Mentalities

Introduction

*T*he Children of Israel spent forty years in the wilderness making an eleven-day trip because they had a "wilderness mentality." We really shouldn't look at the Israelites with such astonishment because most of us do the same thing they did. We keep going around and around the same mountains instead of making progress. The result is that it takes us years to experience victory over something that could have and should have been dealt with quickly.

A wilderness mentality is a wrong mindset. We can have right or wrong mindsets. The right ones benefit us, and the wrong ones hurt us and hinder our progress. Colossians 3:2 teaches us to set our minds and keep them set. We need our minds set in the right direction because wrong mindsets not only affect our circumstances, but they also affect our inner life.

1. Read Deuteronomy 1:2

   Why was an eleven-day journey for the Children of Israel extended to a forty-year journey? _____

   _____

   _____ .

2. Read Deuteronomy 1:6

   a. How are we like the Israelites? _____

      _____

      _____

      _____ .

b. What is God saying to us today that He said to the Children of Israel in their day? _____

_____

_____

_____ .

3. Read Colossians 3:2

a. What is a wilderness mentality? _____

_____ .

b. What should we do to avoid having a wilderness mentality? ____

_____

_____ .

c. Why do we need our minds set in the right direction? _____

_____

_____

_____ .

"My future is determined by my past and my present."

16

Wilderness Mentality #1

1. Read Proverbs 29:18 KJV

   What was the Israelites' problem? _____

   _____

   _____

   _____ .

2. Read Luke 4:18,19 KJV

   When you face situations that are so bad it seems you have no real reason to hope, what must you remember?_____

   _____ .

3. Read Isaiah 11:1-3 KJV

   Can we judge things accurately by the sight of our natural eyes? Why or why not? _____

   _____

   _____ .

4. Read Numbers 14:2,3

   What was the attitude of the Israelites in this passage? _____

   _____

   _____

   _____ .

349

5. Read Numbers 20:2-4

    Where do such bad attitudes come from? _____

    _____ .

6. Read Numbers 21:4,5

    What other bad attitude of the Israelites do we see evidenced in this
    passage? _____

    _____

    _____ .

7. Read Genesis 13:7-11

    What was Abraham's attitude that allowed him to bless his nephew
    Lot in order to stay out of strife? _____

    _____ .

8. Read Genesis 13:14,15; Romans 4:17 KJV

    a. What was the result of Abraham's good attitude? _____

        _____

        _____

        _____ .

    b. In view of Abraham's situation, how should you think and speak
        about your future? _____

        _____

        _____

        _____ .

"Someone do it for me; I don't want to take the responsibility."

Chapter

17

Wilderness Mentality #2

1. Read Genesis 11:31

   a. How is responsibility often defined? _____
   _____ .

   b. What does it mean to be responsible? _____
   _____ .

   c. How did Terah (Abram's father) respond to the opportunity God placed before him?_____
   _____
   _____ .

   d. How are we like Terah? Why do we respond that way? _____
   _____
   _____
   _____ .

2. Read Exodus 32:1-14, 30-32

   a. For what did the Israelites want to take responsibility? Who did it for them? How? _____
   _____
   _____ .

   b. As a parent, what does God want to teach His children? _____
   _____
   _____ .

3. Read Proverbs 6:6-11

   Why is it important to be motivated from within, not from without?

   _____
   _____
   _____ .

4. Read Matthew 20:16

   In regard to responsibility, the last part of this verse can be inter-
   preted to mean that many are _____

   _____
   _____ .

5. Read Joshua 1:1-3

   If we are not willing to take our responsibility seriously and go forth
   to claim our spiritual inheritance, what will be the result? _____

   _____ .

6. Read Ecclesiastes 11:4

   a. How will meeting resistance to taking responsibility help you?

      _____
      _____ .

   b. What will happen if you only do what is easy? _____

      _____ .

7. Read Matthew 25:1-13

   According to verse 13 of this passage, what do we need to do while
   we are waiting for the Master's return? _____

   _____ .

8. Read Matthew 25:14-28; John 15:16

   a. How should you respond to the ability that God has placed in you? Why? _____

   _____

   _____ .

   b. What does the Bible clearly show us about God's will for us? __

   _____

   _____ .

9. Read 1 Peter 5:6,7 KJV

   a. What can we learn about care and responsibility from this chapter?

   _____

   _____ .

   b. What should you remember if God gives you whatever you ask Him for? _____

   _____

   _____ .

   c. Anyone operating in the mind of Christ will walk in _____
      — not _____ .

   d. Give a two-word summary of this entire chapter: _____
      _____ !

Chapter 18

"Please make everything easy;
I can't take it if things are too hard!"

Wilderness Mentality #3

1. Read Deuteronomy 30:11

    Why aren't God's commands too difficult for us? _____
    _____
    _____ .

2. Read John 14:16

    a. When do things get hard? _____
        _____
        _____ .

    b. If everything in life were easy, what effect would it have on our lives? _____
        _____
        _____ .

    c. The Holy Spirit is in us and with us all the time for what purpose? _____
        _____
        _____
        _____ .

3. Read Exodus 13:17; Hebrews 4:16

    a. If you know God has asked you to do something, what should you do when things get hard?_____
        _____
        _____ .

b. Why did God lead the Children of Israel the long, hard way?___
_____
_____
_____ .

c. Did entering the Promised Land mean no more battles for the Israelites? _____
_____
_____
_____ .

d. Why did God lead the Children of Israel the longer, harder route even though there was a shorter, easier one?_____
_____
_____
_____ .

4. Read Galatians 6:9; Luke 4:1-13

a. Why is it important that we not give up in the mind, lose heart, grow weary and faint? _____
_____
_____ .

b. How was Jesus' forty-day fast in the wilderness different from the Israelites' forty-year wandering in the wilderness? _____
_____ .

5. Read 1 Peter 4:1,2

What secret concerning how to make it through difficult things and times does this passage teach us? _____

_____
_____
_____ .

6. Read Philippians 4:12,13 AMP; (in addition, read verse 13 in the *New King James Version*)

   a. What does right thinking do for us? _____
   _____ .

   b. If you are a whiner and a complainer, what should you do? _____
   _____
   _____ .

"I can't help it; I'm just addicted to grumbling, faultfinding and complaining."

Wilderness Mentality #4

1. Read 1 Peter 2:19,20

    It is not suffering that glorifies God, but _____ .

2. Read 1 Peter 2:21-23

    How did Jesus endure suffering? _____

    _____

    _____

    _____ .

3. Read Ephesians 4:1,2

    To the many people in the world who are trying to find God, what is more important than what we tell them?_____

    _____ .

4. Read Psalm 105:17-19; Genesis 39-50

    Why was God eventually able to deliver and promote Joseph who was mistreated by his brothers and unjustly condemned to prison?

    _____ .

5. Read 1 Corinthians 10:9-11

    a. How was Joseph different from the Israelites?_____

        _____

        _____ .

b. What is the message of these passages of Scripture?_____

_____

_____ .

c. What was the difference between the Israelites and Jesus, our example?_____

_____

_____ .

d. What can we see in this contrast? _____

_____ .

6. Read Philippians 2:14,15

According to this passage, why are we to do all things without grumbling and faultfinding and complaining? _____

_____

_____

_____ .

7. Read Philippians 4:6

a. What does Paul teach us in this verse about how to solve our problems? _____

_____

_____ .

b. When does murmuring, grumbling, faultfinding and complaining usually occur in our lives? _____

_____

_____ .

c. What does the Word of God teach us to do during these times?

    _____

    _____ .

d. Patience is not the ability to wait, but _____

    _____ .

e. How can you overcome complaining? _____

    _____ .

"Don't make me wait for anything;
I deserve everything immediately."

Wilderness Mentality #5

1. Read James 5:7

    a. Impatience is the fruit of _____ .

    b. Why should we learn to be patient while waiting? _____
        _____
        _____ .

    c. What lesson do we need to learn about our life's journey? ____
        _____
        _____ .

2. Read Romans 12:3

    a. Why does pride prevent waiting? _____
        _____
        _____ .

    b. A humble person will not display an _____
        _____ .

3. Read John 16:33

    a. If we get the idea in our heads that everything concerning us and
        our circumstances and relationships should always be perfect,
        what are we setting ourselves up for? How can this be stated
        another way? _____
        _____ .

b. All the mishaps in the world cannot harm us if we will_____

_____ .

4. Read Colossians 3:12

   a. How is patience described in this Scripture? _____

   _____

   _____ .

   b. Why should we turn to this Scripture often? _____

   _____

   _____ .

5. Read James 1:2-4; Galatians 5:22

   a. Patience is a fruit of the _____ .

   b. According to the *New King James Version* of James 1, what is the method God uses to bring out patience in us? _____

   _____ .

6. Read Numbers 21:4

   a. According to this Scripture, why did the Israelites become impatient, depressed and discouraged? _____

   _____ .

   b. What will happen if you learn to respond patiently in all kinds of trials? _____

   _____

   _____ .

7. Read Hebrews 10:36 AMP; 6:12 KJV

   a. Hebrews 10:36 tells us that without _____ and
      _____we will not receive the promises of God.

   b. Hebrews 6:12 KJV tells us that it is only through _____
      and _____ that we inherit the promises.

8. Read Proverbs 16:25; John 6:63; Romans 13:14

   a. Why are there multitudes of unhappy, unfulfilled Christians in
      the world?_____
      _____
      _____ .

   b. When you are trying to wait on God, why does the devil pound
      your mind continuously demanding that you "do something"?
      _____ .

   c. Impatience is a sign of pride, and the only answer to pride is ____
      _____ .

9. Read 1 Peter 5:6

   a. What does the phrase "lower yourself in your own estimation"
      mean? _____
      _____
      _____
      _____ .

   b. What happens when we wait on God and refuse to move in
      fleshly zeal? _____
      _____

_____
_____ .

c. What should you do when you are tempted to become frustrated
and impatient? _____
_____
_____
_____ .

*"My behavior may be wrong,
but it's not my fault."*

Wilderness Mentality #6

1. Read Genesis 3:12,13

   Name one major cause for wilderness living. _____

   _____

   _____ .

2. Read Genesis 16:1-6 NKJV

   a. Give an example from your own life of blaming others. _____

      _____ .

   b. Why does Satan work hard on our minds — building strongholds
      that will prevent us from facing the truth? _____

      _____ .

   c. Why do we avoid facing the truth about ourselves and our behav-
      ior? _____

      _____

      _____ .

3. Read Numbers 21:5

   Have you ever gone around and around the same mountains in your
   life? What were your excuses? _____

   _____ .

4. Read Numbers 13:1-3, 25-28

   a. Who plants "ifs" and "buts" in our minds? How should we defeat
      this tactic? _____

_____

_____ .

b. Name one reason our problems often defeat us. _____

_____ .

5. Read Psalm 51:1-6

What does verse 6 mean when it says that God desires truth "in the inner being"? _____

_____

_____ .

6. Read 1 John 1:8-10; Romans 3:20-24

a. What must we do to truly repent? _____

_____ .

b. Where is our justification found? _____

_____ .

c. How are you and I made right with God after sinning? _____

_____

_____ .

7. Read John 1:1-5; 8:32

a. What is one of the most powerful weapons against the kingdom of darkness? Why? _____

_____

_____

_____ .

    b. Jesus said it is truth that sets us free. How is the truth revealed?

_____

_____ .

8. Read John 16:12,13; Hebrews 13:5

    a. Who is "The Spirit of Truth"?_____

_____ .

    b. What is the major facet of His ministry to us? Why? _____

_____

_____ .

    c. What has God promised you to help you hang on to the truth about yourself?_____

_____

_____ .

    d. What is left for you to do now that you are on your way out of the wilderness?_____

_____

_____ .

"My life is so miserable; I feel sorry for myself because my life is so wretched!"

Wilderness Mentality #7

1. Read Numbers 14:1,2

    a. How did the Israelites react to their situation? _____

    _____

    _____ .

    b. What was God's word about such "pity parties"? _____

    _____ .

    c. What is vitally important to understand about this subject? ____

    _____

    _____ .

2. Read 1 Thessalonians 5:11

    a. What does the devil do the minute someone hurts us, the moment we experience disappointment? _____

    _____

    _____ .

    b. What will happen if you listen to the thoughts rushing into your mind during such times?_____

    _____ .

    c. How is self-pity perverted? _____

    _____

    _____ .

    d. What happens when we take the love of God meant to be given away and turn it in toward ourselves? _____ _____ .

    e. What is self-pity? Why is it wrong? _____ _____ _____ .

3. Read Philippians 2:4

    a. How do we stay out of self-pity? _____ _____ .

    b. How is self-pity supported?_____ _____ .

    c. How is self-pity a major trap?_____ _____ .

    d. What rare privilege does a Christian have when he experiences disappointment?_____ _____ .

4. Read Isaiah 43:18,19

As soon as you feel your emotions starting to rise up, what can you do?_____ _____ _____ .

"I don't deserve God's blessings because I am not worthy."

Chapter
23

Wilderness Mentality #8

1. Read Joshua 5:9; Romans 8:17 KJV

   a. The Lord told Joshua that He had "rolled away" the reproach of Egypt from His people. What does the word "reproach" mean?

   _____ .

   b. God wants to give us grace. What does Satan want to give us?

   _____
   _____
   _____ .

   c. What does God's rolling away the reproach from us mean? ____

   _____
   _____ .

   d. Although we know we don't deserve God's blessings, why do we receive them anyway? How do we get them? _____

   _____ .

2. Read Galatians 4:7

   a. Are you a son or a slave — an heir or a bond servant? _____

   _____
   _____
   _____ .

   b. What is the difference between an heir and a bond servant? ____

   _____
   _____

_____

_____ .

c. What does experience with the world teach us? _____

_____ .

d. What is the result of this teaching? _____

_____

_____ .

3. Read Numbers 13:33

a. Because of the reproach upon them, what kind of an opinion did the Israelites have of themselves? _____

_____ .

b. How does Satan try to give you a negative opinion of yourself?

_____

_____

_____

_____

_____ .

c. How is a poor self-image, an attitude of unworthiness and an "I-don't-deserve-God's-blessings" mentality spread from one generation to the next? _____

_____

_____ .

d. God is willing to give you mercy for your failures if _____

_____ .

He does not reward the perfect who have no flaws and never

make mistakes, but _____

_____

_____ .

4. Read Hebrews 11:6

   a. Without _____ you cannot please God.

   b. No matter how many _____ you offer, it
   will not please Him if they were done to _____
   His favor.

5. Read Ephesians 1:4

   According to this Scripture, what does the Lord want for us? _____

   _____

   _____

   _____ .

6. Read James 1:5; Philippians 1:6

   a. What does James 1:5 teach us? _____

   _____ .

   b. If you desire to have a victorious, powerful, positive life, you cannot be negative about yourself. Instead of being negative, what
   must you do? _____

   _____

   _____ .

   c. In Philippians 1:6, what does Paul say about you? _____

   _____

   _____

_____

_____ .

d. After reading this chapter, how should you think and speak
   about yourself?_____

_____ .

"Why shouldn't I be jealous and envious when everybody else is better off than I am?"

Wilderness Mentality #9

1. Read John 21:21,22

   Jealousy, envy and mentally comparing ourselves and our circumstances with others is _____ .

2. Read Proverbs 14:30

   a. How will envy cause a person to behave? _____
      _____ .

   b. Define *envy* and *jealousy.* _____
      _____
      _____
      _____ .

3. Read Luke 22:24-26

   Why is life in the Kingdom of God usually the direct opposite of the way of the world or the flesh? _____
   _____
   _____
   _____ .

4. Read Galatians 5:26; Proverbs 3:3,4 KJV

   a. Where does promotion come from for the believer?_____
      _____ .

   b. God will give us favor with Him and with others if _____
      _____ .

5. Read 3 John 2 KJV

   a. What should you do when you recognize wrong thought patterns beginning to flow into your mind?_____

   _____

   _____

   _____ .

   b. Why is it better to be around for the long haul than to be a "shooting star"? _____

   _____

   _____ .

   c. If you have had a mental stronghold for a long time in this area, what should you do? Why? What will be the result? _____

   _____

   _____

   _____ .

*"I'm going to do it my way,
or not at all."*

Wilderness Mentality #10

1. Read Psalm 78:7,8

   a. What two mindsets did the Israelites display during their years in the wilderness that caused them to die out there? _____
   _____ .

   b. What does God demand that we learn? Why? _____
   _____ .

   c. How are "stubborn" and "rebellious" described? Do either or both of them describe you?_____
   _____
   _____ .

   d. Why is it not enough to reach a certain plateau and think, "I've gone as far as I'm going to go"? _____
   _____ .

2. Read 1 Samuel 15:22,23; Romans 5:17; Revelation 1:6 KJV; Ecclesiastes 12:13

   a. Why do many of God's children fail to "reign as kings in life"?
   _____
   _____ .

   b. How is obedience related to respect and reverence? _____
   _____ .

   c. If Solomon had so much wisdom, how could he have made so many sad mistakes in his life?_____

_____

_____.

3. Read Romans 5:19 KJV

   a. Explain how your choice to obey or not to obey not only affects you, but multitudes of others. _____

_____

_____

_____

_____.

   b. Obedience is a far-reaching thing; it _____

_____.

4. Read 2 Corinthians 10:4,5; Isaiah 55:8

   a. Our thoughts are what get us into trouble quite often. What must we do to avoid this problem? _____

_____

_____.

   b. What should you do if what is in your mind does not agree with God's thoughts (the Bible)?_____

_____.

   c. Satan has launched a war. What is the battlefield? _____

_____

_____.

   d. How will this book assist you to win that war?_____

_____

_____.

Personal Reflection

1. What aspect of *Battlefield of the Mind* was most meaningful for you?

    _____

    _____

    _____

    _____

    _____ .

2. Has reading it changed any of the established mindsets you may have had?_____

    _____

    _____

    _____

    _____ .

3. Has it helped you in any areas of difficulty and if so, what are they?

    _____

    _____

    _____

    _____

    _____ .

Prayer for a Personal Relationship with the Lord

G od wants you to receive His free gift of salvation. Jesus wants to save you and fill you with the Holy Spirit more than anything. If you have never invited Jesus, the Prince of Peace, to be your Lord and Savior, I invite you to do so now. Pray the following prayer, and if you are really sincere about it, you will experience a new life in Christ.

Father,

You loved the world so much, You gave Your only begotten Son to die for our sins so that whoever believes in Him will not perish, but have eternal life.

Your Word says we are saved by grace through faith as a gift from You. There is nothing we can do to earn salvation.

I believe and confess with my mouth that Jesus Christ is Your Son, the Savior of the world. I believe He died on the cross for me and bore all of my sins, paying the price for them. I believe in my heart that You raised Jesus from the dead.

I ask You to forgive my sins. I confess Jesus as my Lord. According to Your Word, I am saved and will spend eternity with You! Thank You, Father. I am so grateful! In Jesus' name, amen.

See John 3:16; Ephesians 2:8,9; Romans 10:9,10; 1 Corinthians 15:3,4; 1 John 1:9; 4:14-16; 5:1,12,13.

Answers

Answers

Part 1: Introduction

1. The mind is the leader or forerunner of all our actions.

2. Our actions are a direct result of our thoughts.

3. We will prove out in our experience "the good and acceptable and perfect will of God" for our lives.

4. By comparing our thoughts with the Word of God. Any thought that attempts to exalt itself above the Word of God we are to cast down and bring into captivity to Jesus Christ.

Chapter 1

1a. With strategy and deceit, through well-laid plans and deliberate deception.

1b. ". . .the father of lies and of all that is false" (John 8:44).

1c. He uses a cleverly devised pattern of little nagging thoughts, suspicions, doubts, fears, wonderings, reasonings and theories.

1d. He is willing to invest any amount of time it takes to defeat us.

2a. Areas in which we are held in bondage (in prison) due to a certain way of thinking. Through careful strategy and cunning deceit.

2b. (Your answer.)

2c. (Your answer.)

3a. We must get the knowledge of God's truth in us, renew our minds with His Word, then use the weapons of 2 Corinthians 10:4,5 to tear down strongholds and every high and lofty thing that exalts itself against the knowledge of God. These "weapons" are the Word of God, praise and prayer.

3b. By "abiding"(continuing) in it until it becomes revelation given by inspiration of the Holy Spirit.

3c. Praise defeats the devil quicker than any other battle plan, but it must be genuine heart praise, not just lip service or a method being tried to see if it works. Also, praise and prayer both involve the Word. We praise God according to His Word and His goodness.

4a. God has promised good news for the poor, release for the captives, recovery of sight for the blind, deliverance for the oppressed and acceptance, salvation and free favors for all.

4b. Continue to study God's Word and act on the truth of His Word. Also, face the truth about themselves and their past as God reveals it to them.

5. God will not allow us to be tempted beyond what we can bear, but with every temptation He will also provide the way out, the escape.

Chapter 2

1. Powerful; creative ability. Our thoughts affect what we become. We cannot have a positive life and a negative mind.

2a. Renewed, God-like thinking.

2b. Tear down the strongholds that Satan has built in it, using the weapons of the Word, praise and prayer.

3a. The help of the Holy Spirit.

3b. It is a vital necessity. Without it there is no life.

4a. Thoughts bear fruit. Think good thoughts, and the fruit in your life will be good. Think bad thoughts, and the fruit in your life will be bad.

4b. Yes. A sweet, kind person does not have mean, vindictive thoughts. By the same token, a truly evil person does not have good, loving thoughts.

Chapter 3

1. If necessary, an inch at a time, always leaning on God's grace and not on your own ability to get the desired results.

2a. "When you pass through the waters, I will be with you . . . . When you walk through the fire, you will not be burned or scorched. . . ."

2b. By going through and not giving up, knowing that God helps us make spiritual progress by being with us to strengthen and encourage us to "keep on keeping on" in rough times.

3a. By renewing our mind to follow after the Spirit and not the flesh, purposely choosing right thinking.

3b. Since our thoughts become our words, we must choose life-generating thoughts. When we do, right words will follow, and we will choose life.

4a. They had a "wilderness mentality." We can avoid a "wilderness mentality" by getting our mind renewed and learning to choose our thoughts carefully.

4b. "You must not quit, or give up until victory is complete and you have taken possession of your rightful inheritance." The same thing.

Chapter 4

1a. Little by little.

1b. Lest the "beasts of the field" increase among them.

1c. Pride.

2. We rejoice more when freedom comes. When we try to do something on our own, fail and then realize that we must wait on God, our hearts overflow with thanksgiving and praise as He rises up and does what we cannot do ourselves.

3a. When a baby is learning to walk, he falls many, many times before he enjoys confidence in walking. However, one thing in a baby's favor is the fact that, even though he may cry for a while after he has fallen, he always gets right back up and tries again.

3b. Through discouragement and condemnation. Remind him and yourself that you do not walk after the flesh but after the Spirit.

3c. Depending on yourself.

3d. Depending on God.

3e. It simply means that you don't do everything right.

4a. Discouragement destroys hope. Without hope we give up, which is what the devil wants us to do.

4b. Use the weapon of the Word to tear down strongholds. Purposely think right thoughts, and go the extra mile and speak them aloud in your confession. Refuse to be discouraged or feel condemned if you make a mistake. Be patient with yourself!

Chapter 5

1. Positive thoughts, full of faith and hope, produce positive lives. Negative thoughts, full of fear and doubt, produce negative lives.

2a. No, it says that all things "work together for good" to those who love the Lord and are called according to His design and purpose.

2b. We are not to fall apart. Instead, we are to be readily adaptable and adjustable.

3. We should not allow the things that have happened to us to keep affecting our new life in Christ.

4a. If Jesus had not gone away, the Holy Spirit, the Comforter, would not have come.

4b. He will convict us of sin and convince us of righteousness.

4c. He is well able to bring it to full completion.

5. By having a ready mind, open to the will of God for us, whatever that will may be.

6a. We realize that no matter how negative the circumstances may seem, God is able to overcome them.

6b. Hope. It keeps us steady in time of trial.

7a. God wants to be gracious to us, to show mercy and loving-kindness to us. Expect it.

7b. Anxious thoughts. By having a "glad heart."

8. Keep our tongues free from evil and our lips from guile (treachery and deceit).

Chapter 6

1. By doing what Philippians 4:6,7 KJV says: being careful for nothing; but in everything, by prayer and supplication, with thanksgiving, letting our requests be made known unto God so that the peace of God, which passes all understanding, may keep our hearts and minds through Christ Jesus.

2. By abiding in the Word of God, which is the Truth that sets us free. His Word will heal us and rescue us from the pit of destruction.

3a. God often gives us faith for things that our minds just can't always come into agreement with, things our minds cannot understand, so we must decide to believe. By praying in Jesus' name and by the power of His blood, coming against "mind-binding spirits."

3b. Ask God for wisdom; He will give it to us and will show us what to do.

Chapter 7

1. The precepts of God — His instructions and teachings. We will prosper and come to maturity.

2a. We will get from the Word of God what we put into it.

2b. They do not delve into the Word of God very deeply. As a result, they get confused about why they are not powerful Christians living victorious lives.

3a. By meditating on it, by pondering on it, by contemplating it, by rehearsing or practicing it in our thinking.

3b. We really do not expect to be experts at anything in life without a lot of practice, so why would we expect Christianity to be any different?

4a. Meditate on the Word of God day and night.

4b. By controlling their thoughts.

5a. Our sensual nature. The impulses of our flesh, the thoughts of our carnal mind.

5b. To make sure we are not thinking all the wrong things.

6a. He literally came through the problem by choosing to remember the good times of past days — pondering the doings of God and the works of His hands. In other words, he thought on something good, and it helped him overcome depression.

6b. It is the power of the Holy Spirit working through the Word of God that brings victory into our lives. But a large part of the work that needs to be done is for us to line up our thinking with God and His Word. If we refuse to do this or think it is unimportant, we will never experience victory.

7a. So that we may prove for ourselves what is the good and acceptable and perfect will of God, even the thing which is good and acceptable and perfect in His sight for us.

7b. God's way of thinking.

8a. Our thoughts affect our attitudes and moods.

8b. By deceiving them into thinking that the source of their misery or trouble is something other than what it really is. He wants them to think they are unhappy due to what is going on around them (their circumstances), but the misery is actually due to what is going on inside them (their thoughts).

8c. It can help you locate some of your problems and be on your way to freedom very quickly.

Part 2: Introduction

1a. "The thoughts (feelings and purposes) of His heart."

1b. A critical, judgmental and suspicious mind.

2. No. They have to be renewed.

3. No. As children of God, it is our privilege to cast all of our care upon Him.

Chapter 8

1a. The mind.

1b. The mind and the spirit work together.

2a. The Holy Spirit knows the mind of God. Just as a person's own spirit within him is the only one who knows his thoughts, so the Spirit of God is the only One Who knows the mind of God.

2b. To reveal to us God's wisdom and revelation.

2c. This wisdom and revelation is imparted to our spirit, and our spirit then enlightens the eyes of our heart, which is our mind.

2d. So we can understand on a practical level what is being ministered to us spiritually.

2e. The natural does not understand the spiritual.

3. In "a still small voice."

4. Both with his spirit and with his mind.

5. The spirit is speaking something, and the mind is given understanding.

6a. So it cannot be free and available to the Holy Spirit working through your own human spirit.

6b. It should be both peaceful and alert.

Chapter 9

1a. Mental attack from the devil.

1b. An undisciplined thought life, vitamin deficiency and extreme fatigue.

1c. A lack of comprehension indicates a lack of understanding; a lack of concentration indicates an inability to focus.

2a. "Don't lose your balance or get off track." A wandering mind.

2b. (Your answer.)

2c. By disciplining it and keeping it on what you are doing.

3a. It leaves a person in indecision, and indecision causes confusion. Wondering, indecision and confusion prevent an individual from receiving from God, by faith, the answer to his prayer or need.

3b. Believe.

Chapter 10

1. They keep us from receiving what we need from God.

2a. Because of wondering and reasoning.

2b. Trying to figure out the "why" behind something.

2c. If what He tells us to do does not make sense, we may be tempted to disregard it.

3a. Obedience in the spirit.

3b. (Your answer.)

4. Mobilize — not rationalize.

5a. We can reason and figure something out that makes sense to us, but what we have reasoned to be correct may still be incorrect.

5b. Logic and order and reason. It leads to choosing what is comfortable but which may be totally wrong.

5c. It bore witness in his spirit.

6a. He resolved not to rely on human philosophy or wisdom but to know nothing but Jesus Christ and Him crucified.

6b. Excessive reasoning is not normal for the Christian who intends to be victorious — the believer who intends to win the war that is fought on the battlefield of the mind.

Chapter 11

1. Doubt causes a person to waver between two opinions, whereas unbelief leads to disobedience.

2a. By attacking us with doubt.

2b. Then we can recognize when the devil is lying to us.

3a. He continued to be steadfast, praising and giving glory to God.

3b. Doubt and unbelief. The mind.

3c. He doesn't want our mind in agreement with our spirit.

3d. He knows that if God places faith in us to do a thing, and we get positive and start consistently believing that we can actually do it, then we will do considerable damage to his kingdom.

4a. Both faced and acknowledged circumstances which seemed impossible. Unlike Abraham, however, Peter allowed doubt and unbelief to press in on him, and as he did, he began to sink.

4b. Tighten the belt of truth around us.

4c. To intimidate you.

4d. By remembering that the mind is the battlefield and by making decisions based on your spirit rather than on thoughts or feelings.

5.   (Your answer.)

6.   Choice. The seed of faith was planted in our hearts by God. Doubt is the devil's warfare tactic against our minds. We choose to doubt or to keep on believing!

7.   It will keep us from doing what God has called and anointed us to accomplish in life. It will also keep us from experiencing the sense of peace that He wants us to enjoy as we find rest for our souls in Him.

8a. The rest of God.

8b. A sabbath rest.

8c. Under the Old Covenant, the Sabbath was a day of rest. Under the New Covenant, the emphasis is on spiritual rest.

8d. Through believing.

8e. Through unbelief and disobedience.

9a. By faith.

9b. Unbelief.

9c. Being double-minded or living in doubt.

9d. ". . . refute arguments and theories and reasonings and every proud and lofty thing that sets itself up against the [true] knowledge of God; and . . . lead every thought and purpose away captive into the obedience of Christ (the Messiah, the Anointed One)."

Chapter 12

1a. Attacks on the mind intended to distract us from serving the Lord.

1b. A fruit of the Spirit.

1c. By abiding in the vine.

2a. Of such high quality that we enjoy it immensely.

2b. To steal our life from us.

3.   There is nothing in life that we are to worry about. We are valuable to God. Worry is useless. God will take care of us and provide for us.

4.   The wrong things will eventually begin to come out of our mouth.

5.   The Lord.

6.   We should use the time God has given us for what He intended.

7. A sword in its sheath won't do any good during an attack. God has given us His Word — we need to use it!

8. The Word coming forth out of a believer's mouth, with faith to back it up.

9a. A person who worries still thinks that in some way he can solve his own problem. The proud man is full of himself, while the humble man is full of God. The proud man worries; the humble man waits.

9b. To lean on God and to enter His rest.

10a. It is one of abiding in Jesus and entering the rest of God.

10b. God's peace is a spiritual peace, and His rest operates in the midst of the storm — not in its absence. Jesus did not come to remove all opposition from our lives, but rather to give us a different approach to the storms of life.

10c. It proves that His ways work.

11a. We do not need to have our minds set on money, worrying how we are going to take care of ourselves, because He will take care of these things for us. Never to leave (fail) us or forsake us.

11b. Don't worry. "Trust (lean on, rely on, and be confident) in the Lord and do good; so shall you dwell in the land and feed surely on His faithfulness, and truly you shall be fed."

Chapter 13

1a. To condemn or sentence them.

1b. God is the only One Who has the right to condemn or sentence; therefore, when we pass judgment on another, we are, in a certain sense, setting ourselves up as God in their life.

2a. Pride.

2b. God has given us grace for it.

3. We must have a "holy fear" of pride and be very careful of judging others or of being critical of them.

4a. He is able to make us stand and to justify us.

4b. No, we cannot always prevent ourselves from having opinions, but we do not have to express them.

4c. It becomes explosive and has the ability to do a great deal of harm in the realm of the relationship as well as in the spiritual realm.

4d. By changing the mind.

5.   We can sow and reap an attitude as well as a crop or an investment.

6a.   That way, we never see or deal with what is wrong with us.

6b.   We cannot change others; only God can. We cannot change ourselves either, but we can cooperate with the Holy Spirit and allow Him to do the work.

7.   When we judge and criticize, we have taken the holy thing (love) and cast it before dogs and hogs (demon spirits).

8a.   We make excuses for our own behavior, but when someone else does the same thing we do, we are often merciless.

8b.   It thinks about what is wrong with an individual instead of what is right.

9.   Judgment and criticism.

10a.   A balanced attitude.

10b.   To use wisdom and discernment in dealing with others, without looking at everyone with a negative, suspicious eye, always expecting to be taken advantage of by them.

11a.   He was not suspicious of others, but knowing human nature, He did not trust Himself to them in an unbalanced way.

11b.   If we go beyond wisdom, trouble will brew, and we will be hurt.

11c.   We open the door for the Holy Spirit to let us know when we're crossing over the line of balance.

11d.   Suspicion comes out of the unrenewed mind; discernment comes out of the renewed spirit.

11e.   Prayer, not gossip.

12a.   They affect our inner man, our health, our joy and our attitude.

12b.   We will step into a whole new realm of living.

Chapter 14

1a.   The opposite of activity. The Word of God clearly teaches that we must be alert, cautious and active — that we are to fan the flame and stir up the gift within us.

1b.   He knows it will spell the believer's ultimate defeat.

1c.   By moving against him, using his will to resist him.

2a.   An empty, passive mind can easily be filled with all kinds of wrong thoughts.

2b.   The empty space that is left must be filled up with right thinking.

3a.   We will not change our behavior until we change our thoughts. Right thinking comes first, and right action follows. Right action or correct behavior is a "fruit" of right thinking.

3b.   Abiding in the vine.

3c.   Being obedient.

3d.   He must be constantly renewed in the spirit of his mind, having a fresh mental and spiritual attitude. To do that, he must first change his thoughts — activating his mind and lining it up with God's Word and will.

3e.   The way for sinful action is paved through sinful thoughts.

4.   You must be active — not passive. Right action begins with right thinking. Don't be passive in your mind. Start choosing right thoughts.

Chapter 15

1.   We have His mind — and a new heart and spirit.

2a.   He knew that we would need them to heed His ordinances and walk in His statutes.

2b.   Death. Life.

2c.   Think positive thoughts.

2d.   A positive outlook and attitude.

2e.   Not operating with the mind of Christ.

2f.   "To lower in spirits: SADDEN."[1] We regularly have the opportunity to think negative thoughts, but they will only press us down further.

3a.   1) Identify the nature and cause of the problem.
      2) Recognize that depression steals life and light.
      3) Remember the good times.
      4) Praise the Lord in the midst of the problem.
      5) Ask for God's help.
      6) Listen to the Lord.
      7) Pray for deliverance.
      8) Seek God's wisdom, knowledge and leadership.

3b.   "Dwelling in dark places as one who is long dead."

4a.   To drag millions into the pit of darkness and despair.

4b.   From negative thoughts.

4c.   Be God-minded.

5a. Meditating on God and His ways and works.

5b. It is one sure way to begin enjoying life.

6a. Our own thoughts.

6b. By thinking about Him.

6c. Be "God-Loves-Me" minded.

7a. By meditating on it.

7b. A "conscious knowing" of God's love.

8. A righteousness-consciousness.

9a. Thoughts of guilt and condemnation are a waste of time and turn into action.

9b. Rebuke the devil and start going forward by thinking right thoughts.

9c. Have an exhortative mind.

10a. Saying something encouraging or uplifting — something that makes others feel better and encourages them to press on.

10b. You will find them behaving in a more lovable manner.

10c. They negate what they have asked for with their own thoughts and words before God ever gets a chance to work in their behalf.

10d. Develop a thankful mind.

11. He will find his thoughts filled with praise and thanksgiving.

12a. By letting His praise continually be in our thoughts and mouths.

12b. It is not only good for the other person, but it is good for us, because it releases joy in us.

13a. By speaking to ourselves (through our thoughts) or to others (through our words) in psalms and hymns and spiritual songs. In other words, by keeping our thoughts and words on, and full of, the Word of God; by offering praise at all times and for everything, giving thanks.

13b. Be Word-minded.

14a. A written expression of His thoughts, how He thinks about every situation and subject.

14b. So people could believe and experience all the good results of it.

14c. By meditating on it.

15. By first practicing it mentally.

16. Health; healing.

17. The greater the amount of time we put into thinking about and studying the Word of God, the more we get out of it.

18. The practice of meditating on it.

19. Through attending to it — by having it on our mind more than anything else.

20. You begin to take every thought captive unto the obedience of Jesus Christ.

Part 3: Introduction

1. They had a "wilderness mentality."

2a. Most of us do the same thing they did. We keep going around and around the same mountains instead of making progress. The result is that it takes us years to experience victory over something that could have and should have been dealt with quickly.

2b. "You have dwelt long enough on the same mountain; it is time to move on."

3a. A wrong mindset.

3b. Set our minds and keep them set.

3c. Wrong mindsets not only affect our circumstances, but they also affect our inner life.

Chapter 16

1. They had no positive vision for their lives — no dreams. They knew where they came from but not where they were going. Everything was based on what they had seen and could see. They did not know how to see with "the eye of faith."

2. Your future is not determined by your past or your present!

3. No. We must have spiritual "eyes to see" and "ears to hear." We need to hear what the Spirit says, not what the world says.

4. They had a negative, complaining attitude. They were ready to give up easily, preferring to go back to bondage rather than press through the wilderness into the Promised Land.

5. They are the fruit of bad thoughts.

6. They had a tremendous lack of gratitude.

7. He knew that if he acted properly God would take care of him.

8a. The devil could not keep the blessings of God from him. God gave him even more possessions than he had enjoyed before the separation, and blessed him mightily in every way.

8b. In a positive way, according to what God has placed in your heart, and not according to what you have seen in the past or are seeing even now in the present.

Chapter 17

1a. As our response to God's ability.

1b. To respond to the opportunities that God has placed in front of us.

1c. Instead of going all the way to Canaan with the Lord, he chose to stop and settle in Haran.

1d. When God speaks to us and gives us an opportunity to do something, many times, like Terah, we never finish what we start. We get into it and realize there is more involved than goosebumps and excitement.

2a. Nothing. Moses. He did their praying; he sought God for them; he even did their repenting when they got themselves in trouble.

2b. To accept responsibility.

3. God sees all and our reward will come from Him if we persist in doing what He has asked us to do.

4. Called or given an opportunity to do something for the Lord, but very few are willing to take the responsibility to answer that call.

5. We will never have the privilege of standing and ministering under God's anointing.

6a. You will build your strength.

6b. You will always remain weak.

7. Watch, give strict attention and be cautious and active.

8a. By doing all that you can with it. So that when the Master returns, you can not only give Him what He has given you, but more besides.

8b. It is God's will for us to bear good fruit.

9a. Not to be afraid of responsibility, to cast our care, but not our responsibility.

9b. There is a responsibility that goes along with the blessing.

9c. Wisdom; emotions.

9d. Be responsible!

Chapter 18

1. He gives us His Spirit to work in us powerfully and to help us in all He has asked of us.

2a. When we are trying to do them independently without leaning on and relying on God's grace.

2b. We would not even need the power of the Holy Spirit to help us.

2c. To help us, to enable us to do what we cannot do and to do with ease what would be hard without Him.

3a. Spend more time with Him, lean more on Him and receive more grace from Him.

3b. They were still cowards, and He had to do a work in them to prepare them for the battles they would face in the Promised Land.

3c. No. After they crossed the Jordan River and went in to possess the land of promise, they fought one battle after another.

3d. He knew they were not ready for the battles they would face in possessing the land. He took them the harder way to teach them Who He was and that they could not depend on themselves.

4a. If we hold on, we will eventually reap.

4b. Jesus drew strength from His heavenly Father and came out in victory.

5. "Think about everything Jesus went through and how He endured suffering in His flesh, and it will help you make it through your difficulties. Arm yourselves for battle; prepare yourselves to win by thinking on what Jesus did. . . ."

6a. It "arms" us for battle.

6b. Get a new mindset that says, "I can do all things through Christ who strengthens me" (Philippians 4:13 NKJV).

Chapter 19

1. A godly attitude in suffering that pleases Him and brings glory to Him.

2. Gloriously! Silently, without complaint, trusting God no matter how things looked, He remained the same in every situation. He did not respond patiently when things were easy and impatiently when they were hard or unjust.

3. What we show them.

4. He never complained, and he had a proper attitude in suffering.

5a.   He did not complain at all, and all they did was complain about every little thing that did not go their way.

5b.   The complaining of the Israelites opened a door for the enemy who came in and destroyed them.

5c.   The Israelites complained and remained in the wilderness. Jesus praised and was raised from the dead.

5d.   The power of praise and thanksgiving and also the power of complaining.

6.   That we may show ourselves to be blameless and guileless,   innocent and uncontaminated, children of God without blemish in the midst of a perverted and wicked generation, among whom we are seen as bright lights in the dark world.

7a.   To pray with thanksgiving in every circumstance.

7b.   When either something or someone has not gone the way we want it to, or when we are having to wait for something longer than we expected.

7c.   Be patient.

7d.   The ability to keep a good attitude while waiting.

7e.   By making the most of the mind of Christ that is within you.

Chapter 20

1a.   Pride.

1b.   Waiting is part of life. We actually spend more time in our lives waiting than we do receiving.

1c.   To enjoy where we are while we are on our way to where we are going!

2a.   The proud person thinks so highly of himself that he believes he should never be inconvenienced in any way.

2b.   Impatient attitude.

3a.   A fall. Satan is setting us up for a fall through wrong thinking.

3b.   Remain in the love of God, displaying the fruit of the Spirit.

4a.   As tireless and longsuffering, and having the power to endure whatever comes, with good temper.

4b.   To remind ourselves of what kind of behavior we should be displaying in all situations.

5a.   Spirit.

5b.   "Various trials."

6a. Because of the trials of the way.

6b. You will find yourself living a quality of life that is not just endured but enjoyed to the full.

7a. Patience; endurance.

7b. Faith; patience.

8a. They are busy trying to make something happen, instead of waiting patiently for God to bring things to pass in His own time and His own way.

8b. He wants to move you in fleshly zeal because he knows that the flesh profits nothing.

8c. Humility.

9a. It does not mean to think badly of yourself. It simply means, "Don't think you can solve all your problems on your own."

9b. There is a "dying to self" that takes place. We begin to die to our own ways and our own timing and to become alive to God's will and way for us.

9c. Begin to say, "Lord, I want Your will in Your timing. I do not want to be ahead of You, nor do I want to be behind You. Help me, Father, to wait patiently on You!"

Chapter 21

1. An unwillingness to take responsibility for one's own actions, blaming everything that is wrong or goes wrong on someone else.

2a. (Your answer.)

2b. The truth will set us free, and he knows it!

2c. It is painful.

3. (Your answer.)

4a. Satan. By keeping our eyes on God and not on the potential problem.

4b. We think they are bigger than God.

5. If we want to receive God's blessings, we must be honest with Him about ourselves and our sins.

6a. Face and acknowledge the truth about what we have done.

6b. Only in Jesus Christ.

6c. Only by the blood of Jesus — not by our excuses.

7a. Truth. Truth is light, and the Bible says that the darkness has never overpowered the light, and it never will.

7b. By the Spirit of Truth.

8a. The Holy Spirit.

8b. To help us face truth — to bring us to a place of truth. Because only the truth will set us free.

8c. "I will never leave you nor forsake you."

8d. Enjoy the Promised Land!

Chapter 22

1a. They felt exceedingly sorry for themselves. Every inconvenience became a new excuse to engage in self-pity.

1b. "You can be pitiful or powerful, but you cannot be both."

1c. We cannot entertain demons of self-pity and also walk in the power of God!

2a. He assigns a demon to whisper lies to us about how cruelly and unjustly we have been mistreated.

2b. You will quickly realize how the enemy uses self-pity to keep us in bondage.

2c. It is taking something that God intended to be given to others and turning it in on ourselves.

2d. It becomes selfishness and self-centeredness, which actually destroy us.

2e. Idolatry. It makes us only aware of our own selves and our own needs and concerns — and that is certainly a narrow-minded way to live.

3a. By looking at the other person's side and not just at our own.

3b. By thinking only of us and no one else.

3c. If we are not careful, we can actually become addicted to it.

3d. He can be re-appointed.

4. Pray, "Oh God, help me pass this test. I don't want to go around this mountain even one more time!"

Chapter 23

1a. "Blame . . . disgrace: shame."[1]

1b. Disgrace, which is another word for reproach.

1c. Each of us must receive for ourselves the forgiveness He is offering for all our past sins.

1d. We are joint-heirs with Christ. He earned them, and we get them by placing our faith in Him.

2a. (Your answer.)

2b. An heir is one who receives something other than by merit, as when property is passed down from one person to another through a will. A bond servant or laborer, in the biblical sense, is one who is weary from trying to follow the Law. The term denotes burdensome toil and trouble.

2c. We must deserve everything we get.

2d. By the time we are finished with the world, the reproach of it lies heavy upon us and definitely needs to be rolled away.

3a. A negative opinion.

3b. He fills your mind (if he is allowed to) with all types of negative thinking about yourself. He began early building strongholds in your mind, many of them negative things about you and about how other people feel about you. He always arranges for a few situations in which you experience rejection, so he can bring the pain of it back to your remembrance during a time when you are trying to make some progress.

3c. It is passed on from a parent to his children.

3d. You are willing to receive it. Those who put their faith and trust in Him.

4a. Faith.

4b. "Good works"; "earn."

5. That we should know that we are loved, special, valuable and that we should be holy, blameless and above reproach.

6a. To receive from God without reproach.

6b. Not look at how far you have to go, but at how far you have come. Consider your progress and remember Philippians 1:6.

6c. ". . . I am convinced and sure of this very thing, that He Who began a good work in you will continue until the day of Jesus Christ [right up to the time of His return], developing [that good work] and perfecting and bringing it to full completion in you."

6d. Positively!

Chapter 24

1. A wilderness mentality.

2a. In a way that is callous and crude — even animalistic at times.

2b. *Envy* is "the feeling of displeasure produced by witnessing . . . the prosperity of others."[1] *Jealousy* is "feelings of envy, apprehension, or bitterness"[2]; being fearful of losing what you have to another; resentment of another's success, arising from feelings of envy.

3. Jesus taught things like (author paraphrases), "Many who are first will be last, and the last will be first" (Mark 10:31), "Rejoice with those who are blessed" (Luke 15:6,9 KJV), "Pray for your enemies, and bless those who mistreat you" (Matthew 5:44). The world would say that this is foolishness — but Jesus says it is true power.

4a. From God and not from man.

4b. We will do things His way.

5a. Talk to yourself a little. Say to yourself, "What good will it do me to be jealous of others? It won't get me blessed. God has an individual plan for each of us, and I am going to trust Him to do the best thing for me. It isn't any of my business what He chooses to do for other people." Then deliberately and purposely pray for them to be blessed more.

5b. "Shooting stars" rise quickly and get a lot of attention, but usually they are around for only a short period of time. Most of the time they fall as quickly as they arise.

5c. Get a new mindset. Set your mind to be happy for others and trust God with yourself. It will take some time and persistence, but when that old mental stronghold has been torn down and replaced by the Word of God, you will be on your way out of the wilderness and into the Promised Land.

Chapter 25

1a. Stubbornness and rebellion.

1b. To give up our own way and be pliable and moldable in His hands. As long as we are stubborn and rebellious, He can't use us.

1c. "Stubborn" is described as obstinate; difficult to handle or work with, and "rebellious" as resisting control; resisting correction, unruly; refusing to follow ordinary guidelines. (Your answer.)

1d. We must be obedient in all things — not holding back anything or keeping any doors in our lives closed to the Lord.

2a. Because of their stubbornness and rebellion.

2b. Without obedience, there is no proper respect and reverence.

2c. The answer is simple: it is possible to have something and not use it. We have the mind of Christ, but do we always use it? Jesus has been made unto us wisdom from God, but do we always use wisdom? Solomon wanted to go his own way and do his own thing.

3a. Your decision to obey God affects other people, and when you decide to disobey God, that also affects others. You may disobey God and choose to stay in the wilderness, but please keep in mind that if you now have or ever have children, your decision will keep them in the wilderness with you. They may manage to get themselves out when they are grown, but they will pay a price for your disobedience.

3b. Closes the gates of hell and opens the windows of heaven.

4a. Choose to examine our thoughts in light of the Word of God, always being willing to submit our thoughts to His thoughts, knowing that His are best.

4b. Cast down your own thoughts and think on His.

4c. The mind!

4d. It will assist you in casting down imaginations, and every high and lofty thing that exalts itself against the knowledge of God, bringing every thought into captivity, into obedience to Jesus Christ.

Personal Reflection

1. (Your answer.)

2. (Your answer.)

3. (Your answer.)

Endnotes

Chapter 15

[1] *Webster's II New Riverside University Dictionary,* (Boston: Houghton Mifflin Company, 1984), s.v. "depress."

Chapter 23

[1] *Webster's II,* s.v. "reproach."

Chapter 24

[1] W.E. Vine, *Vine's Expository Dictionary of Old and New Testament Words* (Old Tappan: Fleming H. Revell, 1940), Vol. II: E-Li, p. 37.

[2] *Webster's II,* s.v. "jealousy."

Do you have a real relationship with Jesus?

God loves you! He created you to be a special, unique, one-of-a-kind individual, and He has a specific purpose and plan for your life. And through a personal relationship with your Creator—God—you can discover a way of life that will truly satisfy your soul.

No matter who you are, what you've done, or where you are in your life right now, God's love and grace are greater than your sin—your mistakes. Jesus willingly gave His life so you can receive forgiveness from God and have new life in Him. He's just waiting for you to invite Him to be your Savior and Lord.

If you are ready to commit your life to Jesus and follow Him, all you have to do is ask Him to forgive your sins and give you a fresh start in the life you are meant to live. Begin by praying this prayer...

> *Lord Jesus, thank You for giving Your life for me and forgiving me of my sins so I can have a personal relationship with You. I am sincerely sorry for the mistakes I've made, and I know I need You to help me live right.*
>
> *Your Word says in Romans 10:9, "If you declare with your mouth, 'Jesus is Lord,' and believe in your heart that God raised him from the dead, you will be saved" (NIV). I believe You are the Son of God and confess You as my Savior and Lord. Take me just as I am, and work in my heart, making me the person You want me to be. I want to live for You, Jesus, and I am so grateful that You are giving me a fresh start in my new life with You today.*
>
> *I love You, Jesus!*

It's so amazing to know that God loves us so much! He wants to have a deep, intimate relationship with us that grows every day as we spend time with Him in prayer and Bible study. And we want to encourage you in your new life in Christ.

Please visit joycemeyer.org/salvation to request Joyce's book *A New Way of Living*, which is our gift to you. We also have other free resources online to help you make progress in pursuing everything God has for you.

Congratulations on your fresh start in your life in Christ! We hope to hear from you soon.

About the Author

JOYCE MEYER is one of the world's leading practical Bible teachers. Her daily broadcast, *Enjoying Everyday Life*, airs on hundreds of television networks and radio stations worldwide.

Joyce has written more than one hundred inspirational books. Her bestsellers include *Power Thoughts*; *The Confident Woman*; *Look Great, Feel Great*; *Starting Your Day Right*; *Ending Your Day Right*; *Approval Addiction*; *How to Hear from God*; *Beauty for Ashes*; and *Battlefield of the Mind*.

Joyce travels extensively, holding conferences throughout the year and speaking to thousands around the world.

JOYCE MEYER MINISTRIES

U.S. & FOREIGN OFFICE ADDRESSES

Joyce Meyer Ministries
P.O. Box 655
Fenton, MO 63026
USA
(636) 349-0303

Joyce Meyer Ministries—Canada
P.O. Box 7700
Vancouver, BC V6B 4E2
Canada
(800) 868-1002

Joyce Meyer Ministries—Australia
Locked Bag 77
Mansfield Delivery Centre
Queensland 4122
Australia
(07) 3349 1200

Joyce Meyer Ministries—England
P.O. Box 1549
Windsor SL4 1GT
United Kingdom
01753 831102

Joyce Meyer Ministries—South Africa
P.O. Box 5
Cape Town 8000
South Africa
(27) 21-701-1056

Other Books by Joyce Meyer

Straight Talk
Teenagers Are People Too!
Trusting God Day by Day
The Word, the Name, the Blood
Woman to Woman
You Can Begin Again

Joyce Meyer Spanish Titles

Belleza en Lugar de Cenizas (Beauty for Ashes)
Buena Salud, Buena Vida (Good Health, Good Life)
Cambia Tus Palabras, Cambia Tu Vida (Change Your Words, Change Your Life)
El Campo de Batalla de la Mente (Battlefield of the Mind)
Como Formar Buenos Habitos y Romper Malos Habitos
(Making Good Habits, Breaking Bad Habits)
La Conexión de la Mente (The Mind Connection)
Dios No Está Enojado Contigo (God Is Not Mad at You)
La Dosis de Aprobación (The Approval Fix)
Empezando Tu Día Bien (Starting Your Day Right)
Hazte Un Favor a Ti Mismo...Perdona (Do Yourself a Favor...Forgive)
Madre Segura de sí Misma (The Confident Mom)
Palabras de Poder (Power Words)
Pensamientos de Poder (Power Thoughts)
Sobrecarga (Overload)
Termina Bien tu Día (Ending Your Day Right)
Usted Puede Comenzar de Nuevo (You Can Begin Again)
¡Viva con Esperanza! (Get Your Hopes Up!)
Viva Valientemente (Living Courageously)

* Study Guide available for this title

Books by Dave Meyer

Life Lines

From Joyce Meyer
#1 *New York Times* bestselling author

THE MIND CONNECTION
STUDY GUIDE

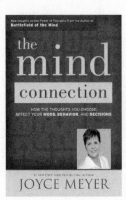

Make the most of what you learn from *The Mind Connection* with this companion study guide. Its engaging lessons and stimulating exercises will help you think with purpose, maintain a positive attitude, and overcome every obstacle you face.

Available now from FaithWords
wherever books are sold.